Luhmann and Socio-Legal Research

This book discusses the designs and applications of the social systems theory (built by Niklas Luhmann, 1927–1998) in relation to empirical socio-legal studies.

This is a sociological and legal theory known for its highly complex and abstract conceptual apparatus. But how to change its scale in order to study more localised phenomena and to deal with empirical data, such as case law, statutes, constitutions and regulation? This is the concern of a wide variety of scholars from many regions engaged in this volume. It focuses on methodological discussions and empirical examples concerning the innovations and potentials that functional and systemic approaches can bring to the study of legal phenomena (institutions building, argumentation and dispute-settlement), in the interface with economy and regulation, and with politics and public policies. It also discusses connections and contrasts with other jurisprudential approaches – for instance, with critical theory, law and economics, and traditional empirical research in law. Two decades after Luhmann's death, the 21st century has brought countless transformations in technologies and institutions. These changes, resulting in a hyper-connected, ultra-interactive world society bring operational and reflective challenges to the functional systems of law, politics and economy, to social movements and protests, and to major organisational systems, such as courts and enterprises, parliaments and public administration. Pursuing an empirical approach, this book details the variable forms by which systems construct their own structures and semantics and 'irritate' each other.

Engaging Luhmann's theoretical apparatus with empirical research in law, this book will be of interest to students and researchers in the field of socio-legal studies, the sociology of law, legal history and jurisprudence.

Celso Fernandes Campilongo is Full Professor and Vice-Dean at the University of São Paulo Law School, Brazil.

Lucas Fucci Amato is Professor at the Department of Legal Philosophy and Jurisprudence at the University of São Paulo Law School, Brazil.

Marco Antonio Loschiavo Leme de Barros is Professor at the Law School of Mackenzie Presbyterian University, São Paulo, Brazil.

Luhmann and Socio-Legal Research

An Empirical Agenda for Social Systems Theory

Edited by Celso Fernandes Campilongo, Lucas Fucci Amato, and Marco Antonio Loschiavo Leme de Barros

Routledge
Taylor & Francis Group
a GlassHouse Book

First published 2021
by Routledge
2 Park Square, Milton Park, Abingdon, Oxon OX14 4RN

and by Routledge
52 Vanderbilt Avenue, New York, NY 10017

Routledge is an imprint of the Taylor & Francis Group, an informa business

A Glasshouse Book

British Library Cataloguing-in-Publication Data
A catalogue record for this book is available from the British Library

Library of Congress Cataloging-in-Publication Data
A catalog record has been requested for this book

ISBN: 978-0-367-43971-2 (hbk)
ISBN: 978-1-003-12039-1 (ebk)

Typeset in Times New Roman
by MPS Limited, Dehradun

Contents

Figures

Contributors

Lucas Fucci Amato is a professor in the Department of Legal Philosophy and Jurisprudence at the University of São Paulo Law School, Brazil. He was a visiting researcher at Harvard Law School, USA, and at the Oxford Centre for Socio-Legal Studies, UK.

Marco Antonio Loschiavo Leme de Barros is a professor at the Law School of Mackenzie Presbyterian University, São Paulo, Brazil. He was a visiting researcher at the University of California, Los Angeles, USA, and at Oñati International Institute for the Sociology of Law, Spain.

Cristina Besio is a professor of sociology, focusing on the sociology of organizations, at the Faculty of Economics and Social Sciences, Helmut-Schmidt University, Hamburg, Germany. She has also taught at the University of Bielefeld, Germany.

Celso Fernandes Campilongo is a full professor and vice-dean at the University of São Paulo Law School, Brazil. He is also a professor at Pontifical Catholic University (PUC-SP) and was a visiting scholar at Salento University, Italy.

Raffaele De Giorgi is a professor emeritus of jurisprudence and legal sociology at the University of Salento, Lecce, Italy, and was a head of the law school there and of the Centre of Studies on Risk, co-founded with Niklas Luhmann.

Mark Hanna is a professor at the School of Law of Queen's University Belfast, UK. He teaches torts, legal theory and legal research, and studies the role of interaction, organisations, social movements and mass media in the development of law.

Bettina Lange is an associate professor of law and regulation at the University of Oxford (Centre for Socio-Legal Studies), UK. She works with environmental law and was a Jean-Monnet Fellow at the European University Institute, Florence, Italy.

John Paterson is a professor of law at the University of Aberdeen, UK. His research has covered systems theory, the regulation of risk, governance in the EU, corporate governance and energy law.

Margrit Seckelmann is the executive manager at the German Research Institute for Public Administration. Her research interests cover the fields of public law, legal history, legal theory, administrative sciences and particularly the regulation of new technologies.

Lukas K. Sosoe is a full professor at the University of Luxembourg. He has translated many of Luhmann's works into French, and works with legal theory, ethics, contemporary political philosophy and European studies.

Gunther Teubner is a professor of private law and legal sociology at Goethe University, Frankfurt am Main, Germany. He has also taught at the European University Institute Florence, Italy, and at the London School of Economics, UK.

Chris Thornhill is a professor and former head of the School of Law at the University of Manchester, UK. He was also the Niklas Luhmann Distinguished Visiting Professor in Sociological Theory at the University of Bielefeld, Germany.

Acknowledgement

The editors acknowledge the support from the University of São Paulo Law School (USP), São Paulo State Research Foundation (Fapesp) and the Brazilian National Coordination for the Improvement of Higher Education Personnel (Capes).

Chapter 1

An empirical agenda for social systems theory?

Lucas Fucci Amato, Marco Antonio Loschiavo Leme de Barros, and Celso Fernandes Campilongo

Introduction

Niklas Luhmann (1927–1998) started by studying the problems of public administration, bureaucracy and organisation and ended by providing a highly abstract and far-reaching theory of society and many of its sub-systems – politics, religion, art, education, science, economy and the law. This is certainly not a 'middle-range theory' (Merton 1968: ch. 2) and therefore is not easily applicable to empirical research. On the other hand, it provides a range of concepts to compare many specialised areas and pays attention to the internal mechanisms and discourses articulated in each of them – their semantics and structures. It is different, therefore, from so-ciological proposals that aim to catch and denounce the distance between the 'formalist', symbolic self-representations of these systems and their 'real' routines in a social field set up by the 'struggle between professionals pos-sessing unequal technical skills and social influence' (Bourdieu 1987: 827).

Every social system (from an organisation such as a court or a bank to a functional system such as the law or the economy) is unavoidably 'em-bedded' in society and cannot disentrench itself from the basic social op-eration, ie, communication. 'Disembeddedness' (in the line of thought by Polanyi 2001) is simply (conceptually) impossible according to Luhmann's theory (2013: 110). More than this: each social system reproduces society when it reproduces its own operations. Hence, one would need some criteria to specify why and how such diverse components (sentences and statutes, payments and borrowings, public policies and discourses) are distinguished and inter-related to form an order, a system. The 'pedigree' for each of these units of communication is not given by some transcendental fiction or shared consensus, such as those usual in jurisprudence (Kelsen's *Grundnorm* or Hart's rule of recognition); nor is it a matter of moral disagreement or authority. Legal communications are different from political or economic messages because of the function that these communications fill in relation to their surrounding social environment; the consequences that the law, politics or the economy produce act as causes, feeding back legal, political or economic communications – this is why these are functional systems. They are not an ideal ensemble, but empirical networks or chains of self-referred communications, organised around some generalised symbols (such as validity, money or power), referring to some problem, codified to distinguish the legal and the illegal, having and not having (money, property), government and opposition. The spheres of self-referred communications are, finally, structured through some programs, such as statutes and case law or investment plans and budgets.

If law – like economy or politics – is a matter of empirical observation, and theories and research are just communications, like sentences or menaces (observed through statutes and case law as crimes, illegal actions), the only difference that a study can claim in the face of its object is to work on a higher order of observation – to observe observations, to communicate about communications. Science builds communications following its own criteria and codes, giving limited answers linked to self-constructed hypotheses and trying to prove them to be true or false. Socio-legal research would encompass, from the viewpoint of social sciences, the basic operations of the legal system (eg, statute projects, judicial claims, defences and sentences), its reflexivity (such as the reflexivity of ordinary laws in the constitutional order, or of rules in principles and policies, or of norms of conduct in norms of process and organisation) and its reflection (self-descriptions through the legal doctrine).

Therefore, part I of this volume is concerned with the theoretical innovations that systems theory presents in relation to sociological and philosophical trends. It starts with a pure epistemological approach by Raffaele De Giorgi (Chapter 2) questioning the possibility of conducting socio-legal empirical research under systems theory, considering the ruptures that Luhmann made with rationalist philosophy based on the subject/object distinction and on notions of linear causality. The sociology of law is traditionally intended to approach – from an external, non-dogmatic point of view – the side of 'is' (versus 'ought'), of efficacy (versus validity) and of society (versus the law). However, De Giorgi shows that these distinctions are also internal to the legal system, and in this way sociology becomes captive to properly legal operations and operational concepts. A more promising path, opened by systems theory and its approach to second-order observation ('observing observers'), would be to really consider these differences as legal forms, as specific ways the legal system persists in its communication, building its own reservoirs of meaning and memory and its own ways of filtering, producing, presenting and approaching conflicts (through procedures). Instead of observing law and society as mutually external 'places', one would avoid what Whitehead (1948: 52) calls the 'fallacy of misplaced concreteness' and would start from the premise that law is a subsystem of society that through its own communications simply enlaces more communications, indications, self-descriptions and external observations (ie, hetero-reference) in order to construct its own reality.

Another venue for social systems theory, opened by legal scholars with affinities with the Frankfurt School (from Adorno to Habermas), is critical systems theory. Indeed, this possibility opens the way for linkages among Luhmann and many other authors, such as Foucault and the critical legal scholars (see, eg, Amato and Barros 2018). One should remember that Luhmann (1994) himself was sceptical about this normative emphasis and recommended avoiding it, while devaluing the gap between theoretical and empirical investigation, since all observation on a system would be an autological process – ie, observations applied to observations: self-reference in any case. Chapter 3 (by Lukas K. Sosoe) takes up exactly this question of the emergence of a proposal for 'critical systems theory', and places in this debate the possibility of using systems theory to observe empirical phenomena such as legal procedures and the role of the courts. Since systems theory observes and describes other systems (such as law, politics or education) and their own self-description, at the limit every systemic-theoretical statement is about empirical operations of communication. There is not a reality to grasp independent of communications; communications refer to themselves in interactions, organisations and functional systems. All these can be grasped by empirical research, but one would need to enlarge the methodological repertoire to couple it with the level of complexity required by a systemic-theoretical construct.

Part I, exploring theoretical bases for systemic empirical legal research, is completed with Chapter 4 (by John Paterson and Gunther Teubner), which discusses regulation and proposes the use of cognitive mapping methodology, presenting an empirical illustration of a particular regulatory situation (occupational health and safety in Britain's offshore oil industry). Unlike simple propositions, theories are general articulations of concepts and cannot be falsified, perishing instead through a test in the face of some contrasting social 'reality' that lies objectively outside them. On the other hand, systems are not simply stipulations made by a researcher but observable self-organising processes taking place in the social world, drawing their own borders and differences and building their own programmes of difference minimisation. Paterson and Teubner advance these positions and claim that if some elements (communications) collected in a somehow controlled or restricted situation or context (empirical research) contrast with the theoretical expectations and explanations, that is a matter of irritation between the self-observed system (in some sense, its 'sample' built by the researcher) and the scientific system, with whose criteria and 'validation' a sociological theory complies. Through this irritation, the theory is pressured to learn, rearranging its concepts and suppositions. Homologously, a system (eg, politics) cannot interfere in another's autopoiesis (eg, economy) but can simply learn and change its own programmes in view of the information gathered through hetero-observation.

Part II turns to exemplifying the concepts, methods and applications of socio-legal systemic research; it is focused on the interface between the legal and economic systems. Chapter 5 (by Bettina Lange) proceeds with a discussion of how to conceive regulation under a systemic-theoretical approach, focusing on the critical topic of the interface between social and natural systems, ie, environmental regulation. It deals with the concept of 'interests'. For Lange, systemic-theoretical ideas on how knowledge about the social world is generated can be related to qualitative empirical approaches, which stress the relativity and subjectivity of the meaning systems of the particular actors studied. These actors (such as regulators and the regulated organisations) are observed as such by a social system – ie, they are addresses of communication – and their discourses express articulations of interests in line with some system of reference, such as the legal system, distinguished by its code, programmes and symbolic medium.

In Chapter 6, Cristina Besio and Margrit Seckelmann propose a case study on the regulation of e-scooters in German cities, focusing on the self-reference that a multitude of organisations build in order to conduct law-making and implementation. Organisations re-specify the irritations from their environment into internal programmes and decisions. The regulated actors seek influence in regulation, and the legislators answer with new follow-up mechanisms in what Besio and Secklemann describe as an open-ended and highly recursive communication network. This chapter therefore provides a provoking example of how to conduct research in public policies with a systemic approach.

Chapter 7 (by Lucas Fucci Amato) presents a theoretical discussion with reference to the relation between the legal and economic systems. A systemic approach is contrasted with the new institutional economics, which provides the main theoretical basis for 'law and economics' studies. Amato claims that the proposed conceptual changes and theoretical refocusing – in the direction of describing the internal structures of each social system, ie, its institutions – may refine the use of systems theory for empirical research on legal-economic operations. This is a way of reducing the complexity and widening the scale of a theory basically built to discern the relation between the global social system (society) and its subsystems (specially the functional systems). Now the focus should be explaining the inter-relations among these subsystems, their structural couplings, internal environments and organisations, and how these typical structures institutionalise the operations of each system.

We then enter part III of the book, which addresses empirical observation of the coupling between law and politics and discusses how to observe normative expectations in contemporary society. Chapter 8 (by Marco Antonio Loschiavo Leme de Barros) focuses on organisational systems as a key viewpoint for observing more empirically detailed communications and events, such as sentences and legal decision-making. It presents a systemic-theoretical framework for analysing courts as organisational systems, ie, a core legal subsystem. It recovers the Weberian tradition of analysis of power and domination within bureaucracies, and then introduces the discussions by Luhmann and his followers on the theme of organisations. The chapter finally provides a typology of courts, classified according to their typical communicative profiles (argumentation forms) in the interface with politics and economy.

The following chapters deal with the study of normative expectations as structures of the legal systems, many times colliding with other (especially cognitive) expectations coming from politics, economy, science, mass media and social movements, among other systems. Chapter 9 (by Mark Hanna) focuses on case studies in legal mobilisation and fundamental rights. Attention is given to the functional method underlying systems theory, from which a 'soft empiricism' emerges: the potential to structure information provided by empirical observation with the conceptual tools of this theory and revise the theory in the face of new data uploaded to it. Through that method, teleology can be dispensed with and causalities can be assumed simply as hypotheticals; the focus is shiften to problem–solution linkages and to the functionally equivalent structures ordering these relations. The chapter considers how this method can be compatible with radical constructivism, namely with the theory of observation. An interesting contrast between the purity of Luhmann's theory – with its scale for typifying the long-lasting emergence of 'modern society' – and the rich and raw communicative material provided by more focused and detailed approaches (ie, empirical and middle-range research questions) is developed through the finding of the integration of many forms of societal differentiation within a functionally differentiated society. The 'constructed types' of a theory (McKinney 1966) are inevitably blurred and combined in describing and explaining complex but situated phenomena.

Chapter 10 (by Celso Fernandes Campilongo) discusses empirical observation of the legal system with reference to the diverse kinds of legal interpretation mobilised by protest and social movements. Its empirical observations mainly refer to contemporary Brazil, where a three-decade constitutional order plays the role of internalising into law many of the conflicts about unrealised expectations which that constitution itself and the following legal order formalised and generalised. Campilongo conceptualises two kind of social movements: those aiming at social integration, using protest performances and claims against the law (and against the differentiation between law, politics, economy etc.), and those that admit functional differentiation and mobilise law and dispute settlement as venues to increment the variation of the legal system, ie, to generate new interpretations to advance their expectations and pressure for the legal evolution.

Chapter 11 (by John Paterson) brings systemic theory to explain conjuncture, namely the procedural and constitutional questions raised by Brexit. The research question central to this chapter is: How generalised are expectations shaped in legal-political procedures, in their self-descriptions and justifying discourses? This interesting problem concerns how the frictions between political and legal institutions and organisations (prime minister, parliament and courts, the formal principle of parliamentary sovereignty and the uses and misuses of referendum) can contrast and frustrate popular expectations instead of congruently generalising norms – what Luhmann (2014: ch. 4, 2004: ch. 3) considered to be the singular function of the legal system.

In Chapter 12, we present an interview with Professor Chris Thornhill discussing as a trend of empirical research the historical-phenomenological observation of the legal-political interface, articulated around democratic constitutionalism. The conversation brings a consideration of the instability of contemporary democracies beyond a Eurocentric viewpoint. Evidence from the legal system shows how democracy at the level of nation states is a contemporary and ongoing construction, and how this process is interwoven with the transnational dynamics of law in a world society.

We intend this volume to present an up-to-date map of the applications of systems theory to socio-legal research, bringing to the reader both epistemological and conceptual discussions, as well as examples of current political and economic phenomena that are observed by the legal system in world society. The authors contribute to expand the horizons of systemic research throughout many countries and academic traditions.

References

Amato, L.F. and Barros, M.A.L.L. (eds) (2018) *Teoria crítica dos sistemas? Crítica, teoria social e direito* (Porto Alegre, Fi) [online] Available at: https://3c290742-53df-4d6f-b12f-6b135a606bc7.filesusr.com/ugd/48d206_55ed2ac8fe01488b89718288359b90c8.pdf (accessed 14.03.20.).

Bourdieu, P. (1987) 'The force of law: toward a sociology of the juridical field' *38 Hastings Law J.* 805–853.

Luhmann, N. (1994) '"What is the case?" and "what lies behind it?" The two sociologies and the theory of society' *12*(2) *Sociol. Theory* 126–139.

Luhmann, N. (2004) *Law as a Social System* (Oxford, Oxford University Press).

Luhmann, N. (2013) *Theory of Society II* (Stanford, Stanford University Press).

Luhmann, N. (2014) *A Sociological Theory of Law*, 2nd ed. (New York, Routledge).

McKinney, J.C. (1966) *Constructive Typology and Social Theory* (New York, Appleton Century Crofts).

Merton, R.K. (1968) *Social Theory and Social Structure* (New York, Free Press).

Polanyi, K. (2001) *The Great Transformation: The Political and Economic Origins of Our Time*, 2nd ed. (Boston, Beacon).

Whitehead, A.N. (1948) *Science and the Modern World* (New York, Pelican Mentor Books).

Part I

Theoretical bases for systemic empirical studies

Chapter 2

The sociological investigation of law in systems theory[1]

Raffaele De Giorgi

Introduction

A theoretical perspective of observing the world or researching it is very much of interest – in our case, the world of law. The topic, therefore, refers to the theoretical and epistemological assumptions of the construction of the object of observation. Here, however, the object is the research itself, not the object of research. But research always observes its object, and here its object is the legal system. Research is understood just like the observer. The main question here is: who is the observer? Luhmann (2003: 127) once replied: 'someone who is observed as an observer'. Heinz von Foerster 1993 would have added: *an observer is one who builds a reality*. If we combine the two responses, the result is that the observer is constituted with the construction of the object. In this manner the research is itself part of the object it observes.

This perspective allows us to affirm that our contribution contains nothing more than a reflection regarding the construction of objects. We understand that this perspective has a universal reach, since, as observers, we are all object builders – *hacedores*, as Borges (1960) said; we are also part of the world that we observe (see von Foerster and Bröcker 2002), ie, that we build. This means that our contribution applies to itself, deals with our present and tells us why we are liars when we speak the truth.

I Kantian perspective

In the communicative construction of what we use as reality, we are overwhelmed with redundancy, with meanings that always include more than what is supposed, with meanings that always include contents of sense in which old customs of access to the world are stratified. Indeed, these are simplifications, reductions of meaning that present the world to us in an accessible format and, in this way, make it familiar to us. Thus, we can affirm that if it is true that we are continually exposed to the experience of an unpredictable world, to its continuous variation, it is no less certain that we experience this experience without surprise: the reductions in meaning through which we have access to the world have the function of democratising the experience, so that it can be experienced by everyone without anxiety, uncertainty or disappointment. We have access to the world in a reduced format and we are used to calling it 'reality' (Watzlawick 1976, 1981).

The experience we have of reality is actually *a denomination experience with controlled origin*. It is guaranteed and ensured, because even when faced with variation, the unpredictability of what happens and the multiplicity of what is diverse, such exposure to complexity occurs through domesticated access, through channeled observations, consolidated reductions of meaning – ie, it happens through those redundancies of meaning with which we are overwhelmed. Provided by tradition and stabilised by self-evidence, these reductions give us certainty for experience and ensure stable guidelines for action.

With this, however, the possibility for variation is also reduced – ie, the opportunity of alternatives to access the world is limited (Luhmann 2000). In relation to this, we usually act considering a particular habit. It is a custom that leads us to treat the world as objectivity, exteriority, an external obstacle to us, an objective extension on which experience is practiced. We will not be responsible for this consideration in any way; we act within it and are not the object of our action. We are not part of it. As commonly specified, we are subjects.

This notion describes the conceptual core of what constitutes Western culture in modern society. It is an idea that, in the Kantian sense, is both theoretical and practical; in the modern saying, it is simultaneously *the cognitive and moral foundation of the 'subject/object' distinction*. We practice an exasperated subjectivism (see Marquard 1981, 1973), we act because the world is there before us; or rather, we act as if the world were there before us and action were just a matter of 'understanding and transforming it', to refer to an expression that is still used. As subjects, we exclude ourselves from the world, because only then it is possible to justify the construction of theories that tell us how to apprehend, ie, how to know and transform.

We operate with meanings, with descriptions, interpretations, which we consider to be self-evident and treat them as if they have objective consistency. Obviously, precisely for this reason, we exonerate them from any empirical evidence. They lead us to believe that we are observers of an external world: *reality observers*, as usually affirmed. In order to understand this empiricism and organise our world, we use categories, schemes. According to some, these categories would be transcendental, conditions for the possibility of empirical experience. It cannot be said, however, whether the difference between empiricism and transcendence is an empirical or a transcendental distinction. (An issue that I often discussed with Luhmann. More than considering it an issue, we considered it as a joke.) Likewise, it is not possible to say whether the difference between subject and object is a subjective or objective distinction – for von Foerster (1993), it was, of course, a subjective difference. In essence, we use distinctions that make a difference, that distinguish the world, but that later are not distinguished, do not apply to themselves. So at least from that point of view, they are not credible. For that reason, we prefer to say that they are paradoxical.

We don't know, but we act. We observe, describe, confront, transform meanings that we treat as objects, as reality. It is a Kantian heritage from which we have not been able to break. This heritage resisted the great Hegelian effort to think about the unity of the rational and the real (Hegel 1979: 24), but also Hegel's criticism of 'ought to be' (see Marquard 1973), the self-consummation of the philosophies of history and even Marx's (1932) great attempt to rescue reflection about the unity of the difference between subject and object from the foundation of the idea of gender (*Gattung*, in his language). This heritage still resists, because around it an inexhaustible semantics has been consolidated: even if empty, as Hegel would have said, it is highly productive, since until the first half of the last century, several modern forms of self-understanding of knowledge were extracted from it. In addition, one can define in this perspective the pedigrees of the differences through which the disciplining of knowledge is justified, as Foucault (1966) lucidly demonstrated.

II Disciplining knowledge and knowing reality

In a magnificent conference on a theme related to our discussion, Luhmann (1997) stated that without having to wait for sociology, humans had already made their reflections on the reasons why they act, on the ways of their action; they made it through isolating knowledge, and this was called 'culture', and related to the exteriority in which their action was produced and justified. Knowledge related to the meaning of economic action was specified and outlined as economic rationality; knowledge of education was defined as pedagogy; knowledge of the state and political organisations was articulated in protective categories such as sovereignty and legitimacy; moral and theoretical knowledge of the difference between good and evil was called ethics. Humans beings developed a concept of society based on the old ideas of 'civil society' that, incorporated into contractarian economic-political representations, seemed to be able to access the descriptions of modern society (see Luhmann and De Giorgi 1992: ch. 4). The unity of the object, ie, the unity of society, was represented as the result of a normative and moral integration or, as they still say, an integration between norms and values. Both kept the factuality of modern society, the accident, the infinity referred to by Hegel as the contingency of acting or, as Foucault said, the threatening savage exteriority. To this universe of divergence and the incongruous perspectives of singular action, norms and values provided horizons of integration and stable orientations to act.

Thus, notwithstanding the divergence of perspectives, the different criteria for guiding the action and the possibility of using different forms of rationality in acting, it became possible to isolate a unitary concept of society. Normative integration and the connection of values defined a single space that contained and justified the divergences. It was the space of action, the universe in which action could be extended and in which it could orient itself according to an economic logic of ends and means. This space was the domain of modern Enlightenment reason: a world organised by an ordered reason or, in Kantian terms, the universe of an ordering reason (Kant 1974). Theoretical reason and practical reason, norms and maxims, internal and external, truths and values, empiricism and transcendence – the observation of this world, its description, should use and presuppose that universal idea of order that was the great acquisition of the Enlightenment. Sociology, Parsons once told Luhmann, was born as a sociology of law.[2] An absolutely understandable statement.

This sociology, which finds in the legacy of the old Enlightenment the semantic universe of its self-constitution, becomes possible because the representation of the order which justifies it is closely connected with the representation of the act, which in turn was born from a precise semantics of the movement, *Semantik des Bewegungsbegriffes*, as Koselleck (1979) called it. Since Hobbes, acting was already interpreted as a movement toward the world, as a productive activity of events, as the event itself, ie, as one that could be observed from the point of view of the economic logic of its production and therefore could be coordinated with other events of the same nature. The order of the world could be understood as the order of the actions of individuals (see De Giorgi 1984: part 1).

In this way, it is finally possible to secularise the old notion of society that for centuries was determined by the idea of creation. Now, society itself is interpreted as a universe that realised jointly by the actions of individuals. As can be seen, both the Kantian elaboration of cause and the Hegelian criticism through the representation of the object of the will have a long history.

Sociology could define society as its unitary object, understand it as a universe of action by individuals, observe the regularity of actions, elaborate generalisations, and with that – according to some – it could even arrive at a formulation of general rules. In any case, if such a formulation could appear to be an excessive or ideologically compromised pretense, sociology would still be able to offer prognoses about acting, determine causal connections or at least present objective probabilities, as was said at the beginning of the past century (Weber 2013). In other words, sociology could describe the act, observing the connections of meaning that guided it.

As a sociology of law, sociological knowledge was interested in acting in relation to law, in the normative orientation of action and in the determination of the legal sense of action. Let's see how.

III Socio-legal research and sociologies of law

If on the one hand we can agree with Parsons that sociology was born as a sociology of law, on the other hand we must remember that sociology of law arranges its self-understanding as scientific knowledge only as a reaction to the *jurisprudence of concepts*, the *Begriffsjurisprudenz* (Krawietz 1976) of the second half of the 19th century. Initially, both (sociology and sociology of law) were divergent ideas around which different responses were made to the differentiation of the legal system and to the assertion of its artificiality. If Marx offers law a position in the semantics of power and in the structure of economic-social relations of production, since Jhering the idea of the separation between law and society has become a commonplace which will form the inevitable assumption of all socio-legal research (see De Giorgi 1980). From the generic consideration of 'social conditions' to the investigation of 'interests' as a methodological guideline in the application of law, or the acquisition of voluntary references, such as those of the German historical school of jurisprudence, to numerous contraceptive manifestations, socio-legal research will seek to obtain recognition through justification of the autonomy and the original character of its knowledge regarding legal phenomena.

The first half of the last century was particularly rich in theoretical efforts. Consider, for instance, Ehrlich's constructions and his debate with Kelsen (see Carrino 1992), institutionalism (Romano 1945), American-based sociological jurisprudence and legal realism (see Castignone et al. 2002), legal socialism (particularly in the field of criminal law; Quaderni Fiorentini 1974–1975), the Scandinavian schools (Olivecrona 1939; Ross 1946), the work of Schelsky (1980) and those close to him, and even attempts of an analytical-linguistic origin (MacCormick and Weinberger 1985).

These studies contributed to stabilisation of a non-dogmatic knowledge about the law, a non-systematic-conceptual, non-legal approach. They occupy a wide spectrum of reflection and analysis, from the extent to which the study of the fundamentals of law is understood as covering social facts to considerations about the economic and political determinations of legal phenomena. They also unfold an examination of the nature of the claims of individuals in relation to law and in the analysis of languages through which the immanent expectations to such claims are consolidated in discourses of social movements, as Campilongo has shown (see Chapter 10 in this book). However, execpt the brief season of studies on knowledge and opinion about the law (Podgorecki 1968), the aspect that has characterised recent sociological research on law is, on the one hand, as they say, research on the impact of law on society and, on the other, critique of law.

The first orientation is more widespread and practised, and according to some it deserves more than any other approach to be considered the sociology of law. Using methodologies of empirical data analysis, this field describes the modalities of expression about legally compliant action and the intensity of its occurrence, interprets it from the perspective of the legal system and deals in a considerable way with legally non-compliant action, which has been called 'deviant'. The description of deviant action often uses theories that have the intention of making it the object of theoretically founded knowledge (see De Giorgi and Nuzzo 2015). At this point, with significant interludes, the spectrum of theoretical resources used ranges from the positivism of ignoble memory to the refinement of psychoanalysis and the interesting constructions of the political economy of punishing.

The second guideline organises different perspectives of criticism of the law and deals with the modality of production of legal decisions, the analysis of its consequences, the form of the distribution of resources through the law and the construction of hierarchies between legal values. The expression 'socio-legal research' thus congregates multiple meanings and orientations that cannot be reduced to one unit, because they use different cognitive resources, are born of different intellectual motivations and follow different paths. They include epistemological assumptions that would be incongruous with each other and that could acquire congruence only from the perspective of a non-legal analysis of the law (Luhmann 1986). However, such a perspective would certainly not undo the differences. On the contrary, it would justify them insofar as it allowed them to appear as legitimate reactions to the legal observation of the law. In this sense, we can affirm that even if all the different sociologies of law have different perspectives, they are justified on the basis of another assumption: they assume the distinction between law and society as self-evident.

It is a constitutive distinction of the object, the law, the observer and the sociology of law. Combined from this perspective, the different branches of socio-legal research differ by the fact that some consider society as the starting point, others the legal system. All, however, admit the distinction between law and society and claim to be able to prove that society determines the legal system or that the legal system determines society. In this claim, they fall into the paradox that nullifies the assumption of their own existence. Moreover, they show a complex of other distinctions that bring them back to the old bed of an unacceptable Kantian heritage. Let us see briefly what the distinctions are that the first distinction produces.

IV The unity of distinctions

The paradox of non-legal analyses of law, ie, of socio-legal studies, consists in the fact that they use the distinction between law and society as a constitutive distinction of the object. Hence, they recognise the internal perspective of law just to observe it, from an external point of view, as an object (see Rehbinder 1970, 1995). It is undoubtedly a paradoxical approach, which leads to conclusions that are also paradoxical. In fact, the distinction between what is and what should be, an internal difference about what law creates to make its operation possible, becomes constitutive of the existence of this type of research – see the classical works by Kelsen (1911, 1922) at the beginning of the last century. It is in this way that the sociology of law also makes it possible for itself to operate, because otherwise there would be no scope to which it could direct its activity. Socio-legal research is directed to the factual side of the 'ought', observing its factual reality.[3] The paradox, however, lies in the fact that apart from legal reflection about the legal system, there is no sociological theory capable of determining the legal proposition ('ought') in society.

If socio-legal research became the object of itself, it could observe that its observation about 'being outside the law' is semantically within the law. Ranulph Glanville (1981) wrote an article title 'The same is different'. Here, on the contrary, it must be said: *the different is the same*. In society, there is only room for empirical factuality – only that which can be observed empirically has social existence, and it has social existence only because it can be empirically observed, ie, because it can operate as a reality and be observed in contrast to anything else.

Thus, regarding the legal system, it is possible to say what it is, not what it should be. Or, better: it can be said how it operates, how it builds itself, what will be used as a reality and thus how it differs from other spheres of social action. All this, however, can be seen only by the external observer. For the observer, the 'ought' appears as a paradox, as something that hides from itself the fact that it is as it is. The legal proposition ('ought') is a protective shell of a semantic nature which the rule covers to hide from itself the fact, the pure factuality, that it has no right to be right. This, of course, holds true for modern positive law. Other types of law used different semantics and constructed in a different way what they used as reality.

The other distinction that arises from the first constitutive distinction (between law and society) – and shares with it explorations and paradox – is the difference between validity and efficacy. It is a fundamental reference for traditional socio-legal research, which deals precisely with the efficacy of law, ie, its impact on society, its integrative function, the social control that would be performed by it or its 'resource allocation' potential. The reason this distinction is useless lies not only in what Max Weber noticed a century ago – ie, the impossibility of establishing objective causalities in acting – but in the fact that what jurists call 'validity' is nothing more than a symbol that moves in the legal system and has the function of fixing in the system's temporality what can be different from what it is: a form that unites the difference between actuality and potentiality (Luhmann 1993: 98–110). In other words: validity is a factual symbolisation of the legal proposition ('ought'), ie, the normativity of the law. It is the result of including the temporality of 'ought' in law. As such temporalisation always operates, and always in the present, the legal system builds a memory through validity, ie, it becomes present for itself. The legal system has a memory (De Giorgi 2006: 37–61) and is the recipient of it (von Foerster 1996). In this sense, the representation of efficacy hides the paradox of validity, since it subtracts from the observer the power to be different from what is used as it should be, gives it the value of a value and justifies the image according to which the law applies to reality, producing observable consequences – empirically observable and statistically detectable. A major theoretical and practical problem with each sociological observation of law is the idea of 'application', which is also present in legal reasoning, logic and interpretation. In fact, the reality which the legal system would subsume is that the system is built through applications. It is really very difficult to understand how there could be a reality of law that is outside the system, or a content of rules external to its application.

'Conformity' and 'deviation' is another distinction that socio-legal research admits and that leads to the ultimate consequences – until the elaboration of a theory of deviant action and the claim to determine the causes and factors of deviation. Here, there is evidence that modern theories of deviation have suppressed their positivist ancestry. The difference between conformity and deviation is a legal distinction in action, not a sociological one. This is the paradox of the excluded third who is included. The object of criminology is not, as is generally thought, deviant action, but criminological observation itself.

Finally, there is the myth of sociological observation of the social integration function that the law would have. Sociological research would have the potential to describe such a function. It is not simple, however, to understand what social breakdown means and how one could achieve what is called integration. In order to keep this myth alive, sociological research considers as disaggregated those regions of society – such as, for example, the multiple spaces of the South of modern society – in which the legal system has only one expressive function: to make visible the power that has the power to resort to law or circumvent it. In reality, such spaces are not disaggregated but, on the contrary, hyper-integrated, since in them one depends on the other and the possibilities of acting depend on this reciprocal dependence. In a different way, in societies where the legal system has reached a high degree of differentiation, dependence is linked to autonomy. On the other hand, beyond this discussion it is not possible to explain how the legal system can have an integrative function if, in its normal operation, it uses differences and stabilises them as subjective areas of action, recognised precisely by the law itself. There is no doubt that the 'integration'/ 'disaggregation' distinction has to do with the concepts that Bateson (1987: 48–69) called explanatory, ie, concepts by which one can explain everything, because they themselves are not explainable, they do not describe any object.

It is in this sense that sociological research of the law uses, in reality, the concepts and distinctions internal to the law – legal distinctions – as if they were external differences, constructions of an external observer, distinctions through which sociology observes the law. Thus, a main question is: why does sociology continue to have this difficulty with the legal system? Why should we still use observations that hide the paradoxical construction of law and resign ourselves to keeping the old semantics of the Enlightenment alive? Luhmann stated that it is a theoretical abstinence from sociology that leads it to refuse to be a theory of society and prevents it from understanding the extent to which modern society is, in itself, the realisation of a semantics that has great pretensions. How can socio-legal research access such semantics?

V Socio-legal research in systems theory

Sociological research manages to apprehend the observation of law as long as it distances itself from the distinctions through which the legal system hides its constitutive paradox, and builds its conscious knowledge of the structural limits of law, which is a self-referent structure, in simultaneous production of the legal and the illegal. This structural deficit offers sociological research the opportunity for confrontations and comparative analyses of the possible ways of constructing reality through which law develops its constitutive paradox. Such research can observe the asymmetries of the legal system, its circularity, and identify how it resorts to different strategies of temporal relocation of its operation. For example, it is possible to observe how the law uses end-oriented strategies to include the future in its cognitive operations. Sociological research can therefore formulate assessments and observe the real role of the techniques of invention of causalities in the future to which the law resorts. In this way, it refrains from considering the future as a specific area of legal operations and from appreciating differences from the consequences. With this, it does not block itself in the face of the universe of distinctions consolidated by the semantics of causality, it does not fall into the empirical fallacy of traditional sociological analyses and it gives itself the luxury of theory's cognitive techniques. Sociological research evaluates the alternatives and observes the strategy of making the law asymmetric from a realistic perspective, which in turn allows it to observe and describe other possible mechanisms for constructing reality by law. In other words: it sees what traditional research cannot see.

From this background, sociological research can observe the control strategy realistically. It is not possible to continue to describe it as an intervention of law in the environment and to speak of functions that the legal system cannot perform. Research needs to consider control as a technique for immunising the law in relation to the simultaneity of its environment. The issue becomes much more complex. There is control, because the legal system establishes all the events of the present through the filter of its past. By the past, we mean the time in which a sense is thickened by the remembrance of the legal system. Through this control activity, law selectively reactivates memories, leaves open the possibility of forgetting and builds its memory. In other words: the law represents its own being present to itself and temporalises the existence of the environment. In this way, sociological research can formulate an authentic sociology of jurisprudence through observation of the continuous reconstruction of the activity of memory of law. It is therefore a sociology of the memory of law, ie, sociological observation of the continuous reproduction of memory. What we observe as jurisprudence is in reality a condensed legal sense that apparently leaves the legal system to act on it (De Giorgi 2015). It is, in fact, what Hofstadter (1979) calls 'tangled hierarchies'. This observation orientation opens the way for research to describe the ways in which the legal system makes its own evolution possible. The assumptions of evolution are in the memory of the system. They are born from the fact that in each activity, the legal system acts as memory but at the same time it is its addressee. Operations and results of operations are actually the same thing. Localised self-reference always emerges, but in this case it predisposes itself to evolution.

From these first indications, it is already possible to notice how diverse the field of socio-legal research would be if it managed to free itself from the bonds that force it to employ the semantics used by the legal system to enable its action and, on the contrary, adopted the perspective of observing a complex theory of society. Not only would the field of research be different, but it would be much broader, to the point where the necessary knowledge to understand the legal system of modern society was reached.

Such sociological observation, which finds its origins in a theory of society, allows research to assess the cognitive capacity of learning that the legal system has, ie, to evaluate to what extent the legal system is able to control the conflicts that it produces. These are channeled by the system as it proceduralises them and turns them into legal problems. This is accomplished by procedures. A sociological observation of the procedure is able to observe that the route through which the conflict that represents a social problem is transformed into a legal problem is possible due to an acknowledgement about the asymmetry of the circularity of law, ie, the distinction between rule and decision. The decision allows the rule, which in turn makes the decision possible. Apart from the sociological view, the question of the construction of reality by law becomes a strictly legal discussion of the argument, a search for reasons. Even so, however, the legal system opens up to evolution.

This type of knowledge deals with another circular issue, which concerns the relationship between law and politics. Like the legal system, politics is about conflict. Its maintenance is, however, totally different. Politics seeks to reactivate the conflict and learn from this reactivation. Law, on the other hand, deals with the stabilisation of expectations, generalises them and tends to resist learning. In other words, the legal system is concerned with not questioning the assumptions of its operations every time it operates. Politics, on the contrary, can become unstable and reconstruct, at each moment, the unity of the distinction between its interests and its evaluations. Sociological observation of the production of conflicts, of the different functions that conflict acquires in law and in politics, provides this other way of investigating the evolution of law.

Sociological research can also deal with another strategy of relocating the self-reference of the law, namely the use of the idea of 'interest' and the assessment of interests. Contrary to what happens within the legal system and the semantics of interest that has been affirmed in jurisprudence, the sociological orientation is directed to describing the construction of differences and hierarchies that the legal system uses in relation to interests and values. The law resorts to the operationalisation of the unity of the difference between interests and values because in this way an interest acquires a value, because it has a value. In reality, the value of an interest is born out of an interest in a value. The function of interests and values is to keep open the variation of both parties, the interest part and the value part. Law's memory is reactivated, referring continuously to the selective remembering and forgetting of the unity of the respective difference. As the law is always and simultaneously reproduced in relation to its environment, permanent self-application of the unity of the distinction between interest and value explains the system's ability to immunise itself from a threatening environment and keep it under control. Socio-legal research must be able to observe such a strategy and avoid considering interests and values as objects, data, objectivity that the law receives from the environment where they supposedly exist, in an open manner. Once again, we are faced with assumptions of evolution that use assumptions of evolution.

If understood as indicated, sociological observation of law can describe the complex paths by which, through the activation of its memory, the legal system is capable of producing identity and difference, ie, of recognising itself by its transformations, evolving from itself and achieving stability from contingency. In this sense, sociological research opens up to great perspectives: it does not repeat what law uses as reality, it does not repeat legal semantics and their distinctions, but it observes what such semantics cannot describe, reveals what cannot be seen, and it names what cannot be named. In other words, it can name the constitutive paradox of law and observe the reality of the reality of law. It can describe, from an external perspective, what Schelsky (1980) calls 'juridical rationality' and identify how this rationality describes the dramaturgy of the paradox, ie, how it is the dramaturgy of its realisation.

Traditional sociological research repeats the law to give it meaning, criticises it to indicate a better law. This kind of research does like Prometheus in Dürrenmatt's (1992) Dramaturgy of a Rebel (Dramaturgie eines Rebellen: Prometheus), who sought to make sense of his divine existence by trying to create rational gods. It was his big mistake, said Dürrenmatt. Prometheus did not consider the fact that, rational or not, a god has no meaning. Systems theory assumes as its point of observation the deficit in the rationality of law. In its structure, law has tautology and paradox, undecidability and closure to the external. Logic also had to learn to live with Gödel, just as society learned to live with its legal system, an organism with its immune system.

Notes

1 Translated by Marco Antonio Loschiavo Leme de Barros. Originally published in Portuguese as 'A investigação sociológica do direito na teoria dos sistemas' (2016) 2(2) *Univ. Brasília Law J.* 103–119.
2 The episode was told to me by Luhmann, but he also alluded to it at his conference in Würzburg (Luhmann 1986).
3 *Rechtstatsachenforschung* in German, the language in which the first works appeared at the beginning of the last century which constituted the point of reference for all successive literature.

References

Bateson, G. (1987) *Steps to an Ecology of the Mind: Collected Essays in Anthropology, Psychiatry, Evolution, and Epistemology* (Northvale, Jason Aronson).
Borges, J.L. (1960) *El hacedor* (Madrid, Alianza).
Carrino, A. (ed) (1992) *Ehrlich-Kelsen: Scienza giuridica e sociologia del diritto* (Napoli, Edizioni Scientifiche Italiane).
Castignone, S., Ripoli, A.M. and Faralli, C. (eds) (2002) *Il diritto come profezia: Il realismo americano* (Torino, Giappichelli).
De Giorgi, R. (1980) *Wahrheit und Legitimation im Recht* (Berlin, Duncker & Humblot).
De Giorgi, R. (1984) *Azione e imputazione: Semantica e critica di un concetto nel diritto penale* (Lecce, Milella).
De Giorgi, R. (2006) *Direito, tempo e memória* (São Paulo, Quartier Latin).
De Giorgi, R. (2015) 'Giurisprudenza: È una commedia? È una tragedia?' in De Giorgi R., *Temi di filosofia del diritto II* (Lecce, Pensa MultiMedia), 33–43.
De Giorgi R. and Nuzzo, L. (2015) 'Criminology: what is it about?' in Crewe D. and Lippens R. (eds), *What Is Criminology About? Philosophical Reflections* (Abingdon, Routledge), 84–100.
Dürrenmatt, F. (1992) *Gedankenfuge* (Zürich, Diogenes).
Foucault, M. (1966) *Les mots et les choses: Une archéologie des sciences humaines* (Paris, Gallimard).
Glanville, R. (1981) 'The same is different' in Zeleny M. (ed), *Autopoiesis: A Theory of Living Organizations* (New York, Elsevier), 252–262.

Hegel, G.W.F. (1979) 'Grundlinien der Philosophie des Rechts oder Naturrecht und Staatswissenschaft im Grundrisse' in Moldenhauer E. and Michel K.M. (eds), *Hegel Werke* (Frankfurt, Suhrkamp), vol. 7, 1–456.

Hofstadter, D.R. (1979) *Gödel, Escher, Bach: An Eternal Golden Braid* (New York, Basic Books).

Kant, I. (1974) 'Kritik der reinen Vernunft' in Weischedel W. (ed), *Werke in 12 Bänden* (Frankfurt, Suhrkamp), vol. 3–4, 1–744.

Kelsen, H. (1911) *Über Grenzen zwischen juristischer und soziologischer Methode* (Tübingen, Mohr).

Kelsen, H. (1922) *Der soziologische und der juristische Staatsbegriff: Kritische Untersuchungen des Verhältnisses von Staat und Recht* (Tübingen, Mohr).

Koselleck, R. (1979) '"Neuzeit": Zur Semantik moderner Bewegungsbegriffe' in Koselleck R., *Vergangene Zukunft: Zur Semantik geschichtlicher Zeiten* (Frankfurt, Suhrkamp), 260–277.

Krawietz, W. (ed) (1976) *Theorie und Technik der Begriffsjurisprudenz* (Darmstadt, Wissenschaftliche Buchgesellschaft).

Luhmann, N. (1986) *Die soziologische Beobachtung des Rechts* (Frankfurt, Metzner).

Luhmann, N. (1993) *Das Recht der Gesellschaft* (Frankfurt, Suhrkamp).

Luhmann, N. (1997) 'Kultur als Historischer Begriff' in Luhmann N., *Gesellschaftsstruktur und Semantik: Studien zur Wissenssoziologie der modernen Gesellschaft* (Frankfurt, Suhrkamp), vol. 4, 31–54.

Luhmann, N. (2000) *Vertrauen: Ein Mechanismus der Reduktion sozialer Komplexität* (Stuttgart, Lucius & Lucius).

Luhmann, N. (2003) 'Sthenographie' in Luhmann N., Maturana H., Namiki M., Redder V. and Varela F., *Beobachter: Konvergenz der Erkenntnistheorien?* 3rd ed. (M. München, Wilhelm Fink), 119–137.

Luhmann, N. and De Giorgi, R. (1992) *Teoria della società* (Milano, FrancoAngeli).

MacCormick, N. and Weinberger, O. (1985) *Grundlagen des institutionalistischen Rechtspositivismus* (Berlin, Duncker & Humblot).

Marquard, O. (1973) *Schwierigkeiten mit der Geschichtsphilosophie* (Frankfurt, Suhrkamp).

Marquard, O. (1981) *Abschied vom Prinzipiellen* (Stuttgart, Reclam).

Marx, K.H. (1932) 'Ökonomisch-philosophischen Manuskripte aus dem Jahre 1844' in Marx K.H., *Marx-Engels-Gesamtausgabe* (Berlin, Dietz), vol. 3, 29–172.

Olivecrona, K. (1939) *Law as Fact* (Oxford, Oxford University Press).

Podgorecki, A. (1968) *Knowledge and Opinion about Law* (London, M. Robertson).

Quaderni, Fiorentini (1974–1975) *'Il socialismo giuridico: Ipotesi e letture' Quaderni Fiorentini per la Storia del Pensiero Giuridico Moderno.*

Rehbinder, M. (1970) 'Die Rechtstatsachenforschung im Schnittpunkt von Rechtssoziologie und soziologischer Jurisprudenz' *1 Jahrbuch für Rechtssoziologie und Rechtstheorie* 333–359.

Rehbinder, M. (1995) *Abhandlungen zur Rechtssoziologie* (Berlin, Duncker & Humblot).

Romano, S. (1945) *L'ordinamento giuridico* (Firenze, Sansoni).

Ross, A. (1946) *Toward a Realistic Jurisprudence: A Criticism of the Dualism in Law* (Copenhagen, E. Munksgaard).

Schelsky, H. (1980) *Die juridische Rationalität* (Opladen, Westdeutscher).

von Foerster, H. (1993) *Wissen und Gewissen: Versuch einer Brücke* (Frankfurt, Suhrkamp).

von Foerster, H. (1996) 'Was ist Gedächtnis, dass es Rückschau und Vorschau ermöglicht?' in Schmidt S.J. (ed), *Gedächtnis: Probleme und Perspektiven der interdisziplinären Gedächtnisforschung* (Frankfurt, Suhrkamp), 56–95.

von Foerster, H. and Bröcker, M. (2002) *Teil der Welt: Fraktale einer Ethik. Drama in drei Akten* (Heidelberg, Carl Auer).

Watzlawick, P. (1976) *Wie wirklich ist die Wirklichkeit? Wahn, Täuschung, Verstehen* (München, Piper).

Watzlawick, P. (1981) *Die erfundene Wirklichkeit: Wie wissen wir, was wir zu wissen glauben?* (München, Piper).

Weber, M. (2013) 'Die Objektivität sozialwissenchaftlicher und sozialpolitischer Erkenntnis' in Weber M., *Gesammelte Aufsätze zur Wissenschaftslehre* (Paderborn, Salzwasser), 146–214.

Chapter 3

Is there a need for a critical systems theory?

Lukas K. Sosoe

Introduction

This chapter aims to show how important topics the sociology of law in Niklas Luhmann's earlier works, such as *Legitimation durch Verfahren* (Luhmann 1984), were empirically informed or can be submitted to important empirical research in addition to their critical potential; even chapters such as 'Evolution of law' and 'Place of the courts in the legal system' in *Law as a Social System* (Luhmann 2004), for instance, can be submitted to empirical tests. However, Luhmann's attitude toward empirical research is quite ambiguous. Although empirical elements can be found in his works, their place is highly restricted because of the structure of his system theory. This chapter will express this ambiguous – even ambivalent – attitude and position through three claims:

1   Luhmann uses empirical research in many contributions and refers to it when necessary.
2   He mentions the need for empirical data to confirm our theories.
3   But he believed that there was no need for empirical research because sufficient empirical research had already been done, so we have stocks of facts at hand and know their consequences (to the point that such facts are even known to common sense).

I

Since his famous debate with Habermas at the beginning of the 1960s, published under the title *Theorie der Gesellschaft oder Sozialtechnologie* (*Social Theory or Social Technology*; Habermas and Luhmann 1971), Luhmann has acquired the reputation of a conservative thinker in sociology, engaged in an uncritical description of society. It is said that under the guise of scientific discourse, he was only reinforcing the powers of social oppression by renouncing every kind of contemporary political debate. As a reaction against this kind of 'neutrality', a group of sociologists have launched an assault under the name of Kritische Systemtheorie (critical systems theory), declaring their intention either to complement or to pursue a further development of systems theory. What this intention really covers is not easy to spell out in detail. Its formulations are rather vague and sometimes irritating, even puzzling. How might the following aim of one of the books on the perspectives of critical systems theory be understood? 'This volume contains perspectives defending very different critical positions (or not really) and which have in common to reflect the aforementioned double pre-formation' (where 'pre-formation' means latent social functions; Möller and Siri 2016: 10). It is said that the contributions in that volume endeavor to 'examine the concrete common point between systems theory and other current theoretical approaches as well as concrete research fields' (Möller and Siri 2016: 10).

To what extent the contributions are critical and what the object of the critique is, however, are quite unclear. It is said instead that the intention of the book is 'less for showing a critical attitude toward Luhmann than asking the question as to how we are to understand the relation between the object/ the empirical and the critique' and 'which kind of presuppositions should be made in a modern theory' (Möller and Siri 2016: 10). Other contributions overtly list a number of elements for the purpose of transforming the purely descriptive character of systems theory into a critical systems theory (Amstutz and Fischer-Lescano 2013: 14–16).[1]

Unless 'empirical research' and 'descriptive approach' have different meanings, the new challenge of the empirical agenda of systems theory runs obviously against critical systems theory. Hence the questions raised by the agenda of empirical research within systems theory. How are we to understand it in the light of the belief that Luhmann's approach is only descriptive and that it leads to the legitimation of unjust existing social and political structures? If 'descriptive' means 'empirical', is the new agenda of empirical research not claiming what is criticised and partly rejected by the programme of critical systems theory? (1) What is the purpose of the empirical agenda on the threefold levels, beginning with the early publications of Niklas Luhmann? (2) How are we to consider the publications where Luhmann explicitly claims to use an empirical method or draws attention to the need for an empirical approach to confirm an idea? (3) What does the agenda of empirical research imply if we take into account the epistemology underlying Luhmann's systems theory? In other words, how do we make sense of the empirical research agenda in the context of an autological theory?

Whether the setting of the empirical agenda is a continuation of the programme of critical systems theory or not is difficult to know exactly, even if the reproach of the mere descriptive character of Luhmann's work may have something in common with it: reconsidering or evaluating Luhmann's systems theory in the light of the need (or not) for empirical research design. Even if it seems opposed to the claim about the uncritical character of Luhmann's theory of social systems, it may still have an element in common with that claim. It may insinuate that systems theory may be perhaps a good theory for some people but is not very useful for those engaged in empirical research. Must a good theory be necessarily a theory for empirical research? Is the criterion for a valid theory its appropriateness for empirical research? Should the value of a theory be measured by its ability to favour empirical research?

Setting an empirical agenda for systems theory may have two different meanings or motives: a stronger and a weaker one. According to the stronger meaning, the agenda may presuppose what many commentators have already said about Luhmann's works in general (eg, Blankenburg 1984). Rottleuthner (1989a, 1989b) asks whether Luhmann's sociological works can tell us something sensible or useful about modern societies and let us understand something which has not even been discussed. It is said that systems theory is not useful for empirical research in social sciences and humanities, as though social research must be empirical in order to be good or valid research. For some critics, systems theory does not even deserve to be called scientific because it is not empirically verifiable; it cannot be falsified, in a Popperian sense. It is even said that it is not useful at all. Some commentators, like Di Fabio, mitigate their judgment and refer only to Luhmann's introduction of the concept of autopoiesis, highlighting the usefulness of, for instance, *Legitimation durch Verfahren* for the German Federal Tribunal (Di Fabio 2000: 140).[2]

While the stronger motive is entirely negative and based on a narrow and specific conception of a scientific theory, the second one admits that a part of Luhmann's work is truly helpful. It is impressive and gives trust. But would an empirical agenda be a remedy to the supposed difficulties in understanding Luhmann's work? Since Di Fabio's (2000) article is about jurists' reception of Luhmann in Germany, the expectation was practice oriented. The stronger motive could have as an implication the development of an agenda of empirical research. Its critique is based on the missing empirical falsifiability of Luhmann's systems theory. It has been pointed out in relation to this critique that

> whether or not a statement is capable of refutation through empirical testing may depend not upon the content of the theory, but upon the methods that are available to the researchers. Some statements may not be capable of refutation simply because existing research methods are not able to determine their validity empirically.
>
> (King and Thornhill 2005: 207)

The second way of understanding the setting of an empirical agenda, the weaker one, is that it is only a part of Luhmann's work, not the whole – specifically the latest publications – that cannot be useful for empirical research. This opinion does justice to much work published by Luhmann in the sociology of law and of organisations and administration. An important part of these publications is unknown to the large public, even to 'Luhmannians' (Luhmann 2018, 2019a, 2019b, 2020). As far as his earlier works are concerned, the title of the first volume in a recently published series is interesting in this perspective (Luhmann 2018): *Schriften zur Organisation 1: Die Wirklichkeit der Organisation* (*The reality of the organisation*).

Would it be incorrect, according to the weaker motive, to take into account the application of systems theory in different disciplines where many scholars have been conducting applied and empirical research? In education, for instance, or in social work, or in the sociology of development, as Mascareño (2010) and others (see Gripp-Hagelstange 1997) are doing? If this is not sufficient evidence that systems theory can be used in a certain way for empirical research, why shouldn't we take their contributions seriously? In this case, what is behind the new agenda for empirical research if the work of these scholars is, as far as we know, not discredited by the scientific community? Is the empirical agenda an attempt to transform Luhmann's systems theory or to apply it to existing problems?

If we consider Luhmann's first publications, dedicated to the sociology of organisation and administration – which can be considered empirical research on these topics – it will be difficult to contend that his systems theory in general cannot be useful for empirical research. Perhaps the first publications are not known, or they are not taken into account because it may be argued that Luhmann had not begun developing his theory of social systems at that time but used other categories instead. One would affirm that his systems theory really started with the concept of autopoietic systems and his later theoretical construction. However, there is no doubt that *Grundrechte als Institution* (Luhmann 1965) and *Legitimation durch Verfahren* (Luhmann 1984), published in the 1960s and 1980s, are systemic-theoretical analyses of fundamental rights and of the major institutions of a democratic society. But if Luhmann has published empirically relevant works or drawn upon empirical research for his works, why set an empirical agenda? For what and for whom?

A closer look at Luhmann's publications in general suggests that the opinion that his works cannot be empirically useful in social research does not consider a few of his works based on empirical theories. Of course, it is one thing to use empirical research done by other people in one's publications, and another to conduct empirical research oneself. Luhmann's use of empirical data not only in the application of systems theory but in the study of different social subsystems is sufficient evidence that he did not always and in every study underestimate empirical research or consider it useless, as his statements sometimes suggest. He even draws upon a few empirical theories in the treatment of topics like elections and judicial procedures in a democratic society. Is empirical research merely quantitative research? Could we not consider research based on empirical concepts to be empirical research?

The best example is Luhmann's analysis of democratic legal and political structures in the book *Legitimation durch Verfahren* (Luhmann 1984), which has become, as already stated, a reference book in the doctrine of the German Federal Republic. Unless empirical research is defined differently or is taken to mean quantitative analysis, no reader would hesitate to consider this book empirical research, since the interpretation of the different social structures reconstructed by Luhmann is based on a theory of social learning. It is worth saying a few words on the content.

Electoral procedures for the legislative have an official intention: their aim is to find 'specially qualified people able to occupy posts of public decisions, people able to decide correctly, ie according to the will of the people and who will be in this sense the true representatives of the people' (Luhmann 1984: 155). Since the people need to be seriously informed about everything, Luhmann's question was: how can a people's will be expressed by elections and satisfy the aim of elections? The information needed to reach the goal of elections will exclude everybody. No one can be totally informed as elections expect us to be. And the conditions for the choice of the best person to occupy a public office is a chimera. We do not need much empirical research to know that, we just need to have a look at the political arena and see whether our heads of state are the best among all countries (Luhmann 1984: 160). Even if we do not conduct an empirical study to know this, no one will say that it is not a part of our day-to-day experience in modern democracies. But if elections do not help in choosing the best people able to govern, what are their functions? For Luhmann, they have a latent function: they help among, other things, to canalise discontent and absorb protests.

Luhmann's (1984) thesis is that traditional theories of democracy are outdated and no longer appropriate for the description and understanding of modern societies. The political reality they have contributed to creating can no longer be grasped adequately from their own perspective. So what is called 'the crisis of democracy' is not a real crisis but the impression transmitted by a false representation of the political reality in a functionally differentiated society. Every kind of legitimation of the state based on traditional theories of democracy is necessarily mistaken. But if reference to these contributions is insufficient to prove Luhmann's ambiguous attitude toward empirical research, a short presentation of the basic elements of the epistemology of systems theory will let us understand the place he assigned to empirical research.

II

Luhmann's relation to empirical research is highly complex and ambiguous, not only because of his polemics against empirical research but because of the very premises of systems theory and its conception of what reality is. What does it mean to set an empirical agenda in the context of an autological theory?

Autological theories are theories which justify themselves. They are self-referential. They do not presuppose an object and a knowing subject. To proceed autologically means, for Luhmann, 'to take one's own conclusions (seriously) into account. Such a circle is not "vicious". And the empirical theory must be complex enough in order to accomplish the autological conclusion' (Luhmann 1994: 9). Consequently, self-referential theories have no pre-given object to be known, and they have no determined point of departure. All that they have are self-referential relations to which they themselves belong (Gripp-Hagelstange 1997). They are not to be conceived deductively, as empirical research presupposes.

Even while describing his theory as autological, Luhmann still refers to empirical theory as a constitutive element of the kind of theory he is talking about. The only condition is that the empirical theory must be complex enough. Does this argue for the need for an empirical theory? On the one hand, it seems that talking about empirical research based on Luhmann's systems theory suggests that we are still in the classical ideas that there is an outside world independent of social theories and that the task of research consists in comparing our theories with reality and seeing whether they are correct. This is not the conception put forward by Luhmann's systems theory. But why is he speaking about an empirical theory which must be complex enough? Is it meant ironically?

A closer look at Luhmann's works and the epistemology of his systems theory gives us a differentiated idea of what he did and thought about empirical research. He resorted to empirical research for some of his works. In his works, he developed ideas that empirical research has to confirm. Furthermore, many social scientists and sociologists have tried to apply Luhmann's systems theory, so that the relation between systems theory and the other disciplines must be carefully studied. How is the relation of the application of systems theory to other fields to be considered? Could these fields be conceived as application fields of systems theory? In this case, could systems theory itself be seen as a kind of meta-theory or super theory applied to different, more or less specific fields of knowledge? Since our topic is empirical research, must these branches of knowledge not be considered as the realities that systems theory is trying to grasp? If systems theory considers other systems – the legal system, the educational system, the economic system, etc – as different realities, should we then not enlarge or redefine our concept of empirical? This cannot be the same concept as in traditional sociological theories. What does our agenda of empirical research take to be reality?

III

In systems theory, reality is defined by a self-referential operation. That means that by defining its environment, a system defines what is reality and what belongs to a mere possibility. Systems construct their reality by making sense of themselves and the environment. The world and its reality are the result of a system's operations. There is nothing given which is not the result of system information, 'an effect of cognitive construction. There is not "one" reality, not one realm of "being" as in the traditional old European ontology but rather a plurality of realities created through cognition. Cognition produces reality by producing system/environmental distinctions' (Moeller 2006: 70). If reality is constructed by a system, then the empirical agenda raises some problems.

The setting of an empirical agenda for systems theory must clarify its intention. Why do we need an empirical agenda for systems theory? The agenda must be able to say whether its purpose is an answer to those who believe that Luhmann's systems theory cannot be used for empirical research or an attempt for further development of systems theory in an empirical perspective. Believing that Luhmann's systems theory cannot be a useful empirical tool is different from attempting to point out the fact that he ignores or does not sufficiently develop the empirical dimension of his theory, although this development is possible. In this last sense, the empirical agenda will just go further in the sense of Luhmann's systems theory and not change it, but keep its fundamental concepts. Setting the agenda will promote Luhmann's systems theory. But what does it mean to develop a suspected missing empirical aspect of a theory criticised for being only an uncritical description of a particular vision of social reality? What are we to understand by the expression 'uncritical' in the context of a theory of social systems? Are the basic concepts of systems theory not critical enough, beginning with the term 'description' itself or, in a Luhmannian language, 'observation'?

In his later writings, Luhmann's systems theory takes its distance from empirical research as well as from the idea that there is a reality which sociology has to describe, because the sociologist's position and the objects the sociologist studies are not justifiable. Sociologists believe themselves to be in a higher position. Luhmann writes that the

> sociological, the methodological confrontation between quantitative and qualitative methods distracts from the real problems. It leaves unclarified how one could transform the distance to the object into a gain of knowledge and how one could at the same time confirm and surpass socially competent people (who are supposed to answer questions) in social communication.
>
> (Luhmann 1997: 37)

Of course, for Luhmann, the fact that the corresponding statements 'are treated as data does not give any answer to the question' (1997: 37). Systems theory takes its distance because traditional sociological methods, including empirical research, instruct researchers to behave as if they were a unique subject in order to make the traditional logical and ontological difference between thinking and being (Luhmann 1997: 36). This goal may be good. But what gets lost with this difference in research is that 'the modern society in which the researcher also has to do his job is a polycontextural system which allows a plurality of descriptions of its complexity' (Luhmann 1997: 36). From the perspective of systems theory in Luhmann's later works, empirical research is not really useful because 'many facts are already known and there is no need for more empirical research; and facts which are known have more serious consequences as common sense knows and empirical sociology can discover' (Luhmann 1997: 42–43). Nevertheless, he is not against the use of empirical data. He even insists on its importance as a complement of social research. We need data. But research based on empirical data alone is trivial and poor. To what extent do we need data if common sense knows already the facts and their serious consequences? But if we need empirical data, how are they to be conceived in order to be adequately and fruitfully used by systems theory? The problem is whether there are sufficiently adequate empirical methods to use in the context of systems theory. Luhmann denies it: 'the repertoire of empirical methods in present day sociology is very limited and completely inadequate for [...] self-observing objects with highly structured complexity' (1992: 1428).

Does this mean that an agenda of empirical social research is a call for 'impoverishing' social reality, which is the subject matter of social studies? This conclusion should not, perhaps, be the last word. We may continue doing empirical research if necessary, and this is not only, as Luhmann says, as a complement which assigns to it only an ancillary function. But it would be an epistemic choice between a strong acceptance of the premises of Luhmann's systems theory and a decision to embrace a kind of ecumenical or pluralistic methodology able to do justice to the complexity as well as the nature of the problems of modern society, which may need empirically specialised study. The result would be using systems theory as a tool to help grasp the polycontexturality of modern society without disregarding the usefulness of some empirical approaches. Luhmann's position can be understood as a kind of irritation at the way and ease with which empirical research programmes are funded and the credibility they enjoy in our society. Appreciating and using systems theory should not be a prison keeping us from looking for appropriate approaches according to the problem at stake. The ambiguity in Luhmann's attitude can be understood as a reaction against the fact that we do not yet have empirical studies which are good enough to be useful for systems theory.

Notes

1 It is said that 'the systems theory of the world society articulates itself as critical systems theory in going beyond the mere description of the structural problems of social structures and submits the social structures to a critique which has a

connection to the present post-materialistic critique' (Amstutz and Fischer-Lescano 2013: 14–16). In the same passage, the common points between systems theory and critical systems theory are mentioned.

2 Di Fabio (2000) insists, among other things, on how Luhmann's ideas have been adopted into the doctrines of the German Federal Constitutional Court in its case law concerning the protection of human-rights administrative procedures. The court has raised *Legitimation durch Verfahren* to the level of discussions on constitutional law. But with the autopoietic turn, judges who were expecting elements of systems theory to apply to legal issues with which they were confronted have ceased to follow the intermediary and later publications. They are no longer able to follow a theory which understands law as jurists understand it – and this does not necessarily mean that jurists understand the theory which understands them.

References

Amstutz, M. and Fischer-Lescano, A. (eds) (2013) *Kritische Systemtheorie: Zur Evolution einer normativen Theorie* (Bielefeld, Transcript).

Blankenburg, E. (1984) 'The poverty of evolutionism: a critique of Teubner's case for the "reflexive law"' *18*(2) *Law Soc. Rev.* 273–289.

Di Fabio, U. (2000) 'Luhmann im Recht: Die juristische Rezeption soziologischer Beobachtung' in Gripp-Hangelstange, H. (ed), *Niklas Luhmanns Denken: Interdisziplinäre Einflüsse und Wirkungen* (Constance, Universitätsverlag).

Gripp-Hagelstange, H. (1997) *Niklas Luhmann: Eine erkenntnistheoretische Einführung* (Paderborn, Wilhelm Fink).

Habermas, J. and Luhmann, N. (1971) *Theorie der Gesellschaft oder Sozialtechnologie: Was leistet die Systemforschung?* (Frankfurt, Suhrkamp).

King, M. and Thornhill, C. (2005) *Luhmann's Theory of Politics and Law* (London, Palgrave).

Luhmann, N. (1965) *Grundrechte als Institution: Ein Beitrag zur politischen Soziologie* (Berlin, Duncker & Humblot).

Luhmann, N. (1984) *Legitimation durch Verfahren* (Frankfurt, Suhrkamp).

Luhmann, N. (1992) 'Operational closure and structural coupling: the differentiation of the legal system' *13*(5) *Cardozo Law Rev.* 1419–1441.

Luhmann, N. (1994) *Die Wissenschaft der Gesellschaft* (Frankfurt, Suhrkamp).

Luhmann, N. (1997) *Die Gesellschaft der Gesellschaft* (Frankfurt, Suhrkamp).

Luhmann, N. (2004) *Law as a Social System* (Oxford, Oxford University Press).

Luhmann, N. (2018) *Schriften zur Organisation 1: Die Wirklichkeit der Organisation* (Berlin, Springer).

Luhmann, N. (2019a) *Schriften zur Organisation 2: Theorie organisierter Sozialsysteme* (Berlin, Springer).

Luhmann, N. (2019b) *Schriften zur Organisation 3: Gesellschaftliche Differenzierung* (Berlin, Springer).

Luhmann, N. (2020) *Schriften zur Organisation 4: Reform und Beratung* (Berlin, Springer).

Mascareño, A. (2010) 'Soziologische Erkenntnisblockaden und der lateinamerikanische Weg der Moderne' *26 Leviathan* 336–356.

Moeller, H.-G. (2006) *Luhmann Explained: From Souls to Systems* (Chicago, Open Court).

Möller, K. and Siri, J. (eds.) (2016) *Systemtheorie und Gesellschaftskritik: Perspektiven der Kritischen Systemthorie* (Bielefeld, Transcript).

Rottleuthner, H. (1989a) 'A purified sociology of law: Niklas Luhmann on the autonomy of law' *23*(5) *Law Soc. Rev.* 779–797.

Rottleuthner, H. (1989b) 'The limits of law: the myth of a regulatory crisis' *17*(3) *International J. Soc. Law* 273–285.

Chapter 4

Changing maps

Empirical legal autopoiesis[1]

John Paterson and Gunther Teubner

I

The idea of self-organisation was simultaneously invented in different fields of knowledge, in the natural as well as in the social sciences. Under such exotic titles as *entre le cristal et la fumée* (Atlan 1979), dissipative structures (Prigogine 1976), synergetics (Haken 1977), self-referential processes (Hofstadter 1979), self-substitutive orders (Luhmann 1981), autopoiesis (Maturana and Varela 1980), morphogenetic fields (Sheldrake 1988), holographic order (Bohm 1981), and second-order cybernetics (von Förster 1981), new theories on the spontaneous emergence of order were spontaneously emerging. Then these ideas began to influence each other in a transdisciplinary discussion and form a common web of theoretical constructs. Today, rather than merging into a unified theory of self-organisation, these interconnected constructs rotate freely in a theory space, *la galaxie 'auto'* (Dumouchel and Dupuy 1983). And finally, this self-organising 'heaven of concepts' confers its blessings on down-to-earth empirical research: scientific foundations are funding significant projects in which self-organisation stimulates different research questions and the development of new empirical tools.[2]

While such projects are flourishing in areas as diverse as economy, psychotherapy and flamenco, in 'law and society' there has so far been a paucity of empirical research on self-organisation.[3] Is this just the usual theory hostility of empirically minded scholars? Is it American empirical imperialism? Is it the *Berührungsangst* of speculative Euro-wimps? Perhaps explanations such as these are somewhat too superficial to account for the anomalous situation in law and society. Rather, the anomaly can be traced back to certain peculiarities of legal sociology as a field of knowledge. It seems that the long-lasting and deep hiatus between theory construction and empirical research is actually deepened by the emergence of theories of self-organisation and autopoiesis. This is our first thesis. Second, if we look more closely at concrete, detailed, historical research carried out in the name of autopoiesis, we can discern clear discontinuities with 'normal' practices of empirical research. Autopoiesis calls for a re-definition of empirical work and requires different empirical tools – tools which are capable of analysing *the transformational dynamics of recursive meaning processes*. As a consequence, everything changes: research questions, the phenomena to be identified, the concepts to be made operational and the analytical instruments. But, as if that weren't enough, there are even stronger anomalies in the socio-legal relationship between the empirical and the theoretical. The constructivist orientation of legal autopoiesis, we submit in our third thesis, works against the omnipotence fantasies inherent in the process of empirical falsification. Legal autopoiesis is not anti-empirical, but it does suggest a role for empirical research which is different from straightforward Popperian theory-killing. It suggests, instead, a quasi-therapeutic relationship between the speculators and the data collectors. But who, then, is the therapist and who is the patient?

II

Why is there a structural hiatus between theory and empirical research in law and society? In the classics of legal sociology, Marx's historical methods, Durkheim's *choses sociales* and the ideal-typical method in Weber's interpretive sociology were guarantees of the unity of empirical research and grand theories of law. But then the 'theory disaster' happened with the introduction of modern empirical methods. 'The dissolution in data and their recombination with the help of newly developed methods of data analysis destroyed the high level of theorising which had been built up in the classics without being able to substitute it adequately' (Luhmann 1990: 410). Today, the field is still suffering from this deep hiatus, which renders theory rather empty and empiricism rather blind. Or to put it more mildly, empirical research in law and society has developed a highly sophisticated methodology which is, however, based on poor and rather ad hoc theorising, while theorising about law and society has become more and more philosophical and speculative – relying, however, on poor and rather ad hoc empirical support.

And today the hiatus is deepening. Desperately seeking theory, empirical legal sociologists are giving in to the temptation of trying economic models and theories for their data, with the predictable result that they are losing their sociological identity. The theory camp, on the other hand, is tempted to follow the famous 'linguistic turn' in sociology, and thus sober law-and-society people are transformed into esoteric literary critics and Nietzsche-Heidegger-Derrida-style philosophers who express their sarcastic contempt for systematic data collection and patient data analysis.

Usually it is the micro-macro problem that is held responsible for the empirico-theoretical gap. Empirical methods are good at gathering individual data at the micro level of legal action and aggregate data at the macro level of socio-legal relations. But they fail when it comes to analysing law's 'organised complexity', which good theory regards as central to understanding law as a social phenomenon. Without denying the importance of the micro-macro difference, we prefer to name, blame and claim another famous *petite différence* as responsible for the great hiatus: the difference between law as operation and law as observation (von Förster 1981). This little difference has sharply divided socio-legal theoreticians and empiricists. Empirical analysis has opted for first-order observation of the law. It takes legal action as simple operations, as spatiotemporal events, which can be correlated in their empirical models with other social events. This drives empirical analysis of law in two directions: toward models of logical and mathematical formalisation on the one hand and toward attempts at causal explanation and prediction on the other (Black 1989). In contrast, ambitious sociological theories of law – whether from Paris, Frankfurt, Edinburgh or Bielefeld–are usually second-order observations. They see legal action itself as observation, as a trinity of utterance, information and understanding, as the recursive transformation of differences, as constructing a special space of meaning and an autonomous world of knowledge. This drives socio-legal theories deeper and deeper into the hermeneutic tradition, in a tradition that allows for sophisticated analyses of 'the operation called *Verstehen*' but ridicules attempts at formalisation, causal explanation and prediction. And attempts to combine both traditions are sucked into the black hole at the centre of the Bermuda Triangle of formalisation, causal explanation and hermeneutics.

If this is an adequate sketch of the intellectual map, how do self-reference and autopoiesis change the somewhat desperate outlook for law and society? At first sight, it looks like Columbus's egg, as Ewald (1987) has called it. It nourishes hope for a recombination of both the empirical-analytical and the normative-hermeneutic traditions. It seems to promise a bridge between law as operation and law as observation, since it compels us to combine first- and second-order analyses. Since law is defined as a closed system of self-reproductive observing operations, legal action is seen as being at the same time both operation and observation. This requires the normative tradition to leave Popper's World 3 and to search for 'law in action' as its social base, and it requires the empirical tradition to include in its observations the complex chains of normative observations of the 'law in the books'.

But a closer look reveals that autopoiesis offers no easy synthesis. It burdens the three traditions – the hermeneutic, the formal and the causal orientation – with an almost unbearable task: how to cope with self-reference? Hermeneutics, with its long tradition of dealing with self-referential relations, reflexivity, paradoxes and hermeneutic circles, is obviously in the best position. This explains the rapid development of autopoiesis – a theory that paradoxically was invented as a 'mechanical' explanation of emergent phenomena such as life and cognition against mystifying vitalistic and holistic proposals – in hermeneutically oriented theories of law. In a view of law as a concatenation of communicative events based on a code which deparadoxifies a basic self-referential relation, autopoiesis has strong (s)elective affinities with discourse analysis as developed by the *maître-penseurs* of poststructuralism: Foucault, Lyotard and Derrida.[4]

The tradition of formalisation in legal theory has much greater difficulties with autopoiesis. The reason is that the paradoxes of self-reference pose an enormous challenge for a formal calculus. It is true that Hofstadter's famous book on the enigmas of reflexivity and self-reference has had a certain impact on legal theory (Hofstadter 1979: 692ff., 1985: 70ff.; Suber 1990). However, sophisticated attempts to come to terms with self-reference like *Laws of Form* by Spencer-Brown (1972), the development of a multi-value logic by Günther (1976a, 1976b) and 'A calculus for self-reference' by Varela (1975) have up to now found only one resonance in legal sociology, which is Niklas Luhmann's discussion of the legal paradox and the binary coding of law (Luhmann 1988, 1992a, 1992b, 1993a, 1995).

However, the situation for causal explanation and prediction, the precious hope of orderly empirical work in law and society that would transform it into a real science, is disastrous. For causal analysis, self-reference is an explosive. The blast comes from a theory of recursive systems and from a concept of non-trivial machines; and the blast is so strong because these explosive concepts were developed not just from the hermeneutic softies of the *Geisteswissenschaften* but from the hard-liners of the exact sciences. According to the sociologists Krohn and Küppers (1990: 114), who deal with problems of the legal regulation of social fields, the results look like this:

> [i]n non-linear systems with a recursive dynamics [...] there are only few cases in which prediction of the system's development is possible, even if their mechanism is known, the systems are deterministic and disturbances do not occur. [...] Due to recursion, even very small deviations in the initial conditions are reinforced in such a way that similar starting constellations are leading after a very short time period to totally opposite system developments. [...] In the case of a non-linear and recursive system dynamics [...] no prediction of the system's development is possible.

And if law as a social system is correctly defined as one of these non-trivial machines (that is, as one of the deterministic systems whose input-output relationship is not invariant but is determined in a self-referring way by the machines' previous output), then, in the words of von Förster (1981: 201), 'for all practical reasons they are unpredictable: an output once observed for a given input will most likely not be the same for the same input given later'. The only hope for causal explanation and prediction is a trivialisation of law and society, their social construction as trivial machines – something which happily coincides with the triviality of certain results of attitude and impact research, results that everyone familiar with the fields already knew in advance.

So what does this mean for the chances of empirical research in the autopoietic framework? Well, they look excellent for all kinds of historical analysis, for genealogical and archaeological digging in historical texts and for qualitative research techniques, case studies of formal organisation, ethnomethodological types of socio-legal interaction, discourse analysis, for 'critical empiricism'. And indeed these are the research techniques that are mainly used in the empirical projects. For static correlations (of 'the more x, the more y' variety), however, the chances look rather bleak – except perhaps for a vague hope nourished by cognitive psychologists that one day they will be replaced by ambitious 'empirical systems research', which would be able to model the recursive interaction of macro-parameters in order to identify bifurcations and attractors in dynamic systems (Schiepek 1989).

III

But before we get carried away, is not autopoietic empiricism simply an oxymoron in any event? Have we not been told about autopoieticists, 'they do not need any empirical evidence' (Rottleuthner 1989: 281)? Is it not the case that autopoiesis is simply incompatible with the dominant working orientation of orderly empirical research – where the task of theory is causal explanation and prediction of empirical facts, and the task of empirical research is the reality test of hypotheses derived from theoretical constructs? Indeed, it is incompatible. Viewed from the constructivist position of autopoiesis, every element of this statement about the empirico-theoretical relationship – causal explanation, prediction, reality tests – is flawed.

To put the counter-position bluntly:

1. Empirical research is by no means closer to the reality of the outside world than theory. Even from empirical experience, we know that often the opposite is true. The hard facts about the external world that empirical research pretends to produce are in reality highly artificial constructs, excessively selective abstractions, mere internal artefacts of the scientific discourse that are both as real and as fictional as are theoretical constructs.
2. The real role of empirical research does not lie in dull falsification. It is in the surprise value of its self-produced data. Empirical world

constructions in law and society do not need to be destructive of theories. Rather, they could play a maeutic role in the birth of theories in the spirit of empiricism.

3. Causal explanation and prediction are grossly overestimated in law and society. They are only special cases of theoretical work that are indeed very rare, and – what is more important – they by no means exhaust the potential of theoretical explanation.

4. For autopoiesis, theoretical explanation of empirical results means that the theory reformulates these artefacts of perception in new contexts in order to analyse – let us repeat the central formula – the transformational dynamics of recursive meaning processes.

Let us take a concrete example of the social effects of legislation in order discuss this counter-position. Occupational health and safety in Britain's offshore oil industry constitutes a well-defined area, which has seen considerable regulatory development over its 30-year history. Traditional empirical research on the effectiveness of law and implementation research suggests the construction of a network of dependent and independent variables among which we can identify correlations and find out their causal connections (eg, Rottleuthner 1987: 54ff.). The usual causality chain – as Mayntz (1983), for example, tells us – works like this: political goal definition → legislative act → legal norm → motivation of implementation staff → motivation of actors in the field → deviation/sanction/incentive → social behaviour → social effects. In our concrete example of offshore health and safety regulation, it is possible to trace this sort of causality chain as follows.

During the early days of the offshore industry in the mid-1960s, there was no detailed regulation of occupational health and safety, simply an instruction from the government that those involved should follow an industry code of practice. When a serious accident occurred in 1965, the inadequacies of this approach became evident and an inquiry chaired by a lawyer recommended that 'a statutory code with credible sanctions' be implemented to provide for the safety of workers in the industry (Ministry of Power 1967, para 10.2(i)). This recommendation was accepted by the government of the day, which introduced a bill to Parliament that eventually became law as the Mineral Workings (Offshore Installations) Act 1971. This provided a framework for the development over a period of years of detailed regulations by the regulators (mainly the Petroleum Engineering Division of the Department of Energy), covering every aspect of the industry from the design and construction of offshore installations to the content of first aid kits.[5] These regulations were then implemented, and the oil companies they were aimed at complied with or deviated from them, ultimately producing an effect on the level of safety that existed in the industry.

We might summarise this on the basis of the foregoing causal chain as: political goal definition by the Ministry of Power inquiry → introduction of a bill to Parliament by the government → passing of the Mineral Workings (Offshore Installations) Act 1971 → development and implementation of detailed regulations by the regulators → compliance/deviation by the industry → effects on safety. In accordance with this understanding of the regulatory chain, when questions are asked about continuing safety problems in the industry we find concern about delay in getting detailed regulations into place[6] and about the toughness of the regulators' enforcement (Carson 1981). In other words, control of safety will be achieved when detailed regulations are in place telling the industry what it must do and when these are being enforced by the regulators.

Autopoiesis, however, forces us to break up this causal chain of events and replace it by – let us condense everything into one formulation – *a multitude of autonomous but interfering fields of action in each of which, in an acausal and simultaneous manner, recursive processes of transformation of differences take place*. To put it more simply, a single *horizontal* chain of causal relations is replaced by a multitude of *vertical* chains of recursions. We can indicate this shift graphically as in Figure 4.1.

Moreover, our framework gives us a new understanding of social regulation through law. Understanding these vertical chains of recursions as operationally closed means that each constructs information internally – there are no input-output relationships between, say, the regulators and the industry. As a consequence, attempts by the regulators to steer the industry by means of prescriptive regulations backed by sanctions and incentives must be understood in a fundamentally different way. Such attempts can only ever be a multitude of *self*-steering processes. More specifically, this self-steering must be understood

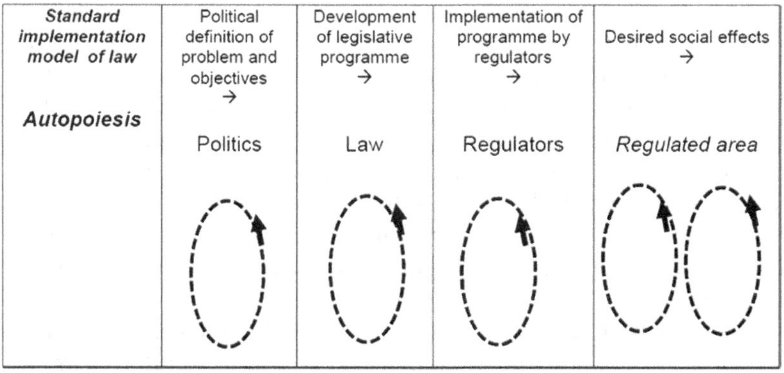

Figure 4.1 The shift from a horizontal chain of causal relations to vertical chains of recursions.

as the *minimisation of a difference*, an attempt to reduce the difference between the current situation and the desired one. This definition is consistent with all forms of steering, but in the context of a recursively closed system of communicative operations the difference is itself internally constructed. Thus, offshore safety regulators construct the current situation according to their own code and similarly construct a desired situation and apply their own *programme of difference minimisation* in an attempt to arrive at it. Given that the industry constructs reality according to its own code and steers according to its own difference-minimising programme, the limits of regulatory ambition become clear. In other words, regulation is possible only as self-regulation within each of these recursive processes. Regulation over the boundaries of action fields is impossible. Chains of causality need to be replaced by simultaneous events of structural coupling.

This is not to say, of course, that regulatory attempts produce no effects, only that those effects cannot properly be regarded as steering in the sense implied by traditional theories. Instead, these effects arise from the construction of differences by the regulators and their attempts to minimise them, but depend on the internal construction of differences by the industry and its attempts to minimise them.[7]

This is a suggestive idea, but can it be made empirical? The task for empirical research in these circumstances would become one of enquiring into several chains of difference minimisation and into their interferences. We would have to retell in detail several divergent stories of self-regulation in the political arena, in the legislative chambers and courtrooms, in the offices of the regulatory agencies and the managerial suites of corporate actors and on the platforms of the oil rigs. The question would be one of how, in each of these stories, the events common to them are idiosyncratically reconstructed and processed in the meaning context of their specific difference-minimisation programmes. To be clear, such a division of the regulatory chain into divergent stories does not imply that autopoiesis is bound to discover regulatory failure. Autopoiesis is not in some sense the opposite of regulatory success, as Nahamowitz (1992) seems to believe. Instead, understanding steering as self-steering means that the theory accounts for regulatory failure and success in ways different from theories where linear causality is assumed. So if we find that our different stories of recursive operations travel together for a time in a common direction instead of diverging, then we can readily speak of regulatory success.

The crucial question, then, is how to disentangle the connections of these multiple cascades of concatenated differences. To repeat, we do not mean causal influences, but the acausal synchronisation of ongoing parallel processes. And our theory tells us that there is not one magic formula of structural coupling; rather, there are several types of synchronisation. In order to find out how the different recursive processes are interrelated, we need first of all to find out how they are closed to each other. *L'ouvert s'appuie sur le fermé* (Morin 1986: 203ff.) – this is not a matter of theoretical definition but a matter of empirical variation. Autopoiesis theory suggests a variety of closure mechanisms in the relations between meaning systems, to which correspond a variety of ways in which they are open to each other: from ad hoc contacts to systematic linkages and long-term co-evolution. Success or failure of regulation depends – this is our guiding hypothesis – on the specific qualities of interwovenness of several recursive meaning processes, which in turn depend on the qualities of their mutual closure.

This compels us to ask a twofold question when it comes to detailed empirical research:

1   How can we identify concretely the multitude of elementary acts – meaning operations – that constitute the autopoietic closure of the various processes involved?
2   How can we identify the different types of mutual re-contextualisation that are responsible for a meeting of these closed discourses?

Applying the first question to our example: are the legislative process and the implementation field autopoietic systems? Although we have so far spoken as if they are, for the sake of the argument, this is not in fact a question we can answer theoretically, but only by empirical observation. Autopoiesis theory does not impose a set of pre-existing systems but rather compels us to observe the concrete interactions in legislative chambers, lobby halls and the technological processes in our implementation field in order to discover the systemicity of our research object. Strangely enough, this reliance on empirical knowledge runs counter to the opinion of empirically minded researchers who tend to treat this as an 'analytical' question, namely the identification of a 'system' as the somewhat arbitrary conceptual selection of the field of enquiry according to the concrete research interests. In contrast, the system concept of autopoiesis is much closer to empirical reality than the abstract models of empirical research.

Unlike the semi-autonomous fields which, as Griffiths (1986: 35) tells us, owe their systemic character only to the research designs of legal sociologists, our decision about their systemicity is dependent upon observable self-organising processes in the social world. Autopoietic systems are produced by self-organising processes in the social world, not by scientific observers. We need careful empirical observation, therefore, in order to find out which operations are recursively linking up to other operations in our field so that in their concatenation they gain the autonomy of an autopoietic system. In the area of the social effectiveness of law, we researchers are by no means free to define the concrete legislative process as a system. Empirical observation would rather compel us to split it up into four or five more or less loosely coupled recursive processes: the ongoing power game of the political actors, the quasi-scientific policy talk of the experts, the profit-oriented calculations of the lobbyists and the doctrinal arguments and constructions of the lawyers. If we are interested in regulation, we have to identify not only the concrete binary codes that are used in each of these processes and the concrete rules of the game which they have developed over time but especially the specific programmes of difference minimisation that they follow at any given moment: strategies of interest and power, reputational gains, policy objectives, risk minimisation, reduction of deviance.

In addition, we will have to split up our regulated field into a similar multitude of recursive processes. For example, when the object of regulation is a specific technology in economic organisations, such as offshore installations, does the concrete technology form a system? Autopoiesis would qualify the usual definitions of technology, 'man-machine systems', as irresponsibly loose talk.[8] Can we identify in the real world elementary operations like 'legal acts', 'theoretical statements' or 'economic transactions' that would process technological differences in a binary code? Probably not. What we will find is a concrete technology as a social field in which formal organisation ties together – with varying degrees of strength – the scientific, economic and political processing of distinctions related to technical artefacts (see Grundmann 1991: 147ff.). And as regards regulation, it would again be important to investigate each of these processes to discover their established difference-minimisation programmes: organisational goals, accumulation of knowledge, profit orientation and so on.

IV

The question arises, however, as to just how we might go about an empirical study guided by autopoiesis. What sort of systematic observation must we carry out? What sort of tools can we use? At the most basic level, by being open to the possibility that more than one recursive difference chain will be in play across the entire range of regulatory process, autopoiesis can direct existing analytical tools to the most appropriate places. Thus, instead of economic analysis seeking to account for the entire field – as attempted, for example, by the Chicago School – autopoiesis can limit it to those recursive processes where the economic code and programmes are in evidence. Similarly, instead of political analytical tools coming to a study with ready-made concepts into which the entire field must be squeezed, autopoiesis asks it more modestly to restrict itself to those systems where the power code of politics is in evidence and where steering is according to political difference-minimising programmes. But beyond this more appropriate deployment of different types of analysis, the question remains of developing a methodology that can more broadly accommodate the analysis of several systems operating on the basis of different codes and steering by distinct difference-minimising programmes.

It is probably the case that only through consideration of individual concrete examples can researchers decide upon a methodology that is appropriate to each case. If a narrative style seems appropriate, then perhaps techniques such as multi-voice or reflexive texts (Woolgar and Ashmore 1988) may provide an answer. Such an approach, however, would appear to suffer from the restrictions of text in that demonstration of the simultaneous processing of events will be problematic if not impossible. King and Piper (1990) successfully rely on a descriptive technique, but both Heller (1987) and Clune (1992)evince a desire for something which might represent more *graphically* what it is that autopoiesis claims to offer to legal sociology.

Santos (1995: 456ff.) provides us with a compelling graphical metaphor for law when he describes it as a 'map of misreading', distorting reality systematically through the mechanisms of scale, projection and symbolisation. Depending on the scale employed, different features of the landscape which law attempts to map will appear or disappear; the particular projection used will emphasise some features over others; and the symbolisation says much about the cultural background of the law and its intended purpose. Now, whereas Santos (1987: 281) believes that laws misread reality in order to establish their exclusivity, understanding law as an autopoietic system reveals that the misreading is not calculated in this way but is rather the *inevitable* result of law's autopoietic nature – reality is constructed on the basis of the selections made by law according to its code ('legal'/'illegal') as it seeks to achieve order from complexity. In other words, it is impossible to avoid a misreading, and law can only observe what its code allows it to construct. But the map metaphor remains useful, since in much the same way, a map – because it cannot reproduce the world – must offer a selective and incomplete view of that world, and consequently there is a sense in which that which is not included on the map is not real (Wood 1993: 85–87). Indeed, there is in cartography an analogue of the binary code of autopoietic systems, namely the *tectonic code*, 'which configures graphic space in a particular relation to geodesic space' (Wood 1993: 124).

The map metaphor is, then, a powerful one, but its true potential is only released when the following points are taken into account:

1. Law's map is but one of a potentially very large number of similar maps arising from the selections of different recursive systems according to their own codes, their own attempts to achieve order from complexity.
2. Because law (and other recursive systems) is in a state of constant change, we must not see the map metaphor as introducing an unwarranted element of stasis, but rather think of changing or evolving maps.

3. The second consideration should not, however, lead us so far away from the idea of a map that we lose the insight that maps are multiply connected; once a particular tectonic code is employed, local changes cannot easily be made without having knock-on effects globally; there are, therefore, built-in constraints limiting the extent to which changes can unproblematically be made – a fact recognised by cartographers, who concentrate on redundant information, thus over-determining the main features (see Ziman 1978: 82).

If we can, then, see the different autopoietic systems as maps evolving through time with the codes and programmes represented by different tectonic codes, constraining by this internal multiple connectivity the changes that can be made as the maps are recursively redrawn, then we can perhaps get a first idea of what the results of autopoiesis research might look like. Such results would allow a comparison of the ways in which the same events (whether, for example, new regulations, a fall in the price of oil or a major accident) appear on the maps of the different systems in our concrete example. Equally, they would allow examples of closer communication between systems to be identified. If such results could be attained, then what Luhmann (1993b: 108) calls second-order observation would be achieved – ie, the observation of 'what others observe and what they cannot observe'. But can the map metaphor be made more concrete?

One existing technique (suitably stripped down) appears singularly appropriate in this regard, not least because it allows us to retain the graphical metaphor of the map. More importantly, it is appropriate because it maintains an insistence on systematic empirical observation while allowing a representation of the multitude of autonomous but interfering fields of action into which autopoiesis proposes to break the causality chain: *cognitive mapping*.

This technique was developed from graph theory by Robert Axelrod (1976c) primarily as a means of examining decision-making processes with a view to improving the performance of policy makers, and it possesses many features which render it useful in the present context. The basic idea is extremely simple. In analysing, for example, a text or a series of texts, the concepts or constructs employed are represented as points, while the causal assertions used to link the concepts or constructs are represented as arrows between the points (Axelrod 1976b: 5). Positive and negative causal assertions are signified by the addition of a positive or negative sign, respectively, to the arrow concerned (Axelrod 1976a: 60). A positive assertion is one where one construct reinforces another, and a negative assertion is one where one construct operates in the opposite direction to another. The basic format of the cognitive map is, therefore, as shown in Figure 4.2.

The cognitive map is thus for Axelrod a graphical representation of a belief system. In other words, concept or construct A is an explanation of B

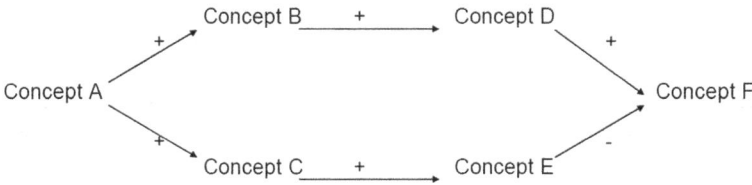

Figure 4.2 Format of a cognitive map.

and is an answer to the question 'How or why did (or does) B happen?' Similarly, concept B is a consequence of A and answers the question 'What were (or are) the consequences of A?' (see Jones and Brooks 1994: 6). The details of the technique as developed by Axelrod (for example, the mathematical approach to the process) are not being discussed here because the value of the technique in the present context does not depend on the exact methodology he proposed, but rather on its ability to provide a graphical representation of autopoietic systems.[9] Indeed, the mathematical element of Axelrod's methodology implies a view of information and its transferability that is at odds with that of autopoiesis.

In the context of autopoiesis research, cognitive mapping provides a means of representing graphically the world that a system has constructed, the concepts its code gives it access to and the causal relations that complete its model of reality. In other words, it allows a picture to be produced of the order that a system has created by means of its selections from the noise of complexity. In this way, one could imagine cognitive maps being produced in our concrete example for legislators, regulators and different sectors of the industry, which would allow us to observe not just the economic and power relations that other approaches impose on the situation but rather the world construction of each system – what each can and cannot observe as a result of the application of its code. Similarly, perhaps even finer detail can be resolved in the form of the programmes by which each system steers itself, which differences it constructs and seeks to minimise. If this could be achieved, then a potentially rich account of the development of occupational health and safety offshore would emerge. Our explanation of regulatory success or failure would not be restricted to the dominant rationality of more traditional empirical tools but would depend much more upon what the regulators and the regulated could and could not observe.

In this spirit, we can now understand Figure 4.1 as displaying the cognitive maps respectively of traditional implementation theories of law and of autopoiesis. But what about the concrete example of health and safety in the offshore oil industry? It is to that example that we now turn.

V

The brief discussion of this topic that follows is drawn from a larger study (Paterson 1997) and, due to the present space restrictions, necessarily presents a rather truncated and incomplete picture of the subject. The intention, however, is primarily to demonstrate the usefulness of cognitive mapping in carrying out an empirical study guided by autopoiesis and to demonstrate how a more adequately complex picture of the study area can emerge in terms of different codes and individual difference-minimising programmes.

As was mentioned earlier, occupational health and safety in Britain's offshore oil industry was initially not the subject of any detailed state intervention. Only in the aftermath of a serious accident and a public inquiry (Ministry of Power 1967) were moves made to introduce prescriptive regulations. Again, as was seen previously, the inquiry criticised the lack of a clear code of statutory authority regulating the question of safety offshore, and this was precisely the issue which the government attempted to address in drafting the legislation. The process which saw the passing of the Mineral Workings (Offshore Installations) Act 1971, as well as subsequent parliamentary debates, provides us with a view of how politics constructed this issue and how it sought to improve safety in what it saw as a technologically complex and rapidly developing industry operating in a hostile environment.

These sources reveal that the discussions of the legislators are very much influenced by the findings of the public inquiry.[10] In place of the previous non-interventionist stance, a detailed enforceable code is envisaged. Requirements are to be set out clearly and penalties are to be graded. The fact that the industry is comparatively new and developing rapidly means that there must, however, be flexibility. A comprehensive set of regulations is to be made in due course within the framework of the act. These regulations are seen as being more easily adaptable than primary legislation and can thus keep pace with technological change. They are envisaged as providing the basis for detailed inspection and enforcement by the regulators. Equally, concern is expressed that the regulations should not cramp development nor cause waste and extravagance for no good reason.

From these deliberations, we can construct a cognitive map for legislators at the time of the passing of the 1971 act (Figure 4.3).

From the cognitive map emerges a fairly standard view of regulation and its impact on the area of society at which it is aimed. Perceiving a need to act on this issue as determined by the political power code, legislators set up the framework for a detailed regulatory response. In other words, they deploy a programme of legal instrumentalism. A difference is constructed between the current unregulated situation, where a number of accidents have occurred, and the desired situation of improved occupational safety. The programme by which this difference is to be minimised is one of detailed regulatory intervention. Regulators will develop detailed norms of action

Figure 4.3 Cognitive map for politics.

which will tell the industry what to do. Provided these norms are followed – and if they are not, then the regulators can impose sanctions – the difference between the current problematic safety situation and the desired situation can be minimised.

There is nothing particularly surprising here. Not only could we expect to find this basic code and programme repeated in many legislative chambers, but it is of course the code and programme which underlies many legal theoretical and sociological approaches. Thus, it is not surprising to find that in subsequent debates on the issue of offshore safety, legislators maintain very much the same code and programme and thus construct a relatively stable picture of the problems they confront and the range of appropriate solutions.[11]

But if this was the understanding of the legislators, what was happening when the task was passed on to the regulators? Drawing on material produced by the regulators (especially Street 1975), it is possible to construct the cognitive map in Figure 4.4.

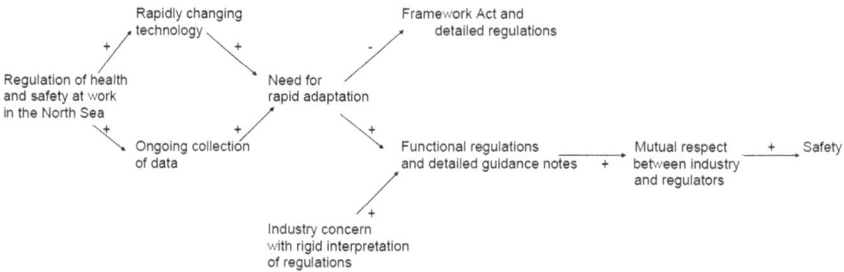

Figure 4.4 Cognitive map for regulators.

In place of the legislators' ongoing optimism about the capabilities of a programme of detailed regulatory intervention, the regulators are aware, from the very earliest stages, of the struggle they will have in keeping up with the industry. On the one hand, there is continual development of the technology, and on the other, there is a lack of environmental data from the untried waters of the North Sea. Both of these factors make even the most rapidly adaptable detailed regulations difficult to achieve. Consequently, at a comparatively early stage the regulators abandon the idea of providing detail at the level of the regulations, as these are simply too cumbersome to adapt to new data and new technology. This is a telling point, given that the regulations would be subject only to minimal negative resolution procedure. But instead, the regulations are described as 'functional', laying down only broad principles, with detail being provided at the level of non-mandatory Guidance Notes, which can be withdrawn, replaced or amended with a minimum of fuss.

The regulators are thus operating in a way that would probably trouble the legislators. The very fact that the detail is to be at the level of Guidance Notes means that failure to comply with such a requirement would not constitute a breach of the law unless it could be shown that the failure to comply also contravened the broad principle laid down in the regulation. Dubious though this might appear to legislators, it can be seen to be a step that is based on the same sort of rationale that motivated them. In other words, in the same way that the legislators were unable to provide the degree of detail at the level of the 1971 act, so the regulators, faced with a rapidly developing technological industry and ever-greater refinement of models based on the ongoing collection of environmental data, found that even the relatively broad confines of negative resolution procedure were not suited to the speed and flexibility which they required. Their response was to develop detail at the yet lower level of Guidance Notes.

But the programme of legal instrumentalism envisaged by the legislators has very clearly become something quite different in the hands of the regulators. Faced with technical problems in the form of a lack of data and rapidly developing technology, the regulators are also trying to minimise the difference between two safety situations (the current one and an improved one), but the programme of legal instrumentalism no longer appears appropriate. Instead, lacking the cognitive resources to develop regulations with any degree of certainty – and in any event unable to keep pace with developments – they adopt a programme of fostering the respect of the industry as a means of ensuring that the requirements of Guidance Notes are complied with. The ongoing lament of a variety of commentators about a lack of tough enforcement of detailed regulation (eg, Carson 1981) now appears in a rather different light.[12]

But if this degree of shift is evident between the legislators and the regulators, what happens when we reach the regulated area? Although the regulated area is more complex, for the sake of the current argument two dominant recursive systems will be considered: industry management and engineering.

Studying the recursive system of industry management at this period, it is immediately clear just how peripheral the issue of occupational health and safety is in the context of the entire system. Nor is this as pejorative as it may initially sound. The industry does not primarily exist to carry out functions associated with the improvement of safety. It exists to explore for and produce offshore oil, and it is on the basis of this fact that the entire system operates. It is accordingly possible to construct the detailed cognitive map for this system shown in Figure 4.5.[13]

It is not necessary here to go into this map in detail. It is sufficient to note that the system stresses certain features of the product it seeks to produce (concealment, state ownership and fluid nature), which in turn determine the way in which it must operate (broadly: spreading the risk of failed exploration; in accordance with state licensing programmes; and continuously). These operational 'facts', combined with the added complexity of the offshore environment (long lead-in time and extremely high front-end loading of costs), mean that the industry is confronted by large economic risks. In other words, the self-steering programme of industry management is related not to two situations of occupational safety but to two situations of economic safety. But we must beware of understanding this too simplistically. This does not mean that the industry seeks first and foremost to cut costs. While profit is undoubtedly the proximate goal, the industry sees this as most likely to be achieved by reducing the time between expenditure and payback – that is, by implementing a programme of rapid production. Industry management assesses operations on the basis of the net present value of money, not on the gross amount it will ultimately receive. In this regard, it is worth noting that other legislative interventions (eg, regarding taxation, state participation and depletion policy) are constructed by the

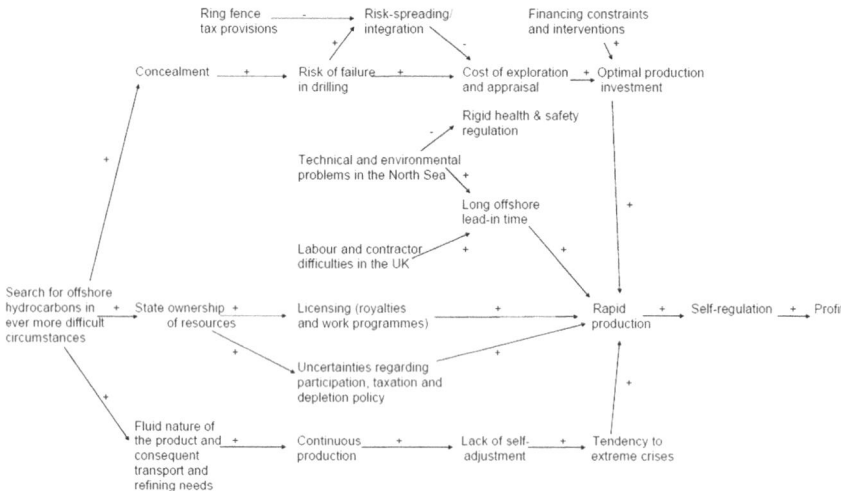

Figure 4.5 The recursive system of industry management.

industry as increasing economic risk and necessitating the application of the same difference-minimising programme.

Now, whereas other commentators have noted the detrimental effect of speed on the occupational health and safety situation (eg, Carson 1981; Wright 1986), it is now possible to see why this speed occurs. It is also possible to see how *any* rigidity in health and safety regulation is constructed by industry management as being fundamentally at odds with their need to move as quickly as possible in order to minimise economic risk, and how external interventions of any kind are seen as second best to its own ability to regulate its own affairs toward this end. The regulatory ambition of the legislators takes another knock, and the approach of the regulators looks somewhat better adapted, if still fundamentally at odds with the self-steering programme of management.

Of course, as was mentioned previously, autopoiesis forces us to consider the possibility that the regulated area is defined not by one system but rather by many – the exact number being a matter for empirical observation. The other dominant system emerging from study of the offshore oil industry is that of engineering, and it is to this cognitive map that we turn next (Figure 4.6).[14]

Despite the broad range of issues regarding occupational health and safety with which the regulators are concerned at this time, we find in the initial decade of the development of Britain's offshore oil a preoccupation in engineering with the design and construction of the installations, to the practical exclusion of other matters. The North Sea represents the largest

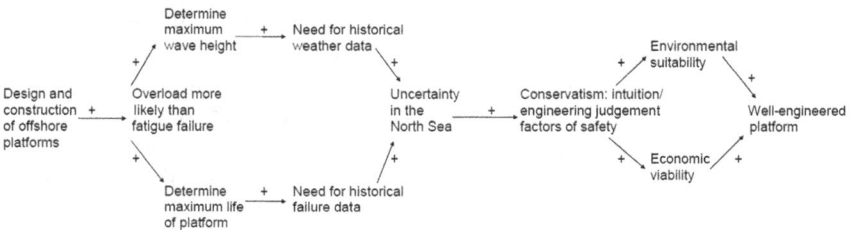

Figure 4.6 The recursive system of engineering.

challenge engineering has ever faced, but it deals with this simply by scaling up techniques developed in less-hostile environments. Thus, it assumes that structural overload is the principal problem (as it was in the hurricane-prone Gulf of Mexico) and sets about design and construction on the basis of expected maximum wave height and the period that installations will be operational. Engineering is seeking a well-engineered platform – one that is both economically viable and capable of operating in its required environment. The lack of data from the new province means, however, that there is a degree of uncertainty, and as a consequence, a programme of scientific conservatism is adopted. In this way, it is hoped that over-design and margins for error will accommodate the uncertainty.

Two issues are of particular importance here. First of all, the concentration on installation design and construction means that engineering cannot observe other health and safety issues – notably the more mundane occupational problems which produced such a toll of death and injury during this period. Safety is constructed purely in terms of the integrity of the installation. Second, the assumption on which this approach is based (the primacy of the problem of structural overload) means that engineering cannot observe other factors affecting structural integrity. And indeed, this systemic blindness was exposed on two occasions during the 1970s, as first fatigue and then dynamic response emerged as more significant problems in the North Sea.

In short, the difference-minimising programme of engineering (scientific conservatism) is certainly directed to safety, but it is a narrower construction of that concept than those of the legislators or the regulators. Furthermore, the definition of a well-engineered platform as one that is both economically viable and suited to its environment reveals the location of engineering at the junction of science and economics. Thus, for as long as cost is not a significant factor during the initial decade of North Sea development, engineering is free to employ a programme of scientific conservatism – as we have seen, industry management at this time is happier to incur costs than to lose time. But once cost pressures increase – not least as a result of the redesign and modification necessitated by the emergent problems of fatigue and dynamic response – the programme of conservatism (involving over-design, larger margins of error, introduction of redundancy and so on) is no longer an option, and a programme which could help to reduce both technical and economic risks is required. In this way, engineering switches from the deterministic techniques of conservatism to probabilistic techniques, which could rationally accommodate more factors – economic as well as technical. When that happens, the steering is in relation to different calculations of overall risk – still quite different from what the legislators and regulators observe.

This has been just a brief and simplified snapshot of a larger study, but it has served to demonstrate how autopoiesis reveals the shortcomings of linear-causal assumptions about the regulatory process. The legislators certainly understood their programme of legal instrumentalism in this way, but in the eyes of the regulators these aims seemed hopelessly optimistic, and different strategies had to be adopted. For the regulated area, regulation was at this early stage either constructed as at odds with the programme of minimising economic risk by a programme of rapid production, in the case of industry management, or barely constructed at all, in the case of engineering.

And of course, freed from the constraints of a linear-causal approach to the regulatory process, interactions among regulated systems, for example, also become visible. Thus, the management programme of speed as the answer to all problems (which were always constructed as problems of economic risk) meant that yet more pressure was put on engineering. Furthermore, management constructed engineering solutions as final and fixed, and it was thus unable to observe the uncertainty which engineering was so concerned about. But of particular significance to regulators and legislators is the finding that throughout the cognitive maps of the regulated area there is simply no mention of *occupational* health and safety in any way equivalent to their concerns. But what the autopoietic approach reveals is that it is no longer sufficient simply to call for tougher enforcement of detailed regulations. Implementationists would disagree, of course; if industry management is set on a course of rapid production to minimise economic risk and this is detrimental to the safety of workers, then a tough stance is exactly what is needed. But it seems clear from this approach that the codes and self-steering programmes of the industry – especially of management – are deep-seated, internally coherent and not something which can simply be pushed aside by interventionist regulation or prosecution. In other words, autopoiesis research produces something more than 'the triviality that the legislator has to take into account certain facts about the addressees of his regulations' (Rottleuthner 1989: 274). But what precisely does autopoiesis have to say about what regulators can do in the face of such closure and self-steering?

VI

As we have said, regulatory success or failure depends on the second question mentioned earlier: how are the diverse processes of difference minimisation 'structurally coupled'? To render this notion operational, we must observe concretely how the regulatory act is re-contextualised within the different cascades of differences and unfolded in their minimisation programs. Regulatory success depends then on the ability of the regulatory system to re-contextualise in its turn the re-contextualisation in the regulated system. In other words, the regulators must direct their attention to the codes and programmes of the systems they seek to regulate. This observation will still of course be on the basis of their own distinctions, and so the theory offers no hope of direct intervention. But as problematic as this sounds, it is important to realise that failing to problematise the situation appropriately is only likely to make matters even worse.

It would seem, therefore, that during this initial period of the development of the occupational health and safety regime in the North Sea, while the different systems constructed events according to their own codes and steered according to their own programmes, there was precious little in the way of a *re-contextualisation by the regulators of the re-construction of the regulations by management and engineering*. While these systems operated to programmes of rapid production in the case of management and of scientific conservatism – followed by tentative steps towards probabilistic techniques under cost pressures – in the case of engineering, the regulators maintained a straightforward attempt to prescribe everything that the industry should do. There was, as a consequence, no adaptation to the complexity of the regulated area and indeed no ability to adapt for as long as the programme remained one essentially of prescription – albeit that this was at the level of Guidance Notes. These systems, then, continued to evolve in rather path-dependent ways, steering according to their own difference-minimising programmes and largely indifferent to the self-steering of others. It comes as no surprise then to discover that in due course, following the world's worst offshore accident in 1988, a further public inquiry (Cullen 1990) found little to praise in the regime and plenty to condemn. This was regulatory failure on a grand scale. Significantly, however, the inquiry did not call for more prescriptive regulation and tougher enforcement. Rather, recognising the futility of this programme – even when the prescription was in the form of Guidance Notes – the recommendation was for an entirely new approach.

Implemented in full, these recommendations have produced a regime which may be briefly summarised as follows: the existing prescriptive regulations have been replaced with 'goal-setting' regulations,[15] and the owners and operators of offshore installations are required to submit to the regulators 'safety cases', without which an installation may not operate.[16] Among other things, these safety cases should demonstrate that a safety management system is in place which is adequate to ensure compliance with statutory health and safety requirements, and that all hazards which have the potential to cause a major accident have been identified, their risks evaluated and measures taken to reduce the risk to a level that is as low as reasonably practicable. It is possible to see in these changes a recognition of some of the problems revealed by the cognitive mapping approach, such as the inability of the regulators to keep pace with developments and the need to encourage a less-deterministic approach in engineering. The question is, however, whether this recognition translates into mechanisms that can foster structural coupling of the different systems, can encourage ongoing mutual re-contextualisation of each system's re-constructions and self-steering. Four different scenarios of structural coupling can be distinguished.

Scenario one: Tangential response

In many situations, despite sensitivity to regulatory impulses, the regulated area will not respond in a predictable way. As was seen in the case of engineering, a variety of difference-minimising programmes are possible in response to the irritations of events. Had we continued the study for a longer period, we would have seen a series of further changes of programme in this system as well as the system of industry management, where the programme of rapid production was in due course replaced by a programme of cost reduction. And yet throughout all of this, a continuing problem of accidents and injuries was alleged (Carson 1981; Wright 1986). The interesting point for observation in the context of autopoietic research is the reaction of the regulatory system when it confronts only such ongoing chaotic reactions on its internal screens. There are several ways in which this chaotic re-contextualisation can itself be re-contextualised by the regulators. If their internal difference minimisation allows for 'symbolic politics', then they may simply ignore the chaos and continue with their regulatory efforts. Alternatively, they may try to strengthen their cognitive and material resources: more money, more legislation, more social-science analysis of causal processes. In the case of the offshore regulators, it appears that they ultimately concentrated on the prevention of catastrophic accidents, and in this way the ongoing toll of more mundane accidents could fade from view. The cumulative catastrophic effects of such minor issues, however, were also obscured until the Piper Alpha disaster in 1988.

In such circumstances of ongoing chaotic reactions to regulatory impulses, however, one response seems to be especially promising for regulators. This is the situation when the regulators re-contextualise the reactions as non-understandable, non-predictable, idiosyncratic 'tangential responses' and give up any attempt to establish stable structures in the regulated system or systems. Instead, they change the strategy and adapt their stimuli to the tangential response character. They limit their efforts and try only punctual intervention, wait until any of the usual idiosyncratic re-actions appears on their screens and then try a punctual stimulus of a dif-ferent kind, and so on and so on, until the regulated systems have moved somewhat in their desired direction.

Although this approach respects the limits of autopoietic systems self-steering according to their own programmes of difference minimisation, and may indeed be more successful than the futile prescriptive race often run by regulators, it is clearly an extremely minimal response, and one that carries with it a high degree of risk. While it may, therefore, be suited to some circumstances (such as the control of currency values), it is probably of limited value in the domain of occupational health and safety or other si-tuations of technological complexity, where stronger structural coupling is called for.

Scenario two: Bifurcation and attractors

There is perhaps a danger that the static format of a cognitive map may lead us to believe that we can at least predict how a given system will react to given inputs. But here the simplification which we must inevitably engage in is apt to mislead us. Because in such chaotic situations, the causal chains revealed by cognitive maps are not the totality of the picture. As a non-trivial machine, a regulated system will react with different outputs even if we know the deterministic relations within the field and keep the input constant. The chances for empirical research grow, however, if our field is, in spite of chaotic macro-relations, self-organising in such a way that its macro-structures develop alongside bifurcations and attractors.

This seems to offer an opportunity for re-reading in the regulatory system. Indeed, contrary to the expectations of critics, it opens up the possibility of social control through law! Assume that recursive and self-organising sys-tems can arrive at new attractor states on the basis of external interference. Then, through general norms or specific legal acts, the law can try to pro-duce this external interference, irritating the system in such a way, and in spite of all chaos, that it moves from its attractor state to one which is at least compatible with the aims of the legislators (Krohn and Küppers 1990: 20). By analogy with systems therapy in psychology (Schiepek 1989; see also Willke 1992), we can envisage the problems with such an attractor strategy lying in the process of trial and error. Only in this way, it seems, can we probe for sensitive intervention points that will provoke the desired in-stability.

While again the trial-and-error nature of this approach raises doubts over its suitability or perhaps acceptability in high-risk settings, it may indeed have a resonance with aspects of the new offshore safety regime. There has been considerable interest in the industry in the apparent discovery that the requirement for systematic risk assessment actually results in lower costs.

There can be little doubt that after the heady days of huge profits and (at times) quite extraordinary disregard for cost, the continuing decline in the price of oil and the twilight of the UK's larger oil fields has led to an industry-wide programme of cost reduction (CRINE 1994). It is perhaps fortunate for the regulators that the procedures demanded by the new regime (representing an attractor state of reduced risk) have apparently coincided with those which the industry was already disposed to follow to the attractor state of reduced costs without any need for trial and error. Generalisations here are dangerous, but there may be other situations in which the sort of proceduralisation now operating in offshore health and safety will represent an advance over existing prescriptive approaches in areas of complexity and uncertainty.

Scenario three: Synchronising difference reduction

The usual situation in a given social field is that several self-regulating processes are going on at the same time. When several differences are minimised simultaneously, they will partially reinforce, partially sabotage each other. Our regulatory system will not be in a position to install an additional difference-minimisation programme in the field; it only minimises its own differences. But the regulatory messages are re-read, re-constructed, re-contextualised in the implementation field. Legal norms may make one of the internal programmes much more costly, or produce incentives for another one. Generally speaking, the interference will change the competitive situation between different minimisation programs; it will increase the attractiveness of one, decrease the attractiveness of others (Luhmann 1997b). Thus, our interference may lead to systematic control results in the critical case when self-regulation processes in different social fields tend to work in the same direction and thus reinforce each other. Some might call this coincidence effectiveness of law, and attribute it to causal processes.

In the context of the new offshore health and safety regime, there is an interesting requirement that, although applicable mainly to circumstances involving technology and risk, is beginning to enjoy more widespread use (see HSE 1996). This is the demand that each safety case include a detailed quantitative assessment of the risks affecting the installation, and that the risk in each case be reduced to a level which is as low as reasonably practicable. While the new regime cannot impose this mathematical difference-minimisation programme on the regulated area to the exclusion of its own steering programmes, it can nevertheless encourage change in desired directions, since it requires those preparing safety cases to be explicit about their assumptions and to make manifest the degree of uncertainty with which they are operating. In this rather indirect way, therefore, self-steering programmes that become difficult or even impossible to justify in terms of risk minimisation are disadvantaged, while those that minimise risk and are open to learning are favoured.

Scenario four: Binding institutions

This is the case where wildly flowing meaning cascades are channelled parallel to each other and mutually interconnected in such a way that a regulator can produce systematic effects. Formal organisations when they are multi-lingual tend to work as binding institutions. They force the spontaneous uncontrolled flow of parallel differences together for a certain amount of time so that they have to be compatible with each other. Of special interest is intra-organisational juridification, ie, when organisational processes are legally re-constructed in such a way that they themselves become sources of law. These processes have been analysed in detail elsewhere (Teubner 1991). The result is a close structural coupling of law and other social processes within the organisation. And here we have a case where the self-regulation programs of the law can be directly linked with the legal self-regulation within the organisation. In such situations, we can expect a high degree of regulatory success.

If we again try to observe how the regulatory system re-contextualises this situation, we will be surprised how little the system needs to know about intra-organisational dynamics. No legal economics, no organisational knowledge needs to be produced. The question is only one of how legal norms are changing legal norms. The only caveat is a need to pay attention to the limits of structural coupling, for the links in the organisation between its internal law and other ongoing processes will break if the external law demands too much. And this would be the strategic task for empirical research: to find and even predict the rupture points in concrete structural couplings. While this remains a problem of trial and error, it can be seen that this approach to structural coupling has a much greater ability to deal with complex and high-risk situations.

This scenario is, therefore, of particular interest for our concrete example. Traditionally this has been a difficult area for trade unions to gain a foothold, and there have been persistent allegations of victimisation of the workforce where there have been attempts to unionise.[17] Equally, the industry is notable for the large proportion of work which is contracted out, resulting in potentially complex employment situations on an individual installation (see Woolfson et al 1996; Wright 1986; Woolfson 1996). There is then the potential for a number of different meaning systems to be involved in a relatively confined and extremely volatile environment, each operating according to its own difference-minimising programme. With factors such as these in mind, the new regime requires that each safety case detail the *safety management system* in place on the installation, which system must include provision for workforce involvement in both the development and the ongoing review of the safety case. Other regulations put in place just before the new regime became operative provide for workforce safety representatives and safety committees.[18] Equally, the safety management system must detail the way in which it is interfaced with the safety management systems of contractors working on the installation. Here, then, is an example of a binding institution that goes beyond formal contact between regulator and regulated, and sets goals for all those involved in the regulated area to set up their own auditable structure which binds together the disparate strands of which it is composed. While the regulatory system in this auditing role cannot be totally ignorant of what is involved, it no longer needs to seek to attain the impossible levels of knowledge required to prescribe in advance what must be done in every situation. But as optimistic as this assessment may appear, we can already see or predict rupture points in what on the surface has all the appearance of a very closely structurally coupled area. Two of these are discussed here by way of illustration, together with proposals as to how such problems can be ameliorated. Interestingly, the results of autopoiesis research imply recommendations also for regulated systems as well as for regulators.

1   Although the new approach to health and safety offshore calls for closely coupled workforce involvement, and although there has been a general welcome from the workforce and the unions, there are equally fears that the new structures will be no more than formal, with many of the old problems of relations between workforce and management remaining. One safety representative, for example, identifies physical, semantic and psychological barriers which separate the workforce from management and which must be addressed if workforce involvement is to have any impact (Molloy 1993). It is possible to see in this the beginnings of an unravelling of the binding institution that promises so much. An autopoietic approach reveals, however, that the answer lies as much in the hands of the workforce and the unions as with the management or with the regulators. For example, by observing how management steers itself, which differences it seeks to minimise, unions can rapidly appreciate the limits of confrontational approaches and can instead seek to emphasise the potential cost and time savings associated with such factors as their own training programmes for safety representatives, workforce involvement in safety case preparation and review and so on. To this end, one union's approach to the question of safety committees and safety representatives represents a clear recognition of the limits of fighting for a change of the entire system and of the value of working within a system that has the backing of management.[19] Such an approach recognises the limits of structural coupling and adopts a stance that ensures that they are not crossed.

2   Quantitative risk assessment (QRA), with its formal mathematical

substance, is an ideal means of narrowing the divergence between different discourses. By requiring a unique format for the discussion of risks, it appears to be able to introduce the same difference-minimising programme into diverse systems. To understand QRA in this way, however, is to misunderstand seriously what is involved. First of all, QRA does not produce results which can be regarded as absolute. Instead, it allows for an expression of degrees of certainty and uncertainty and inherently requires ongoing reassessment. Second, our understanding of autopoietic systems indicates how wild a dream it would be to expect that systems as diverse as industry management, engineering, regulators and legislators would all construct the process or the results of QRA in the same way. And indeed, observation reveals that there are potentially serious problems. For example, there are indications that for all that engineering may stress the provisional nature of QRA results, management has a tendency to understand them as absolute indicators of levels of safety. Thus, while QRA has the potential to focus attention on risk and to demonstrate the need for ongoing assessment and the questioning of assumptions that this involves, the task for the regulators is to address the problem of its constructive misunderstanding in other systems. The regulatory system therefore needs to observe closely how, for example, management self-steering programmes can be taken advantage of to produce a more risk-aware approach and prevent the establishment of dangerous blind spots associated with absolutist misconstructions. The development by management of risk-minimisation strategies associated with oil-price risk may serve as an analogy that regulators can employ in this regard.

VII

Autopoiesis and empiricism are not, then, as mutually exclusive as might have been suspected. In conjunction with techniques such as cognitive mapping, it is possible to obtain a distinctly different view of a research area which is potentially more adequately complex and not reduced to the dominant rationality of the analysis employed. In other words, changing our map of the regulatory process to an autopoietic view allows the study area to be taken more seriously. While cognitive mapping has been proposed here, perhaps other empirical techniques can also be useful when they are deployed within the context of autopoiesis. Only practice will tell. And indeed, perhaps more sophisticated techniques may become available. Already, for example, cognitive mapping has been enhanced by computer-based techniques (eg, Taber 1992), and perhaps one day Schiepek's hope will become reality: that the interference of recursive meaning processes can be modelled in computer simulations and then confronted with real-world processes. There is already ongoing empirical research on 'the plurality of system-types (eg psychic or social systems) taking into account their specific information processing mechanisms and the ways in which these refer to each other' (Schiepek 1989: 232). But equally, experience may reveal that we will have to drastically lower our expectations as to the sophistication of available instruments and be content with narratives, with storytelling, with case studies, with more or less journalistic types of enquiries. But one thing is clear: autopoiesis theory essentially depends on systematic empirical observation.

In conclusion, however, it remains to answer a somewhat more technical question regarding autopoietic empiricism: in what way does autopoiesis depend on empiricism if falsification is excluded and causal explanation and prediction marginalised? To understand the role of empirical observation in the autopoietic framework, we need to enter somewhat into the nuances of the debates within the epistemology of social constructivism. The starting point, contrary to many myths about constructivism, is: the environment exists! It is not an invention of discourse. The problem is only that the environment cannot be reached by the system's operations, and accordingly, the system is forced to invent internal constructs of the external world in order to cope with it. This is true not only for the cognitive acts of the stomach, the brain and the mind, but also for communicative cognition and empirical observations within the scientific discourse. They can never reach the outside world. They only produce artificial data for science as a social system to enable it to cope with the unknown outside world. And this is the point where the debate within the constructivist camp begins. It concerns the qualities of this 'coping'. Is it the mere survival of certain empirico-theoretical constructs? Is it the pragmatic use of scientific constructs for social action? Is it the resonance of the instruments of science with the music of the outside world?

Amid these turbulent waves of the epistemological debate, autopoiesis tries to steer a stable course avoiding the temptation of both sirens of constructivism: Mary Hesse's 'soft programme' and the 'strong programme' of the Edinburgh School of social constructivism. Bloor's strong programme excludes for complex theories the possibility of a world feedback, so that any science, even that of law and society, is nothing but a 'socially generated imaginative schema like other social myths' (Arbib and Hesse 1986: 7; see also Bloor 1976; Collins 1985). Against this, autopoiesis stresses the theory relevance of empirical observation due to its direct structural coupling to consciousness and its indirect structural coupling to the outside world. Empirical observations are artificial constructs within science, but they have real contacts with the environment insofar as they make themselves sensitive and react to perturbations from the outside world by building up new structures. They are not themselves perceptions, but communications about perceptions. To be sure, this does not allow for correspondence of scientific constructs with outside events, but it binds the system to its environment by self-determined constraints. Thus, autopoiesis remains a coherence theory of truth: we have to look for coherence between two types of internal construct – theoretical concepts and empirical facts – that are constructed according to diverse procedures. But, via perturbation, one of these constructs – the artificial data – is closely coupled to psychic (ie, individual mental) perception of the outside world. Thus, Edinburgh's social idealism, with all its solipsist and monadologist threats, is rejected. And perhaps it comes as a relief that on this basis we do not agree with Feyerabend's 'anything goes' relativism.

So do we agree with Mary Hesse's soft programme of constructivism (Arbib and Hesse 1986: 3): 'we construct the natural world in our science, but s-t (space and time reality) constrains these constructions by feedback'? Our answer is a decisive yes and no. Yes, empirical research is world construction, not a reality test. Yes, empirical research constructs the environment in an internal model and simultaneously produces constraints for its constructive imagination by exposing it to the feedback of perturbations. But here the difference begins. No, the feedback does not come from the external world, it is purely internal. No, spatiotemporal reality itself does not produce any constraint. It is the cognising observer (psychic or communicative) who decides about which constraints to create and to which perturbations to expose the constructive imagination. Thus, feedback is not information from the external world, but rather is internally produced information, stimulated by perturbations.

Thus, it is more than mere viability, the sheer survival of a construct, that gives empirically supported theories their certainty of being in tune with the environment. It is the self-assertion of internal recursive operations that is able to develop stable eigenvalues. And they do this not only as a formal calculus, but in close structural coupling with recursive operations of other cognitive processes, and those exposing themselves to the perturbations of the outer world which will always remain unknown to them. Thus, our highly speculative constructs do know that they are on the right track, but they do not know where they are.

Our constructs feel a resistance from the objects they produce. They expose their self-produced expectations at predefined points to outside perturbations. Everything is in the hands of the recursive operations themselves: the expectations, the conditions under which such expectations are fulfilled or disappointed, the consequences drawn from such an experience. Only the yes and the no make for the crucial point of contact where they lose control, where they make themselves dependent upon their environment.

Theories do not die from falsification via independent empirical facts. We called this the omnipotence fantasies of empirical researchers, which they tend to develop when they feel disturbed by speculative theories. The only thing that empiricism can do is to create counterirritations and compel theory to create new routinisations that may keep itself in tune with other constructed worlds or drive itself into implausibility. This is what we would call a relationship of therapy – of course not the usual interventionist therapies, but a therapy re-thought in the spirit of autopoiesis. Has Marxism, for example, died from its countless empirical refutations? For decades we have witnessed successful immunisation strategies of this grand theory by which it moved into admirably complex constructions. Marxism's disaster had its origins elsewhere, in its loss of resonance with other cultural, political and economic operations – especially with its own communicative political and social consequences – which rendered it more and more difficult to re-integrate them into the theory framework. In many respects (for example, in respect to the analysis of social differentiation, to the concept of systemic autonomy, the circularity of social self-production, the totalising tendencies of social systems, human alienation), theories of social self-organisation are the legitimate heirs of Marxian theories. At the moment, they seem to be in good resonance with other recursive processes in modern society. And only the future will reveal whether they survive their self-produced consequences. But, given their esoteric character, will they have any consequences?

Notes

1 The editors would like to thank both the authors and Sage Publications Ltd for giving us permission to reprint this chapter, originally published in (1998) 7(4) *Soc. Legal Stud.* 451–486.
2 On the history of theories of self-organisation, see CREA (1985), Krohn et al. (1987).
3 King and Piper (1990) are the notable exception.
4 On systems theory and deconstruction, see Cornell (1992), Fuchs (1995: 33ff.), Berg and Prangel (1995), Stäheli (1995), and Teubner (1997).
5 Offshore Installations (Registration) Regulations 1972 (SI 1972/702); Offshore Installations (Managers) Regulations 1972 (SI 1972/703); Offshore Installations (Logbooks and Registrations of Death) Regulations 1972 (SI 1972/1542); Offshore Installations (Inspectors and Casualties) Regulations 1973 (SI 1973/1842); Offshore Installations (Construction and Survey) Regulations 1974 (SI 1974/289); Offshore Installations (Public Inquiries) Regulations 1974 (SI 1974/338); Offshore Installations (Operational Safety, Health and Welfare) Regulations 1976 (SI 1976/1019); Offshore Installations (Emergency Procedures) Regulations 1976 (SI 1976/1542); Offshore Installations (Life-saving Appliances) Regulations 1977 (SI 1977/486); Offshore Installations (Fire-fighting Equipment) Regulations 1978 (SI 1978/611); Offshore Installations (Well Control) Regulations 1980 (SI 1980/1759).
6 For example, see the parliamentary debate following further offshore accidents: Hansard HC (Debs) 16 January 1974 cols. 669–696.
7 For a fuller discussion of the notion of steering in autopoiesis, see Luhmann (1997b).
8 For a systemic-theoretical discussion of technical processes, as opposed to autopoietic systems, see Luhmann (1997a: 517ff).
9 For an example of application of the technique as proposed by Axelrod, see Savelsberg (1987).

10 Earl Ferrers Hansard HL (Debs) 18 February 1971, cols. 741–746; Hon. Nicholas Ridley (Under Secretary of State for Trade and Industry) Hansard HC (Debs) 28 April 1971, cols. 645–649.
11 For example, Hansard HC (Debs) 16 January 1974 cols. 669–696 following the sinking of the Transocean 3 and the disabling of the Transworld 61 in the winter of 1972–1973; and Hansard HC (Debs) 6 November 1980, cols. 1472–1546 following the publication of the Burgoyne Report on Offshore Safety.
12 For the sake of simplicity in the current context, we are overlooking the extremely important issue of the regulators' position within the Department of Energy at this time. The consequent ambiguity between safety and production renders their difference-minimisation programme more complicated.
13 The source for this map is primarily Frankel (1968). For the widespread and enduring acceptance of Frankel's analysis in oil industry management, see Skeet (1989) and Roeber (1993).
14 Although a wide range of offshore engineering sources have been drawn on in the larger study, a convenient overview of its development can be found in Howe (1986).
15 Offshore Installations (Management and Administration) Regulations (SI 1995/738); Offshore Installations (Prevention of Fire and Explosion, and Emergency Response) Regulations (SI 1995/743); Offshore Installations and Wells (Design and Construction, etc.) Regulations 1996 (SI 1996/913).
16 Offshore Installations (Safety Case) Regulations 1992 (SI 1992/2885).
17 Offshore Safety (Protection Against Victimisation) Act 1992.
18 Offshore Installation (Safety Representatives and Safety Committees) Regulations 1989 (SI 1989/971).
19 The Offshore Industry Liaison Committee.

References

Arbib, M.A. and Hesse, M.B. (1986) *The Construction of Reality* (Cambridge, Cambridge University Press).

Atlan, H. (1979) *Entre le cristal et la fumée: Essai sur l'organisation du vivant* (Paris, Seuil).

Axelrod, R. (1976a) 'The analysis of cognitive maps' in Axelrod, R. (ed), *Structure of Decision: The Cognitive Maps of Political Elites* (Princeton, NJ: Princeton University Press), 55–73.

Axelrod, R. (1976b) 'The cognitive mapping approach to decision making' in Axelrod, R. (ed.), *Structure of Decision: The Cognitive Maps of Political Elites* (Princeton, NJ: Princeton University Press), 3–17.

Axelrod, R. (ed) (1976c) *Structure of Decision: The Cognitive Maps of Political Elites* (Princeton, NJ: Princeton University Press).

Berg, H. and Prangel, M. (1995) *Differenzen: Systemtheorie zwischen Dekonstruktion und Konstruktivismus* (Tübingen, Francke).

Black, D. (1989) *Sociological Justice* (Oxford, Oxford University Press).

Bloor, D. (1976) *Knowledge and Social Imagery* (London, Routledge & Kegan).

Bohm, D. (1981) *Wholeness and the Implicate Order* (London, Routledge & Kegan).

Carson, W.G. (1981) *The Other Price of Britain's Oil: Safety and Control in the North Sea* (Oxford, Martin Robertson).

Clune, W.H. (1992) 'Implementation as autopoietic interaction of autopoietic organizations' in Teubner, G. and Febbrajo, A. (eds.), *State, Law and Economy as*

Autopoietic Systems: Regulation and Autonomy in a New Perspective (Milan, Giuffrè), 485–513.

Collins, H. (1985) *Changing Order: Replication and Induction in Scientific Practice* (Beverly Hills, Sage).

Cornell, D. (1992) 'The relevance of time to the relationship between the philosophy of the limit and systems theory' *13 Cardozo Law Rev.* 1579–1603.

CREA (Centre de recherche épistémologie et autonomie) (1985) *Généalogies de l'auto-organisation* (Paris, Cahiers du CREA).

CRINE (Cost Reduction Initiative in the New Era) (1994) *REPORT Published on Behalf of UKOOA by the Institute of Petroleum* (London, Crine).

Cullen (1990) *The Public Inquiry into the Piper Alpha Disaster.* Chairman The Hon Lord Cullen (Cm. 1310) (London, HMSO).

Dumouchel, P. and Dupuy J.-P. (eds.) (1983) *L'Auto-organisation: De la physique au politique* (Paris, Seuil).

Ewald, F. (1987) 'The law of law' in Teubner, G. (ed.), *Autopoietic Law: A New Approach to Law and Society* (Berlin, de Gruyter), 36–50.

Frankel, P.H.. (1968) *Essentials of Petroleum: A Key to Oil Economics & Essentials, Updated 1968* (London, Frank Cass).

Fuchs, P. (1995) *Die Umschrift* (Frankfurt, Suhrkamp).

Griffiths, J. (1986) 'What is legal pluralism?' *24 J. Legal Plural.* 1–55.

Grundmann, R. (1991) *Marxism and Ecology* (Oxford, Clarendon Press).

Günther, G. (1976a) 'Cybernetic ontology and transjunctional operations,' in Günther, G. (ed.), *Beiträge zur Grundlegung einer operationsfähigen Dialektik I* (Hamburg, Meiner), 249–328.

Günther, G. (1976b) 'Life as poly-contexturality' in Günther G., *Beiträge zur Grundlegung einer operationsfähigen Dialektik II* (Hamburg, Meiner), 283–306.

Haken, H. (1977) *Synergetics: An Introduction* (Springer, Berlin).

Heller, T. (1987) 'Accounting for law' in Teubner, G. (ed.), *Autopoietic Law: A New Approach to Law and Society* (Berlin, de Gruyter), 283–311.

Hofstadter, D.R. (1979) *Gödel, Escher, Bach: An Eternal Golden Braid* (New York, Basic Books).

Hofstadter, D.R. (1985) 'Nomic: a self-modifying game based on reflexivity in law' in Hofstadter, D.R. (ed), *Metamagical Themas: Questing for the Essence of Mind and Pattern* (New York, Bantam), 70–86.

Howe, R.J. (1986) 'Evolution of offshore drilling and production technology' *5354 OTC* 593–603.

HSE (1996) *Use of Risk Assessment within Government Departments* (London, HMSO).

Hutter, M. (1992) 'How the economy talks the law into co-evolution: an exercise in autopoietic social theory' in Teubner, G. and Febbrajo, A. (eds.), *State, Law and Economy as Autopoietic Systems: Regulation and Autonomy in a New Perspective* (Milan, Giuffrè), 265–293.

Jones, M. and Brooks, L. (1994). *Addressing organisational context in requirements analysis using cognitive mapping. Univ. Cambridge Res. Pap. Manag. Stud.17,* 1–18.

King, M. and Piper, C. (1990) *How the Law Thinks about Children* (Aldershot, Gower).

Krohn, W. and Küppers, G. (1990) 'Selbstreferenz und Planung' *1 Selbstorganisation* 101–127.

Krohn, W., Küppers, G. and Paslack, R. (1987) 'Selbstorganisation: Zur Genese und Entwicklung einer wissenschaftlichen Revolution' in Schmidt, S. (ed.), *Der Diskurs des radikalen Konstruktivismus* (Frankfurt, Suhrkamp), 441–465.

Luhmann, N. (1981) 'Identitätsgebrauch in selbstsubstitutiven Ordnungen, besonders Gesellsschaften' in Luhmann, N. *Soziologische Aufklärung 3* (Opladen, Westdeutscher Verlag), 228–261.

Luhmann, N. (1988) 'The third question: the creative use of paradoxes in law and legal history' *15 J. Law Soc.* 153–165.

Luhmann, N. (1990) *Die Wissenschaft der Gesellschaft* (Frankfurt, Suhrkamp).

Luhmann, N. (1992a) 'Operational closure and structural coupling: the differentiation of the legal system' *13 Cardozo Law Rev.* 1419–1441.

Luhmann, N. (1992b) 'The coding of the legal system' in Febbrajo, A. and Teubner, G. (eds.), *State, Law, and Economy as Autopoietic Systems: Regulation and Autonomy in a New Perspective* (Milan, Giuffrè), 145–185.

Luhmann, N. (1993a) *Das Recht der Gesellschaft* (Frankfurt, Suhrkamp).

Luhmann, N. (1993b) *Risk: A Sociological Theory* (Berlin, de Gruyter).

Luhmann, N. (1995) 'The paradoxy of observing systems' *31 Cult. Crit.* 37–55.

Luhmann, N. (1997a) *Die Gesellschaft der Gesellschaft* (Frankfurt, Suhrkamp).

Luhmann, N. (1997b) 'Limits of steering' *14*(1) *Theory Cult. Soc.* 41–57.

Maturana, H.R. and Varela, F.J. (1980) *Autopoiesis and Cognition* (Boston, Reidel).

Mayntz, R. (1983) 'The conditions of effective public policy: a new challenge for policy analysis' *11*(2) *Policy Polit.* 123–143.

Ministry of Power (1967) *Report of the Inquiry into the Causes of the Accident to the Drilling Rig Sea Gem* (Cmnd. 3409) (London, HMSO).

Molloy, J. (1993) 'Workforce involvement in safety case development' in IBC, *Offshore Safety Cases: The Living Documents—Where Next?* (London, IBC Technical Services), 2–12.

Morin, E. (1986) *La Méthode: 3. La Connaissance* (Paris, Seuil).

Nahamowitz, P. (1992) 'Difficulties with economic law: definitional and material problems of an emerging legal discipline' in Febbrajo, A. and Teubner, G. (eds.), *State, Law, and Economy as Autopoietic Systems: Regulation and Autonomy in a New Perspective* (Milan, Giuffrè), 515–577.

Paterson, J. (1997) *Behind the Mask: Regulating Health and Safety in Britain's Offshore Oil and Gas Industry* (Dissertation, European University Institute, Florence).

Prigogine, I. (1976) 'Order through fluctuation: self-organisation and social system' in Jantsch, E. and Waddington, C.H. (eds.), *Evolution and Consciouness: Human Systems in Transition* (Reading, Addison-Wesley), 93–133.

Roeber, J. (1993) *The Evolution of Oil Markets: Trading Instruments and Their Role in Price Formation* (London, The Royal Institute of International Affairs).

Rottleuthner, H. (1987) *Einfuehrung in die Rechtssoziologie* (Darmstadt, Wissenschaftliche Buchgesellschaft).

Rottleuthner, H. (1989) 'The limits of law: the myth of a regulatory crisis' *17 Int. J. Sociol. Law* 273–285.

Rottleuthner, H. (1991) 'Grenzen rechtlicher Steuerung' in Koller, P. and Weinberger, O. (eds.), *Grundlagen der Rechtspolitik* (Wiesbaden, Steiner).

Santos, B.S. (1987) 'Law: a map of misreading. Toward a postmodern conception of law' *14 J. Law Soc.* 279–302.

Santos, B.S. (1995) *Toward a New Common Sense: Law, Science and Politics in the Paradigmatic Transition* (New York, Routledge).

Savelsberg, J.J. (1987) 'The making of criminal law norms in welfare states: economic crime in West Germany' *21*(4) *Law Soc. Rev.* 529–561.

Schiepek, G. (1989) 'Selbstreferenz und Vernetzung als Grundprinzipien zweier verschiedener Systembegriffe: Vorüberlegungen für eine sozialwissenschaftliche Synergetik' *2 System Familie* 229–241.

Sheldrake, R. (1988) *The Presence of the Past: Morphic Resonance and the Habits of Nature* (London, Collins).

Skeet, I. (ed) (1989) *Paul Frankel: Common Carrier of Common Sense—A Selection of His Writings, 1946–1988* (Oxford, OUP for the Oxford Institute of Energy Studies).

Spencer-Brown, G. (1972) *Laws of Form* (New York, Julian).

Stäheli, U. (1995) *Latent Places of the Political in Luhmann's Systems Theory: Towards a Politics of Deparadoxification* (Colchester, Centre for Theoretical Studies).

Stichweh, R. (1987) 'Die Autopoiesis der Wissenschaft' in Baecker, D., Markowitz, J., Stichweh, R. and Willke, H. (eds.), *Theorie als Passion* (Frankfurt, Suhrkamp), 447–481.

Street, W.R. (1975) 'United Kingdom regulations for permanent offshore structures' *3 Offshore Technol. Conf.* 731–736.

Suber, P. (1990) *The Paradox of Self-Amendment: A Study of Logic, Law, Omnipotence and Change* (New York, Peter Lang).

Taber, C. (1992) 'POLI: an expert system model of US foreign policy belief systems' *55 Am. Polit. Sci. Rev.* 888–904.

Teubner, G. (1991) 'Autopoiesis and steering: how politics profits from the normative surplus of capital in t'Veld, R., Schaapp, L., Termeer, C. and vanTwist, M. (eds.), *Autopoiesis and Configuration Theory: New Approaches to Societal Steering* (Dordrecht, Kluwer), 127–141.

Teubner, G. (1997) 'The king's many bodies: the self-deconstruction of law's hierarchy' *31*(4) *Law Soc. Rev.* 763–822.

Teubner, G. and Febbrajo, A. (eds.) (1992) *State, Law and Economy as Autopoietic Systems: Regulation and Autonomy in a New Perspective* (Milan, Giuffrè).

Varela, F.J. (1975) 'A calculus for self-reference' *2 Int. J. Gen. Syst.* 5–24.

von Förster, H. (1981) *Observing Systems* (Seaside, Intersystems).

Willke, H. (1987) 'Strategien der Intervention in autonome Systeme' in Baeker, D., Markowitz, J. Stichweh, R. and Willke, H. (eds), *Theorie als Passion* (Frankfurt, Suhrkamp), 333–361.

Willke, H. (1992) 'Societal guidance through law' in Febbrajo, A. and Teubner, G. (ed.), *State, Law, and Economy as Autopoietic Systems: Regulation and Autonomy in a New Perspective* (Milan, Giuffrè), 353–387.

Wood, D. (1993) *The Power of Maps* (London, Routledge).

Woolfson, C., Foster, J. and Beck, M. (1996) *Paying for the Piper: Capital and Labour in Britain's Offshore Oil Industry* (London, Mansell).

Woolgar, S. and Ashmore, M. (1988) 'The next step: an introduction to the reflexive project' in Woolgar, S. (ed) *Knowledge and Reflexivity: New Frontiers in the Sociology of Knowledge* (London, Sage), 1–11.

Wright, C. (1986) 'Routine deaths: fatal accidents in the oil industry' *34*(1) *Sociol. Rev.* 265–289.

Ziman, J. (1978) *Reliable Knowledge: An Exploration of the Grounds for Belief in Science* (Cambridge, Cambridge University Press).

Part II

Analysing law through systemic approaches

The economic and regulatory interface

Chapter 5

Regulation without interests? An introduction to Luhmannian empirical mapping of system-environment relationships

Bettina Lange

A mapping tool for empirical research inspired by systems theory

The high level of abstraction of systems theory and the only implicit role of the concept of interests in its analyses are two challenges that this chapter aims to face together. It begins to tackle these two challenges by outlining in the first section a mapping tool that can be used for generating 'grounded theory' empirical accounts of the self-referential operations of subsystems. The chapter argues that applying this mapping tool may reveal blind spots that are the result of subsystems observing and communicating about other subsystems and their natural environments through the distinct lens of their own self-referential operations. Blind spots, however, can be harnessed by regulatory strategies that seek to strengthen the resilience of each subsystem to external shocks. They are also an aspect of the mediation and potentially constrained impact of interests through limited communication between different social subsystems, which adds a distinct sociological conception of interests to accounts of regulation.

Key features

As a sociologist, Luhmann thought that even abstract systems-theoretical concepts should be linked back to some empirical reality (Baecker 2013: xviii). Discussion in the socio-legal literature on how this can be done has been limited so far (for exceptions see, eg, Bora 2006; Kolben 2011; Koppen 1991; Lange 1998; Paterson 2000), though organisational studies have sought to harness systems-theoretical perspectives for empirical research (see, eg, Hernes and Bakken 2003; Nassehi 2005). In the context of socio-legal research, Paterson and Teubner (1998) developed an empirical mapping tool (Figure 5.1) Figure 5.1 that enables fleshing out of the binary coding, self-referential operations and limited exchanges between different social subsystems. They intended this mapping to aid qualitative empirical research on the implementation of legal regulation (see, eg, Paterson 2000).

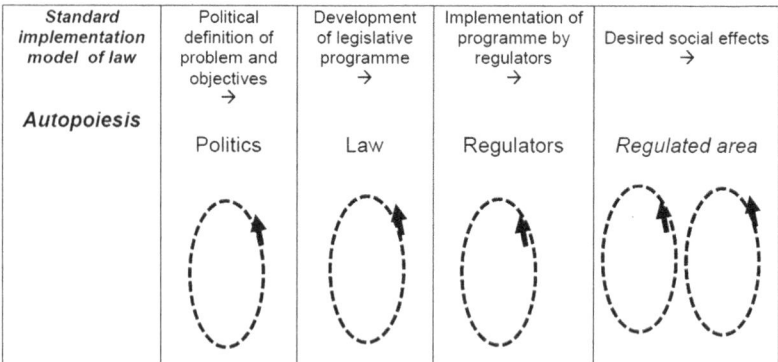

Figure 5.1 The shift from a horizontal chain of causal relations to vertical chains of recursions.
Source: Paterson and Teubner 1998, republished in this book (previous
chapter in this book).

Figure 5.1 shows how Luhmann's ideas about autopoiesis depart from a
conventional analysis of the implementation of legal regulation. The standard
implementation model of law starts with the definition of a regulatory problem agreed upon in a political sphere. This usually entails specifying regulatory objectives. We would then examine the development of a legislative
programme to achieve these regulatory objectives, for instance through empirical examination of the enforcement of the regulatory regime by agencies.
Finally, the standard implementation model assesses whether the legislative
programme has led to the desired societal effects. Systems theory informed by
autopoiesis departs from this linear-causal model. It depicts politics, law,
regulators and the regulated area as distinct, self-referentially constituted
social subsystems. There might be more than one regulated area, since accounts of what constitutes it may vary according to the distinct way in which
each subsystem, such as law, politics and economics, perceives the regulated
area. This schematic account of a systems-theoretical understanding of the
implementation of legal regulation can also serve as a tool for collecting data
in order to empirically flesh out this map of legal regulation. Figure 5.1
prompts the empirical mapping of self-referential operations and self-
observations, ie, first-order observations within social subsystems (Luhmann
1990: 230). For instance, from a systems-theoretical perspective the political-
administrative subsystem is concerned with the determination of goals, while
the legal system is concerned with the stabilisation of expectations, even if
they are not fulfilled in specific cases (Danscheid 2010: 87, 99). Figure 5.1 also
invites an empirical researcher to capture how distinct social subsystems observe other social subsystems. These second-order observations (observations

of observation) may be accessible through oral, written and visual communications about them generated within social subsystems. The researcher then takes a step back from these second-order observations that social subsystems generate of each other and provides her own analysis of the distinct communicative processes that inform them (Danscheid 2010: 22; Luhmann 1997: 875). This can entail uncovering the conditions of possibility of the second-order observation. It may also involve some self-observation from the researcher, a recognition of her own positionality. Differentiating between first- and second-order observations also enables critique of first-order observations (Philippopoulos-Mihalopoulos 2014: 391).

Fleshing out an empirical mapping tool with reference to a 'grounded theory' approach

This systems-theoretical approach chimes with, and can be fleshed out further with reference to, elements of a 'grounded theory' perspective on qualitative empirical research (Corbin and Strauss 1990; Strauss and Corbin 1998, 1997). Like systems-theoretical researchers, grounded-theory researchers develop second-order observations of primary social practices, including observations of social actors in a particular field. Moreover, grounded theory – while rooted in symbolic interactionism and pragmatism – is a flexible approach toward qualitative research that rests on key research techniques that can be harnessed and adapted to different conceptual frameworks for research (Corbin and Strauss 1990: 5), such as systems theory. A key feature of a grounded-theory approach is to build concepts that are anchored in mainly qualitative, sometimes also quantitative, empirical data (Corbin and Strauss 1990: 11). These concepts are derived from coding primary empirical data into more overarching themes. Researchers then constantly compare the main features of concepts, which are built upon themes, in order to refine them, detect variation in them or split them into new concepts to render them more precise (Corbin and Strauss 1990: 9, 13). They then develop categories – and specify their distinct features – into which different concepts can be grouped (Corbin and Strauss 1990: 8). Categories and concepts are finally linked and thereby integrated into an overall analytical scheme. In this way, medium-level theoretical propositions – grounded in the data – are developed. Iteration – ie, frequent revisiting of data by the researcher and revision of research themes in light of an evolving analysis of the data – is a key feature of a grounded-theory approach. It is a research technique that mirrors, and is therefore apt for analysing, the empirical dimensions of the systems-theoretical idea that social subsystems are recursive and self-referential operations.

Moreover, according to systems theory there is not just one version of social reality. Instead, we understand the social world by observing not individual actors or groups of actors but the communication of different social subsystems about their own operations, those of other social sub-systems and the system-environment relationship (Lee 2000: 320). This chimes well with theoretical sampling as an element of a grounded-theory approach. Theoretical sampling of empirical data, in contrast to a re-presentative statistical sample, does not seek to shed light on the social phenomenon as a whole, eg, a population, or a group of social actors, or units of time. Instead it captures data that are relevant for fleshing out the dimensions of specific concepts of analytical interest in the research, such as 'nurses' work' in a health-care system (Corbin and Strauss 1990: 8). More importantly, theoretical sampling enables researchers to address a key challenge for systems-theoretical research: the difficulty of knowing where to draw the boundaries around a social subsystem. How a system is differ-entiated from its environment and how it maintains its boundaries are, for Luhmann, important analytical issues (Lee 2000: 325, 329), though his work provides limited guidance on how to find empirically justified answers. In a grounded-theory approach there is a core category driving the theoretical sampling, eg, 'visible and invisible work'. This can constitute the empirical nucleus of a social subsystem in action (Star and Strauss 1999). This core category may at later stages of the research be further refined through se-lective coding, which entails grouping around the core category all other categories derived from the empirical data. Other categories may represent actions, conditions under which they occur and consequences of actions (Corbin and Strauss 1990: 14). Hence, the techniques of a grounded-theory approach can be harnessed for systems-theoretical empirical research by aggregating the observations of the social world collected by researchers – eg, through interviews, participant observation, and analysis of documents – to accounts of entire social subsystems, including their relationship to their environment.

A grounded-theory approach works, however, with an understanding of the system-environment relationship that, at first glance, looks different from that of systems theory. Grounded theory examines conditions of social practices on both micro and macro levels (Corbin and Strauss 1990: 5, 7, 8, 11). It seeks to capture the dynamic interplay between the perceptions of social conditions by actors and their responses to them, which can entail change to or affirmation of social structures (Corbin and Strauss 1990: 5).

Hence, qualitative empirical data about this interplay, gathered in the context of a grounded-theory approach, may need to be translated into the conceptual language of systems theory. This would entail explaining which aspects of the micro and macro conditions of social practices shed light on the self-referential operations of a social subsystem and, eg, reflect the ap-plication of binary codes. It would also entail stating which aspects of macro-social conditions pertain to the environment of a social subsystem. From a systems-theoretical perspective, a complex environment is necessary for a social subsystem to build up its own operations and internal structures.

Finally, Luhmann's perspective can add further interesting twists to a grounded-theory approach. For Luhmann – who, in contrast to grounded theory, does not work with a notion of innate agency of a unified human actor – it is the observation that constitutes the observer, not the observer who generates the observation. Hence, it is psychic or social systems that do the observing while they are differentiated from their environment. More specifically, social systems observe through the medium of communication, while psychic systems, which are sometimes also referred to as conscious systems, observe through cognition (Arnoldi 2001: 5). From a systems-theoretical perspective, communicative processes within social subsystems are then analysed in terms of the *functions* they play for maintaining the operation of entire social systems. Binary codes that are applied to the self-observations in subsystems are one way of maintaining such functions.

Analysing binary coding in action with the aid of the empirical mapping tool

The empirical mapping tool depicted in Figure 5.1 enables analysis of how social subsystems communicate about each other with reference to binary codes. For instance, the social subsystem of law – which is not just an op-erating social subsystem but also a second-order type of observation of legal processes – works with the binary code of 'legal'/'illegal' (Paterson and Teubner 1998: 453, 461). The social subsystem of the economy works with a binary code of 'to have'/'not to have', eg, money or property (Luhmann 1990: 76). The social subsystem of science works with a distinction between 'true' and 'false' (Luhmann 1990: 150). The binary code of a risk regulatory regime may refer to 'regulation'/'no regulation' (Danscheid 2010: 163), while the social subsystem of politics works with distinctions around access to power, such as 'government'/'opposition' (Luhmann 1990: 76).

Key examples of binary codes can be found in Luhmann's work itself (see, eg, Luhmann 1990: ch. 9), but empirical research can add nuance through an understanding of binary codes in action. As societies evolve and become increasingly functionally differentiated, the operation of codes becomes more complex. Codes become embedded in developing 'success media'. These are generalised media that transmit meaning within a specific social subsystem. Codes produce meaningful difference within each success medium. For instance, money is a generalised success medium for trans-mitting meaning in the economy by drawing on a binary code of 'loss'/'in-come' (Lee 2000: 326).

Some binary coding in action may reflect a degree of structural coupling between a social subsystem and its natural environment. This may help to further flesh out Luhmann's abstract notion of operational chains that link different social subsystems and in which there can be rapid switching be-tween codes, eg, from a legal to a political code or from a scientific to an economic code (Luhmann 1990: 87). For instance, in the context of the legal system, empirical accounts of binary coding can add further nuance to the general code of 'legal'/'illegal' by showing how binary coding may also draw on links with the natural system. In relation to managing water resources, the legal system recognises a multifaceted account of legality, captured through the binary distinction between 'ecological flow'/'water scarcity' (European Commission 2015: 2). Ecological flow exists where rivers carry sufficient water of adequate quality to support a range of flora and fauna. This may – but does not have to – equate to meeting water quality objectives as set out in formal supranational law, such as the European Union Water Framework Directive (2000/60/EC). In contrast to ecological flow, water scarcity refers to a state of water bodies carrying insufficient water of adequate quality to support flora and fauna or insufficient water to enable public water supply. Hence, the binary code 'ecological flow'/'water scarcity' does not necessarily draw on the basic coding 'legal'/'illegal' but refers for its definition on information from the subsystem of the natural environment. The code draws on the impacts that water availability has on the natural and human environment, ie, in supporting ecosystem functions and their services for humans, including public water supply. This may exceed compliance with legal standards or fall short of them.

To summarize, the empirical mapping tool depicted in Figure 5.1 builds on key systems-theoretical ideas, such as autopoiesis, and more specifically observation of observations with reference to binary coding within social subsystems. In order to harness this tool to understand the implementation of environmental regulation, and thus society-nature interactions, it is necessary to add the natural environment as a subsystem.

Adding the natural environment as a subsystem to the empirical mapping tool

Why a Luhmannian approach to society-nature interactions?

Why build on Luhmann's ideas for understanding nature-society interactions? There is already a plethora of academic theory about the subject (see, eg, Beck 1992; Ostrom 2009). But Luhmann's work is distinct also because he is one of the few social scientists whose interdisciplinary perspective builds on his own reading of natural science research, which he incorporated into his sociological theorising. Luhmann's core concepts, such as autopoiesis, draw on the ideas of the biologists and philosophers Maturana and Varela (1980) and can be applied to the operation of both natural and social systems (Paterson and Teubner 1998: 451). Also, Luhmann's understanding of subsystems as 'thermodynamically open' – ie as exchanging inputs and outputs with their environment – reflects the imprint of natural science concepts (Luhmann 1990: 16). This is different from sociological thinking, which has understood the 'environment' of 'society' either in purely social terms, eg, as markets or technological innovations (Luhmann 1990: 18), or as very distinct. In early sociological work, nature was juxtaposed to 'civilisation' (Luhmann 1990: 14). It was perceived as shaped by different laws of natural evolution, or in the case of psychic systems as governed by instinct.

But there is limited discussion of relationships between systems and their natural environments in Luhmann's work. Traditionally, systems theory focuses on meaning-making within social subsystems, although in his book *Ecological Communication* (*Ökologische Kommunikation*), Luhmann (1990) begins to recognize that the material physical (such as spatial and topographical) dimensions of the natural environment also matter (Philippopoulos-Mihalopoulos 2012: 47, 52, 2014: 392). In his later work, Luhmann (2012: 262) emphasise structural coupling that bridges the difference between system and environment as key to the evolution of society (Lee 2000: 325). He briefly discusses the significance of ecological conditions for the self-reproduction of social subsystems (Luhmann 2012: 73–77). In the Anthropocene this also calls for further explicit analysis of relationships between social subsystems and their various natural environments. Moreover, adding a natural subsystem to the empirical mapping tool depicted in Figure 5.1 fits well with the post-humanist, limited anthropocentric orientation of systems theory, which does not focus on humans as a primary unit of analysis (Lee 2000: 322; Schwanitz 1995: 138). It also chimes with Parsons's ideas. He recognises the natural environment as providing distinct types of resources for social systems (Segre 2012: 12). Figure 5.2 provides a schematic account of an empirical mapping tool that includes the natural environment.

There are various ways in which we can begin to conceptualise a natural subsystem from a Luhmannian perspective. For instance, a natural subsystem of animal populations may adopt 'food'/'non-food' as its primary binary coding (Kang 2018: 315). A natural subsystem is distinct from social and psychic subsystems, because the latter operate – in contrast to natural organisms – with reference to meaning (Schwanitz 1995: 141). Hence, social subsystems exchange information with their social environments. In contrast to this, natural subsystems, such as biological systems, operate with reference to exchange of energy (Luhmann 2013: 28), eg, between crops and human food consumption. But like social subsystems, natural subsystems are autopoietic: they produce and reproduce themselves (Arnoldi 2001: 4).

Distinct conceptions of environmental risks and their implications for regulatory strategies

Figure 5.2 illustrates that each social subsystem communicates in distinct ways about the natural environment. Hence, systems-theoretical mapping enables capture of how different subsystems understand in distinct ways what actually constitutes an environmental risk (Danscheid 2010: 59). A risk

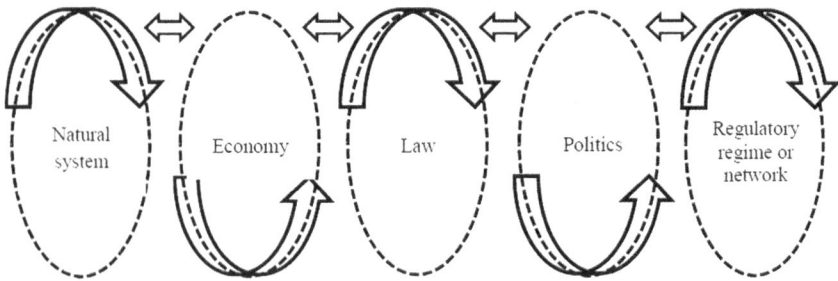

Figure 5.2 Cognitive-affective mapping of the implementation of environmental regulation.[1]

is a possible future event that may cause adverse effects and in relation to which decisions are made (Zehetmair 2012: 276). Consequently, it is decisions that turn dangers, eg, those posed by natural environments, into risks. For instance, rainfall may pose the danger of flooding, but a distinct type of flood risk is created only when planning authorities grant permits that authorise building on floodplains (Zehetmair 2012: 276). Different social subsystems attribute different meaning to environmental risks. For example, some flooding may – from the perspective of a natural subsystem – be creative destruction that stimulates the development and adaptation of flora and fauna, whereas from the perspective of the social subsystem of the economy, flooding may mean substantial losses for insurers.

Figure 5.2 further illustrates that an environmental risk is constructed by all of the communications of all of the subsystems taken together. This reflects Luhmann's (1990: 8) aspiration to develop a theory of society as a whole. Environmental risks are not understood as shortcomings of political governance only or as merely the result of misguided economic activity, nor as the consequence of a lack of moral responsibility.

Mapping how social and natural subsystems – which are themselves often unaware of the limitations in their cognitive capacities (King and Thornhill 2006: 9) – perceive environmental risks in distinct ways can help to develop regulatory strategies. It can help, eg, to identify self-regulatory mechanisms. For instance, from the perspective of the economy, flood risks may simply be translated into increased insurance premiums for houses built on floodplains. But from the perspective of the legal subsystem, flood risk may turn into legal liabilities for those who contribute to its creation. Planning authorities that are in breach of a legal duty to decide upon planning applications with due care and diligence may be incentivised to be more cautious in their decisions to grant planning permission for building on floodplains.

Hence, while systems-theoretical thinking has been referred to in the socio-legal literature in particular to emphasise the limits to legal, political and economic governance of various risks (see, eg, Luhmann 1990: 145; Teubner 1986), we can also harness it for identifying regulatory strategies by empirically mapping the blindness of a distinct social subsystem to the operations of other social subsystems. Such regulatory strategies can focus on reducing blind spots or strategically harnessing them. Regulatory strategies may aim to maintain blind spots because, according to systems theory, they are not necessarily a deficiency but fulfil an important function. They stabilise the operations of existing social subsystems, and thus keep their internal complexity manageable (Danscheid 2010: 115). In the context of the legal system this occurs through 'cognitive openness but normative closure' (Rottleuthner 1989: 789). Stabilising the self-referential operations of existing social subsystems strengthens the resilience of each social subsystem to exogenous environmental shocks. This helps to maintain the distinct contribution that a specific social subsystem, such as politics or economics, can make to environmental risk management.

Moreover, systems theory enables an understanding of the resilience of each social subsystem in a relational way, and empirical research can address the question of why different social subsystems may show different levels of resilience to environmental risks. From a systems-theoretical perspective, resilience is the result of the complexity that one social or natural subsystem can provide for another to develop its own internal operating patterns. For instance, damage caused by a natural hazard may affect the economy to such an extent that it can no longer provide complexity – eg, by enabling payment for services delivered – that enable another social subsystem, such as a health-care system, to build up its own structures, eg, the delivery of vaccination services (Zehetmair 2012: 278). Hence, regulatory strategies may seek to prevent the creation of distinct vulnerabilities, via the reduction in complexity of one social or natural subsystem, in other social or natural subsystems that depend on the complexity of other social subsystems to build up their own structures. This may entail a degree of structural decoupling and thus qualify a preference for integrated environmental risk management.

A Luhmannian understanding of resilience also recognises the significant adaptive capacity of social and natural subsystems to environmental risks since, from a systems-theoretical perspective, social structures have only limited temporal durability. Social structures arise from the limitations of the communicative relations that are enabled by a social subsystem (Luhmann 1984: 384). Hence, social structures manifest themselves as expectations of specific subsequent communications, which are generated by social subsystems. From this perspective, social structures are not necessarily enduring but have limited temporal stability (Zehetmair 2012: 282). Consequently, while social subsystems can be vulnerable to natural hazards, they may also have significant capacity for adaptation, since their social structures may change over time. But what matters for understanding the implications of systems theory for regulatory strategies is not just an empirical analysis of the self-referential operations of subsystems. An empirical take on how structural coupling between natural and social subsystems works is also significant.

A distinct take on structural coupling

The empirical mapping tool enables us to trace the extent and type of structural coupling between social and natural subsystems, indicated by the different horizontal arrows in Figure 5.2. For instance, in the context of international environmental law, recognising biodiversity in watercourses as an important feature of a natural subsystem has led to a legal shift. International environmental law is no longer simply concerned with the balancing of interests, and thus tit-for-tat strategies are appropriate when structural coupling between different social subsystems is at stake. It now also includes non-negotiable norms, such as the 'no significant harm' norm, which protects the biodiversity of natural subsystems such as rivers. This redistributes risk by going beyond a more limited legal expectation of compensation for harms to biodiversity. The system of international environmental law thus seeks to ensure a new complementarity of expectations between states (Kang 2018: 325).

Usually structural coupling is understood as a heterarchical, not a hierarchical, dependence of a social subsystem upon its environment and vice versa. An observer can observe structural coupling with reference to the distinction between subsystem and environment (Luhmann 1990: 267). All observations of each social subsystem are equally significant for constituting society. There is no privileged vantage point of a particular subsystem that makes the observations of that social or natural subsystem more relevant than those of another. But empirical research may qualify this heterarchical perspective of structural coupling. In order to empirically map the implementation of regulation, it may be necessary to *foreground the perspective of the regulatory regime*. This enables a focus on how it observes other social and natural subsystems, such as law, politics and their natural environments (Danscheid 2010: 166).

But how can we foreground communications of, eg, an environmental regulatory regime, thus focusing on *its perspective* of the operations of the subsystems of law and politics, without simultaneously drawing to a significant extent on the internal perspectives of those social subsystems?

For Danscheid (2010: 167), the solution to this conundrum is to adopt a slightly different definition of a social system. While fully fledged Luhmannian social (functional) systems are focused on communications about a functionally differentiated theme, such as politics or law, there are also wider definitions of social systems. These encompass more loosely and sometimes less enduring organised social formations that still have the function of coordinating social action, such as *networks* as a distinct type of social system (see, eg, Tacke and Bommes 2006). Networks do not require actors to be simultaneously present to each other as interaction systems do. They are similar to, but also different from, organisations. They are characterised by an expectation of reciprocal performances based on a past record that is expected to be repeated in the future (Danscheid 2010: 170). Networks can form an institutional framework for the perspectives of different social subsystems that are located within them, such as law and politics. They can facilitate exchanges between different subsystems that ultimately foreground the communications of the network that makes up an environmental regulatory regime (Danscheid 2010: 166). In order to harness the empirical mapping tool for the analysis of legal regulation, we should further probe the strengths and weaknesses of its conceptual, systems-theoretical foundations. Can it shed light on the role of interest in regulation?

What light can the empirical mapping tool shed on the role of interests in regulation?

Interests as a main feature of the design and implementation of regulation

This section further probes the strengths and weaknesses of the conceptual foundations of the empirical mapping tool. Can it provide insights into the role of interests in regulation? Academic regulation literature often asserts that the success or failure of regulation, including environmental regulation, depends on how the interests of various individual and organisational actors are coordinated. This becomes clear, in the first instance, from definitions of regulation. Regulation is usually defined as some form of control over the behaviour of individuals and/or organisations, including business actors – eg, through the setting of standards and objectives – as well as monitoring for compliance (Black 2005: 11). Regulation may also entail attempts by principals, such as government departments setting out regulatory policy, to control how agents, such as agencies, implement statutory mandates for regulation (Pollack 2002; Thatcher and Sweet 2002). These attempts at control raise the spectre of conflicting interests between those who seek to exercise regulatory control and those who may try to resist it. Hence, an understanding of interests can help to explain conflict and consensus regarding the objectives and strategies of regulatory regimes. Both collective action approaches and those that consider regulation to generate 'winners' and 'losers' assume that interests drive the design and implementation of regulation (Trebilcock 1975).

Public and private interest theories of regulation further emphasise the role that interests play in shaping the dynamics of regulatory regimes. Public interest theories suggest that legal rules can be deployed in order to realise wider community interests, such as environmental or consumer protection, or allocative efficiency (Adegbulu 2018). Empirical research in this tradition has analysed the challenges of reconciling different interests in contemporary pluralist societies and the scope for meta-regulation, ie, organisations becoming responsive to expressions of interests in their environment (Simon 2017: 23–25). In contrast to this, private interest (including public choice) theories suggest that both legislators and regulatory agencies, as well as regulated public and private organisations, will develop legal rules which benefit their own self-interests, such as to be re-elected for office as a legislator, to increase resources for regulatory agencies or to retain flexibility in management choices and maximisation of revenue for regulated organisations (Ogus 2004: ch. 4). But public or private interests play only a limited role in Luhmann's and contemporary critical systems theory's understanding of social action and regulation.

A limited role for interests in Luhmann's and critical systems theory

At first glance, Luhmann's theory does not seem to enable analysis of the link between social action and interests. For systems theory, the continuity of social organisation is not a consequence of the resolution of conflicts which are sparked by opposing interests. Instead, systems theory explains the stability of social orders through reference to the self-referential operations of social subsystems and their pattern maintenance over time (Luhmann 2013: 70). For Luhmann, neither individual nor collective actors nor social structures, which can be sources and institutional markers of interests, are relevant categories of sociological analysis. Following systems theory, social subsystems work according to their own functional imperatives (Lee 2000: 325).

One of the reasons for this limited concern about interests in Luhmann's thinking is the influence of Talcott Parsons on his work (Swedberg 2005: 361). Parsons developed a functionalist rather than a utilitarian sociological perspective; he sought to understand how values, rather than interests, can limit freedom of choice in a society by circumscribing what relationships between means and ends are possible (Luhmann 2013: 9). According to Parsons (1963: 46), rules or norms, ie, binding obligations, constrain how an acting unit can purse its interests. Such normative constraints are essential for maintaining the integration of a system (Segre 2012: 9, 29). Normative constraints on actors' interests can also operate on an institutional level, since norms define cultural institutions, which are part of a social system. Institutions define actors' reciprocal role expectations and thereby circumscribe what can be considered a legitimate pursuit of interests in general and how much self-interests should be curtailed with reference to the interests of a collectivity (Segre 2012: 20, 22).

But while interests are not a key explanatory category for Parsons – he focuses instead on a wider range of 'action orientations' – this does not mean that there is no reference at all in his work to interests (Segre 2012: 9). He identified four action orientations. Two of these refer to interests: self-orientation refers to the pursuit of one's own self-interest, and a collectivity orientation refers to the pursuit of the interests of a collective (Segre 2012: 10). Moreover, in his essay on influence, Parsons implicitly discusses interests. For Parsons, influence is a 'generalised medium of persuasion' that has 'effects on the attitudes and opinions of social actors' (1963: 44). As a generalised symbolic medium of interchange, influence, like money, is significant for shaping social action (Parsons 1963: 44; Segre 2012: 11). In the context of economic life, influence draws on the idea of the utility of an object or service, which reflects a particular interest in a social action (Parsons 1963: 39). These interests can be implemented by social actors acquiring control over the object or service to which they attribute utility. Money is then a particular type of language that helps to assert this type of economic influence. It facilitates a distinct type of exchange, ie, market exchanges of objects and services (Parsons 1963: 40). Hence, in order to explain influence, four elements have to be present. The first is that there is a category of value. The second is that there are interests in the properties of an object that are important in the context of the value. The third element consists of a specific definition of the situation that can also promote the implementation of the interest. The fourth element is a normative framework of rules, which enables a distinction between legitimate and illegitimate ways of action in pursuit of the interest. Parsons (1963) then distinguishes between different types of influence. Fiduciary influence, for example, is an interest in control over resources, which is relevant for the attainment of goals where there are a plurality of goals and each is therefore contested. For Parsons this is a classical instance of the operation of interests in social systems.

A key reason for Parsons's rejection of the idea that interests are a key explanatory variable is that he did not start from the idea of a unified human actor to whom specific interests could be attributed. Instead, for him human beings are composed of both behavioural and personality systems (Segre 2012: 6). The latter are action systems of a single actor (Segre 2012: 7). More specifically, for Parsons human beings are composed of distinct social, psychological and biological parts between which there is limited communication. For instance, biological states of human actors, such as their blood pressure, cannot be 'read' and are thus not accessible for meaning generation in the psychological system (Gilgen 2013: xiv). Hence, each of these parts that make up human actors needs to be considered in order to build sociological explanations of social action (Gilgen 2013: xi).

But it is questionable whether we can really draw clear demarcations between biological, psychological and social dimensions of human actors. For instance, thoughts are aspects of psychic subsystems. They may be shared among various social actors and then translate into attitudes and ultimately behaviour, which becomes accessible for meaning-making in a social subsystem. Moreover, social-anthropological research about the social construction of bodies has questioned – especially from a feminist perspective – strict demarcations between social and biological dimensions of human actors (see, eg, Lock and Farquhar 2007).

Parsons's influence on Luhmann's work has meant that there is also no unified human actor with particular interests in Luhmannian systems theory. This aspect of Luhmann's systems theory seems to remain unchanged, slightly surprisingly, by contemporary readings of it that also draw on critical social theory. Critical social theory places a greater emphasis on conflict and paradoxes, potentially driven by opposing interests, as a source of social action. Hence justice becomes 'contingent' and transcendent (see, eg, Philippopoulos-Mihalopoulos 2012: 62). Similarly, critical systems theory recognizes that political conditions can frame processes of communication, which questions Luhmann's account of communication as being self-referentially constituted (Fischer-Lescano 2012: 4). Luhmann (1990: 128) recognises that the environment of social subsystems can be a source of conflicts, and conflicts may help to crystallise interests.

But critical systems theory follows Luhmann's idea that society is not constituted by individual subjects. It perceives society as 'trans-subjective', and thus not constituted by interactions between individual subjects. Social orders are not within the reach 'of the practical intentions of [their] actors' (Fischer-Lescano 2012: 6). This continues to background interests for explaining social action. As the next section further explains, Luhmann's work thus only recognises mediated interests in the background of his theorising.

Mediated interests in the background of Luhmann's work

Mediated interests are interests that do not directly influence social action but are limited by intervening social forces. For instance, values may refract and thereby limit the influence of interests on social action. The degree to which this occurs is a matter of debate. For Max Weber, it depends on whether value-rational or instrumental, interest-driven action is more prevalent in a society. Value-rational action pursues a course of action based on values, with limited regard to its success (Weber 1922: 9, 24). This is one of the ways in which interests can be mediated in shaping social action. Luhmann's work adds to such a sociological understanding of mediated interests another account that is distinct in two ways.

Interests linked back to psychic and other social subsystems, not individual human actors or social structures

Luhmann's notion of mediated interests is distinct firstly because it does not link back to interests held by individual or collective human actors, or interests reflected in and consolidated by social structures, such as class. Instead, from a systems-theoretical perspective mediated interests are linked back to psychic or other social subsystems. Luhmann thus discusses the goal orientation of entire social systems and subsystems. Goal orientation is a communicative process from which 'organised sets of actions emerge' that are self-referential and 'recursively reproduce themselves in their elements' (Teubner 1994: 34). Their objective is to continue their operations and thereby maintain the system.

Luhmann therefore decentres individual and collective human actors. He considers human beings not as part of the system of society but as part of society's environment (Schwanitz 1995: 138). Human beings are only part of society when they communicate (Lee 2000: 322). Luhmann's work departs from a phenomenological tradition that seeks to understand individual actors' meaningful experience. Luhmann is instead interested in the meaning-processing and sense-making activities of entire social systems (Arnoldi 2001: 3–4). While he was initially inspired by Husserl's phenomenological perspective, Luhmann developed a very distinct understanding of meaning with reference to Spencer-Brown's ideas about logic. For Luhmann, meaning in social systems arises from distinctions being drawn: as phenomenon A becomes differentiated from phenomenon B, it is distinct and thereby becomes meaningful (Arnoldi 2001: 4).

By building on Spencer-Brown's formal theory of a system as difference, Luhmann wanted to transcend the potential biological reductionism of Maturana and Varela's notion of the autopoietic closure of a system. He emphasise a distinct *social* dimension of subsystems, including psychic systems (Gilgen 2013: ix). According to Spencer-Brown's theory, social subsystems constitute themselves through the observation of their own operations with reference to their external environment that is different. Hence, the term 'observation' has a specific meaning for Luhmann. It does not mean actual observation of a phenomenon by the *human senses*, but the cognitive process of distinguishing one *social* phenomenon from another by labelling *social phenomena* in distinct ways. Systems theory is therefore concerned not with human behaviour as such but with how social subsystems observe human behaviour (Philippopoulos-Mihalopoulos 2014: 398), a point already alluded to in the earlier discussion of data collection. Moreover, Luhmann does not trace human behaviour back to individual or collective human actors but instead explains social action in contemporary societies with reference to, inter alia, a psychic system. He nevertheless works with a highly socialised understanding of human behaviour by perceiving psychic systems as linked, eg, through observations, to a range of other social subsystems. Psychic systems can thereby become subject to the influence of interests that reflect the rationality of social subsystems, but only in a limited, mediated way due to constrained communication between different subsystems in a society.

Psychic subsystems as social and mediating the influence of interests

Luhmann defines a psychic system as constituted by processes of perception and consciousness. In contrast to this, social subsystems, such as law, economics and politics, are constituted by communicative processes (Luhmann 2013: 187). He works with a highly social conception of a psychic system because human beings are not considered in isolation as distinct, individual human beings, since structural coupling and language link psychic systems with the social system (Luhmann 2013: 193). Complexity in individual psychic systems can only be reduced to manageable structures through the relationships between psychic systems and their environment, ie, other social subsystems. Therefore, social and psychic systems are dependent on each other for their co-evolution (Arnoldi 2001: 6). Patterns of other social subsystems, and their interest in maintaining them, may have a bearing on a psychic system. But this will be mediated by the distinct processes of consciousness and perception that constitute a psychic system. Moreover, the influence of interests on social action is also mediated by limited communication between different social subsystems.

Mediating interests through limited communication between different social subsystems

The second distinguishing feature of Luhmann's notion of mediated interests is that they can shape social action only in a mediated way, since social subsystems communicate with each other on the basis of their internal self-referential operations. Hence, interests are mediated as part of the internal self-reflexive operations of a social subsystem. For instance, within the political subsystem, electoral political preferences – which can be considered as empirical indicators of interest claims of citizens – are adjusted in cyclical movements in response to political programmes (Luhmann 2013: 31). These adjustments can be considered part of the recursive, self-reflexive constitution of the political system.

Interests are also mediated when social subsystems observe their environment. How social subsystems observe differences between themselves mediates the influence that one can exert upon another. The reason for this is that the difference between a social subsystem and its environment will be introduced into the system itself, and the system will constitute itself with the aid of this difference (Miller 1987: 193). Hence, the observations that a social subsystem collates of its environment are in turn the foundation for the internal regulation of information about the system-environment difference (Willke 1987: 254). The *extent* of the difference between a social subsystem and its environment is therefore central for understanding what interests may influence legal regulation in what way (Paterson and Teubner 1998: 460).

For instance, children's welfare or best interests are translated in distinct ways by the legal system, eg, through requirements for procedural fairness in the assessment of special educational needs (King 2006). But this may actually provide only limited recognition of actual, substantive educational needs and thus the interests of the children concerned. Here the law focuses on a 'thin' *procedural legal* account of what is 'right' or 'good'. It stipulates compliance with an obligation of means rather than ends by requiring compliance with specific procedural steps for assembling evidence about special educational needs (King 2006: 36). Hence, from a systems-theoretical perspective, mediation of interests means in the context of legal regulation that we may find procedures empirically for expressing interests but not direct impacts of substantive interests on social action. Organisations, distinct formally organised social systems that operate with the binary code of 'member'/'non-member' (Luhmann 2008: 188), also play an important role in this process.

Mediating interests through organisations

From a systems-theoretical perspective, organisations can mediate interests in three ways. First, they may mediate interests by promoting or even being the result of structural coupling between different social subsystems. For instance, the organisation 'university' is the result of structural coupling between the functional social subsystems of science and education (Danscheid 2010: 42). In this case, organisations enable the performance of a social subsystem through reference to other social subsystems by facilitating communication between different social subsystems. In the case of a university, the goal orientation of scientific endeavour becomes mediated with reference to pedagogical and economic policy goal orientations of a subsystem of education.

Second, organisations may mediate interests by virtue of being mediator organisations. Mediator organisations promote *temporary exchanges* between different social subsystems (Danscheid 2010: 42–34). Here, one social subsystem may become dependent upon another for only for a limited amount of time through expectations of a performance. An example of this may be a stock market as a distinct form of organisation that provides information to the political system about the value of key corporations and thus potential demand for taxation policies that further promote the value of corporations. The interests of the stock market to promote the legibility of the value of corporations as an input in investment decisions becomes mediated by the distinct interest of the political system to understand the spread of value of corporations in order to calculate income to be derived from taxation and macroeconomic impacts of tax policies. Mediator organisations thus promote a degree of alignment of different goal orientations and thus interests of different social subsystems.

Third, in the context of business regulation, corporate organisations' interests are mediated in a particular way. Business regulation is often framed as a struggle to reconcile economic and social regulation for a wider public interest with the corporations' own private interests in maximising revenue and remaining competitive, eg, in market exchange relationships (De Schutter and Lenoble 2010). From a systems-theoretical perspective, the interests of the corporation cannot be understood by linking them back to collectives of individual human beings, such as managers, employees, owners of capital or shareholders. Instead there is a distinct interest of the corporation itself, since the corporation observes itself as a unity (Teubner 1994: 34). This corporate self-interest becomes mediated by a balancing of its function, performance and reflection (Teubner 1994).

The corporation's function refers to its task of maintaining its continued existence. This may be defined in economic terms, eg, as the need to generate sufficient revenue to also support the future needs of society. The corporation's contribution to various subsystems, such as the political and economic subsystems and the natural environment, is referred to as the corporation's performance (Teubner 1994: 43). Reflection captures the corporation's relationship to itself, ie, its self-observation and recursive autopoietic self-constitution. Public interests can influence the corporation's activities in a mediated, though still significant way by shaping the corporation's function and performance (Teubner 1994: 46). For instance, public interests may be integrated into the corporation's internal codes and thus mode of operation (Teubner 1994: 36). Hence, from a systems-theoretical perspective, the interests of the corporation are mediated in the sense that they are defined procedurally rather than substantively (Teubner 1994: 38).

To summarize, from a systems-theoretical perspective, asserting interests is a matter of building up shared rationalities which allow different subsystems to communicate with each other and thus negotiate the terms of intervention into their systems (Willke 1996: 269). The interests of one social subsystem can thus only become influential in a mediated way, ie, if they take into account the other social subsystem's operating code. But what is the contribution of a systems-theoretical notion of mediated interests to regulation literature?

Implications for regulation literature

To begin with, a systems-theoretical notion of mediated interests introduces a sociological approach toward understanding interests to the regulation literature, which usually draws on political and economic conceptions of interests (see, eg, Jolls et al. 2000; Ogus 2004). A political conception of interests focuses on how individual or collective actors assert their preferences and thereby build relationships of power in regulatory regimes (Hancher and Moran 1989). This way of understanding interests has yielded intriguing and counterintuitive insights. For instance, actors with very different political and economic preferences in relation to a regulatory issue may actually all support restrictive regulation. Legal rules prohibiting the sale of alcohol in the United States in the 1920s and 1930s were supported both by bootleggers, who profited from the black-market sale of highly prized alcohol, and Baptists, who supported prohibition on the grounds of their Christian beliefs (Yundle 2011).

Economic conceptions of interests, often closely related to political ones, have also shaped accounts of the design and implementation of regulatory regimes. They focus on economic goals of private corporations and public bodies, such as maximising the wealth of an economy as a whole as well as revenue for the particular organisation, including through taxes and profits. Economic interests are often perceived as objective and measurable (Swedberg 2005: 368).

In contrast to this, a sociological conception of interests highlights that what interests are and how they are expressed is shaped not just by relationships of power and economic objectives but also by distinct social forces, such as social interactions and structures — or, in systems-theoretical terms, structural coupling. A sociological perspective also queries the instrumental character of political and economic conceptions of interests, ie, their focus on the attainment of specific objectives. A sociological take recognises that social action can also run counter to the self-interests of social actors, because of the force of intervening ideas (Swedberg 2005: 380). For instance, the appeal of ideas like 'taking back control' that alluded to the re-establishment of national sovereignty and strengthening of control of the UK government over political and economic governance helps to explain why a narrow majority of the UK electorate voted in the 2016 referendum for leaving the European Union. The voting behaviour of some 'Leave' voters cannot be explained with reference to self-interest, given the real risk of some of these voters losing their jobs due to the relocation of foreign-owned production facilities outside the UK (McKenzie 2017). Hence, a sociological perspective qualifies political and economic conceptions of interests as 'real' and 'objective' (Benton 1981: 164) by recognising the force of intervening ideas. Moreover, a sociological notion of interests can capture the cultural contexts in which interests develop – or, in systems-theoretical terms, the distinct rationalities of each social subsystem. For instance, the very idea of interests, and especially individual interests, may be considered an aspect of Western, Anglo-American versions of liberalism (Swedberg 2005: 365, 384).

More specifically, a Luhmannian sociological conception of mediated interests questions the assumption of public interest theories that politics can develop regulatory programs in the wider, strategic and long-term public interest (Danscheid 2010: 143). It prompts us to abandon an overarching notion of the public interest and invites us instead to analyse empirically whether we can observe communications about a public interest in different social subsystems. If so, we need to ask how a public interest is perceived by the distinct observations of different social subsystems and psychic systems. If we find a high degree of self-referential constitution, eg, of the political subsystem, this may suggest that private rather than public interest theories of regulation have greater explanatory power. Private interest theories of regulation point to the interests of politicians in developing regulatory programs that also secure private interests for themselves, such as re-election to their political office and thus continued access to power (Stigler 1971). Qualitative empirical data can help to develop inductively generated understandings of interests within a social subsystem that are not simply deductively derived from a generalised function of the social subsystem to maintain its own patterns in distinction from its environment. For instance, Paterson and Teubner's (1998: 466) application of their mapping tool depicts regulators as having an interest, among others, 'not to be subjected to inflexible interpretation of legal regulations' in relation to health and safety at offshore oil platforms. Conversely, their map identifies industry interests as related to 'profit' and 'rapid production' (468).

Finally, a sociological systems-theoretical conception of interests questions the idea of interests marking out a battleground for the assertion and potential clash of political and economic interests. From a Luhmannian perspective, we know about interests by observing and thus acknowledging the meaning-making processes and operations of another functional social subsystem and its organisations as well as its natural environments. This perspective is rooted in consensus, in contrast to the conflict orientation of systems theory. Hence, conflicts between different interests may be attenuated through programs of difference minimisation. These can be part of structural coupling, which entails a reconstruction of information from the environment within a social subsystem (Paterson and Teubner 1998: 478).

Abandoning the idea of interests as marking out a battleground for the assertion and potential clash of economic and political preferences also questions the pervasive notion of regulatory agencies being at risk of capture by regulated organisations (Bernstein 1955; Carpenter and Moss 2013; Dal Bó 2006). From a Luhmannian perspective, regulatory failure or success depends on how well structural coupling works. For instance, a regulated organisation may reconstruct state legal regulation within its organisation through close structural coupling between its management systems and state law. Empirical research about this from an organisational-studies perspective has referred to this as legal endogeneity. Here state law, such as anti-discrimination law, is closely embedded in procedures and structures of the regulated organisation (Edelman 2016). In this case the separate social subsystem of the regulatory regime does not need to know much about how the regulated organisation works for regulation to be successfully implemented. This provides a critical take on accounts of regulatory failure in the regulation literature that focus on information asymmetries between regulators and regulated organisations as a reason for such failures (Hawkins 1984; Ogus 2004: ch. 7).

Conclusion

This chapter sought to show the wider relevance of Niklas Luhmann's work – beyond its seminal contribution to social theory – to empirical research about the implementation of legal regulation, including in the context of nature-society interactions. In the regulation literature, Luhmann's work and its interpretation by other systems theorists has often been the basis for exploring the *limits* of regulatory intervention by law or other social subsystems. Overcoming blind spots – which arise from the fact that social subsystems can observe each other only through the distinct and limited lens of their own internal operations – through procedural law has been key to this approach to regulation (eg, Orts, 1995). In contrast, this chapter has suggested that the blind spots created by the self-referential operations of systems – which limit communication between systems and thereby also mediate interests – can be the starting point for developing innovative regulatory strategies that are based on enhancing systems' resilience and adaptive capacity.

This chapter has focused on Luhmannian-inspired systems theory, but there are further approaches in the empirical social-science field that blend Luhmannian ideas with operations research in order to understand how systems work (see, eg, Jackson 1985, 2001). Operations research shares with Luhmann the assumption that systems are highly complex and thus need to be further analysed (Jackson 2001: 233), but it works with a notion of pre-constituted human agency by defining social systems as 'the consequence, intended or otherwise, of the action and interaction of human beings' (Jackson 1985: 137). What recent 'soft' and interpretive perspectives on operations research can add here is that they do not a priori assume that the social world can be understood in systemic ways, but turn this into a question of empirical inquiry (Checkland 1978; Jackson 2001). Soft systems analysis may be particularly relevant for applied research that seeks to inform policy because it works with models, which are fleshed out by quantitative empirical data. These are, however, complemented by reference to stakeholders' subjective perceptions of natural and social systems (Jackson 1985: 143). Systems approaches have become very popular among environmental policy makers in a number of jurisdictions. They seek to build policy on insights about interactions between natural and social systems (see, eg, DEFRA 2014; Pongsiri et al. 2017: 257). A new research agenda into regulation steered by the perspective of empirical Luhmannian systems-theoretical research and cognate fields can therefore build on fruitful foundations and may also matter for public policy makers.

Note

1 Observation: Politics includes public administration offices and political state offices (eg, government departments) at different levels. Figure 5.2 can be adjusted to different empirical scenarios. For instance, in case reliance on science or psychic systems is a significant feature of the subsystem of a regulatory regime, a separate oval shape for the social subsystem of science or psychic systems can be added.

References

Adegbulu, O. (2018) 'Making corporate law great again: deconstructing and identifying public interest in corporate theories and corporate entity theories' *33 Aust. J. Corp. Law* 1–24.

Arnoldi, J. (2001) 'Niklas Luhmann: an introduction' *18*(1) *Theory Cult. Soc.* 1–13.

Baecker, D. (2013) 'Editor's preface to the German edition' in Baecker D. (ed), *Introduction to Systems Theory: Niklas Luhmann* (Cambridge, Polity Press), xvii–xx.

Beck, U. (1992) *Risk Society: Towards a New Modernity* (London, Sage Publications).

Benton, T. (1981) '"Objective interests" and the sociology of power' *15*(2) *Sociology* 161–184.

Bernstein, M.H. (1955) *Regulating Business by Independent Commission* (Princeton, Princeton University Press).

Black, J. (2005) 'What is regulatory innovation?' in Black J., Lodge M. and Thatcher M. (eds), *Regulatory Innovation* (Cheltenham, Edward Elgar), 1–15.

Bora, A. (2006) 'Licensing plant GMOs: a brief overview over European regulatory conditions for the deliberate release of genetically modified plants' in Hausendorf H. and Bora A. (eds) *Analysing Citizenship Talk: Social Positioning in Political and Legal Decision-Making Processes* (Amsterdam, John Benjamins), 50–60.

Carpenter, D. and Moss, D. (eds) (2013) *Preventing Regulatory Capture: Special Interest Influence and How to Limit It* (Cambridge, Cambridge University Press).

Checkland, P.B. (1978) 'The origins and nature of "hard" systems thinking' *5*(2) *J. Appl. Syst. Anal.* 99–110.

Corbin, J. and Strauss, A. (1990) 'Grounded theory research: procedures, canons and evaluative criteria' *13*(1) *Qualit. Sociol.* 3–21.

Dal Bó, E. (2006) 'Regulatory capture: a review', *22*(2) *Oxford Rev. Econ. Policy* 203–225.

Danscheid, M. (2010) *Grenzen und Möglichkeiten von Naturrisikomanagement: Ein systemtheoretischer Ansatz* (Dissertation, Universität Bonn) [online] Available at: http://hss.ulb.uni-bonn.de/2010/2175/2175.pdf (accessed 14.03.20).

De Schutter, O. and Lenoble, J. (eds) (2010) *Reflexive Governance: Redefining the Public Interest in a Pluralistic World* (Oxford, Hart Publishing).

DEFRA (Department for Environment, Food and Rural Affairs) (2014) *Making the Most of Our Evidence: A Strategy for DEFRA and Its Network* [online]. Available at: https://www.gov.uk/government/publications/evidence-strategy-for-defra-and-its-network (accessed 14.03.20).

Edelman, L.B. (2016) *Working Law: Courts, Corporations, and Symbolic Civil Rights* (Chicago, The University of Chicago Press).

European Commission (2015) *Ecological Flows in the Implementation of the Water Framework Directive, Guidance Document No. 31* (Luxembourg: Office for Official Publications of the European Communities) [online] Available at: https://circabc.europa.eu/sd/a/e354116d-f359-4ec9-bdb7-53645df35c90/Guidance%20No%2031%20-%20Ecological%20flows%20(final%20version).pdf (accessed 14.03.20.).

Fischer-Lescano, A. (2012) 'Critical systems theory' *38*(1) *Philos. Soc. Crit.* 3–23.

Gilgen, P. (2013) 'System-autopoiesis-form: an introduction to Luhmann's *Introduction to Systems Theory*' in Baecker D. (ed), *Introduction to Systems Theory: Niklas Luhmann* (Cambridge, Polity Press), iix–xvi.

Hancher, L. and Moran, M. (1989) 'Organizing regulatory space' in Hancher L. and Moran M. (eds), *Capitalism, Culture and Regulation* (Oxford, Clarendon Press), 271–300.

Hawkins, K. (1984) *Environment and Enforcement* (Oxford, Clarendon Press).

Hernes, T. and Bakken, T. (2003) 'Implications of self-reference: Niklas Luhmann's autopoiesis and organization theory' *24*(9) *Org. Stud.* 1511–1535.

Jackson, M.C. (1985) 'Social systems theory and practice: the need for a critical approach' *10 Int. J. Gen. Syst.* 135–151.

Jackson, M.C. (2001) 'Critical systems thinking and practice' *128 Eur. J. Operat. Res.* 233–244.

Jolls, C., Sunstein, C.R. and Thaler, R.H. (2000) 'A behavioural approach to law and economics' in Sunstein C. (ed), *Behavioural Law and Economics* (Cambridge, Cambridge University Press), 13–59.

Kang, K. (2018) 'Making paradoxes invisible: international law as an autopoietic system' *14*(3) *Int. J. Law Context* 315–334.

King, M. (2006) 'How the law defines the special educational needs of autistic children' *18*(1) *Child Family Law Quart.* 23–42.

King, M. and Thornhill, C. (2006) 'Introduction' in King M. and Thornhill C. (eds), *Luhmann on Law and Politics: Critical Appraisals and Applications* (London, Hart Publishing), 1–10.

Kolben, K. (2011) 'Transnational labor regulation and the limits of governance' *12*(2) *Theor. Inq. Law* 403–437.

Koppen, I.J.. (1991) 'Environmental mediation: an example of applied autopoiesis' in T'Veld R., Schaap L., Termeer C. and Van Twist M. (eds.), *Autopoiesis and Configuration Theory: New Approaches to Societal Steering* (Dordrecht, Kluwer Academic Publishers), 143–150.

Lange, B. (1998) 'Understanding regulatory law: empirical versus systems-theoretical approaches?' *18 Oxford J. Legal Stud.* 449–471.

Lee, D. (2000) 'The society of society: the grand finale of Niklas Luhmann' *18*(2) *Soc. Theory* 320–330.

Lock, M. and Farquhar J. (eds) (2007) *Beyond the Body Proper: Reading the Anthropology of Material Life* (Durham, NC, Duke University Press).

Luhmann, N. (1984) *Soziale Systeme: Grundriß einer allgemeinen Theorie* (Frankfurt am Main, Suhrkamp).

Luhmann, N. (1990) *Ökologische Kommunikation, 3. Auflage* (Opladen, Westdeutscher Verlag).

Luhmann, N. (1997) *Die Gesellschaft der Gesellschaft* (Frankfurt am Main, Suhrkamp Verlag).

Luhmann, N. (2008) *Risk: A Sociological Theory* (New Brunswick, Aldine Transaction).

Luhmann, N. (2012) *Theory of Society, Volume 1* (Stanford, Stanford University Press).

Luhmann, N. (2013) *Introduction to Systems Theory* (Cambridge, Policy Press).

Maturana, H.R. and Varela F.J. (1980) *Autopoiesis and Cognition* (Boston, Reidel).

McKenzie, L. (2017) '"It's not ideal": reconsidering "anger" and "apathy" in the Brexit vote among an invisible working class' *21*(3) *Compet. Change* 199–210.

Miller, M. (1987) 'Selbstreferenz und Differenzerfahrung: Einige Überlegungen zu Luhmanns Theorie sozialer Systeme' in Schmid M. and Haferkamp H. (eds), *Sinn, Kommunikation und soziale Differenzierung* (Frankfurt, Suhrkamp), 187–211.

Nassehi, A. (2005) 'Organizations as decision machines: Niklas Luhmann's theory of organized social systems' *53*(1) *Sociol. Rev.* 178–191.

Ogus, A. (2004) *Regulation: Legal Form and Economic Theory* (Oxford, Hart Publishing).

Orts, E. (1995) 'Reflexive environmental law' *89*(4) *Northwestern Univ. Law Rev.* 1227–1340.

Ostrom E. (2009) 'A general framework for analyzing sustainability of social eco-logical systems' *325*(5939) *Science* 419–422.

Parsons, T. (1963) 'On the concept of influence' *27*(1) *Public Opin. Quart.* 37–62.

Paterson, J. (2000) *Behind the Mask: Regulating Health and Safety in Britain's Off-Shore Oil and Gas Industry* (Aldershot, Ashgate).

Paterson, J. and Teubner G. (1998) 'Changing maps: empirical legal autopoiesis' *7*(4) *Soc. Legal Stud.* 452–486.

Philippopoulos-Mihalopoulos, A. (2012) 'Critical autopoiesis: the environment of the law' in de Vries U. and Francot L. (eds), *Law's Environment: Critical Legal Perspectives* (Den Haag, Eleven International Publishing), 45–62.

Philippopoulos-Mihalopoulos, A. (2014) 'Critical autopoiesis and the materiality of law' *27 Int. J. Semiot. Law* 389–418.

Pollack, M. (2002) 'Learning from the Americanists (again): theory and method in the study of delegation' *25*(1) *West Eur. Polit.* 200–219.

Pongsiri, F.W., Bassi, A., Haines, A. and Demassieux, F. (2017). *The need for a systems approach to planetary health. 1*(7) *Lancet* 257–259.

Rottleuthner, H. (1989) 'A purified sociology of law: Niklas Luhmann on the au-tonomy of the legal system' *23*(5) *Law Soc. Rev.* 779–798.

Schwanitz, D. (1995) 'Systems theory according to Niklas Luhmann: its environment and conceptual strategies' *30*(1) *Cult. Crit.* 137–170.

Segre, S. (2012) *Talcott Parsons: An Introduction* (Landham, University Press of America).

Simon, F.C. (2017) *Meta-Regulation in Practice* (London, Routledge).

Star, S.L. and Strauss, A. (1999) 'Layers of silence, arenas of voice: the ecology of visible and invisible work' *8 Comput. Supp. Coop. Work* 9–30.

Stigler, G.J. (1971) 'The theory of economic regulation' *2 Bell J. Econ. Manage. Sci.* 3–21.

Strauss, A. and Corbin J.M. (1997) *Grounded Theory in Practice* (Thousand Oaks, CA, Sage).

Strauss, A. and Corbin J.M. (1998) *Basics of Qualitative Research: Techniques and Procedures for Developing Grounded Theory* (Thousand Oaks, CA, Sage).

Swedberg, R. (2005) 'Can there be a sociological concept of interest?' *34 Theory Soc.* 359–390.

Tacke, V. and Bommes, M. (2006) 'Das Allgemeine und das Besondere des Netzwerkes' in Hollstein B. and Straus F. (eds), *Handbuch Qualitative Netzwerkanalyse: Konzepte, Methoden, Anwendungen* (Wiesbaden, VS Verlag für Sozialwissenschaften), 37–62.

Teubner, G. (1986), 'After legal instrumentalism? strategic models of post-regulatory law' in Teubner G. (ed), *Dilemmas of Law in the Welfare State* (Berlin, Walter de Gruyter), 299–325.

Teubner, G. (1994) 'Company interest: the public interest of the enterprise "in itself"' in Rogowski R. and Wilthagen T. (eds), *Reflexive Labour Law* (Deventer, Kluwer Law and Taxation Publishers), 21–51.

Thatcher, M. and Sweet, A.S. (2002) 'Theory and practice of delegation to non-majoritarian institutions' *25*(1) *West Europ. Polit.* 1–22.

Trebilcock, M.J. (1975) 'Winners and losers in the modern regulatory state: must the consumer always lose' *13*(3) *Osgoode Hall Law J.* 619–647.

Weber, M. (1922) *Economy and Society: An Outline of Interpretative Sociology*, trans Fischoff E. (1978) (Berkeley, University of California Press).

Willke, H. (1987) 'Differenzierung und integration in Luhmanns Theorie Sozialer Systeme', in Schmid M. and Haferkamp H. (eds), *Sinn, Kommunikation und soziale Differenzierung* (Frankfurt, Suhrkamp), 247–274.

Willke, H. (1996) *Systemtheorie II: Interventionstheorie* (Stuttgart, Lucius & Lucius).

Yundle, B. (2011) 'Bootleggers and Baptists in the theory of regulation' in Levi-Faur D. (ed), *Handbook on the Politics of Regulation* (Cheltenham, Edward Elgar), 25–32.

Zehetmair, S. (2012) 'Societal aspects of vulnerability to natural hazards' *70 Raumforschung, Raumordnung* 273–284.

Chapter 6

Free floating or free riding? Recursive norm-building in the German energy transition using the example of the approval of e-scooters in German cities

Cristina Besio and Margrit Seckelmann

Introduction

The energy transition is an important political project in Germany that is meant to make a major contribution to addressing the big challenge of climate change. The success of this project comes down not only to the fact that new technological infrastructure and economic models need to be established but also to the fact that a new normative order is emerging (see also Balasescu and Seguin 2018). This affects several areas: first and foremost, of course, the energy industry, but other important sectors include the building industry, agriculture and mobility. This chapter is concerned with mobility.

In light of the fact that the transport sector is the third largest source of greenhouse-gas emissions in Germany, and the emissions result primarily from road traffic (Bundesministerium für Umwelt, Naturschutz und nukleare Sicherheit 2019, with data from 2018), the plan to launch what is called the 'transport transition' remains crucial (Canzler 2019; Canzler and Knie 2017; Schwedes et al. 2016). German politicians are primarily aiming to achieve this with the 2015 Electric Vehicle Act as well as with measures, including tax measures, intended to give buyers incentives to purchase electric cars, expand the charging infrastructure and add to the federal government's vehicle fleet.

A further milestone in this process is the recent approval (2019) of electric scooters, or e-scooters, in Germany. The federal government (more precisely, the Federal Ministry of Transport) wanted to stimulate the transport transition, pushing it toward electric vehicles. These scooters are seen not only as environmentally friendly but also as a fun alternative to cars. Moreover, the number of registrations for electric cars had been stagnating, and therefore new actions were necessary.

We use the approval, its consequences and the subsequent regulations as an example to show how the emergence of new norms in the context of the energy transition cannot be understood as a top-down process but rather as a process of recursive norm-building, in which not only legislators but also various other actors are involved.

In mid-June 2019, e-scooters were approved in Germany by a regulation from the Federal Minister of Transport, Andreas Scheuer. The aims were to make the use of public transport attractive and to promote the avoidance of cars. Several individual and organisational actors saw this as a new opportunity and began using the new means of transport in line with their interests and goals. However, the consequences have not been as positive as expected. The pictures have been all over the media: more and more e-scooters can be seen on public streets, even in German cities. However, what was intended as a new stage in the 'sharing culture' (Aigrain 2012) threatens to turn into a nightmare. In large cities like Berlin, parked e-scooters are stacked on pavements and represent a serious obstacle for older pedestrians. In addition, it is becoming increasingly clear that large companies such as Lime, Uber Jump, Bird, Tier, Circ and Voi use employment models that suggest that their employees are being exploited and underpaid. Finally, the media have sparked a discussion as to whether the introduction of e-scooters was positive or harmful from an environmental point of view.

We demonstrate that different individual and organisational commercial actors are using the free-floating model (parking e-scooters at any point in the city and not in special parking spaces) in specific ways that we conceive as a sort of free riding. This model was chosen by federal legislators in road traffic law and by municipalities for urban planning in order to make the sharing model more attractive, but it has been interpreted in a way that has caused serious side effects within a short period of time. This in turn has prompted various regulatory bodies to introduce follow-up regulations.

Regulation of the energy transition in Germany

A study recently published by the auditing firm Ernst & Young on behalf of the German government demands that as a measure to accelerate the energy transition, 'legal uncertainties' be eliminated as quickly as possible 'through the final design of essential legal norms that are a basic requirement for the attractiveness of new business models' (Edelmann and Fleischle 2018: 8). Apart from the question of what a 'final design' can be in this context, this demand contains an important idea: the energy transition is dependent on legal conditions that make it attractive for actors to participate in its design.

With regard to the energy transition, there are some studies available on the topic of renewable energies that map the dynamics of the sector well (including Bruns et al. 2011; Fuchs 2014; Fuchs and Hinderer 2014; Fuchs and Wassermann 2008; Giacovelli 2017; Kungl and Geels 2018) and provide a good overview of the development of legal regulations. These studies reconstruct the phases that the energy industry in Germany has gone through in the past decades and show which technological innovations have taken place, which actors (companies, but also civic movements, associations, farmers, municipal utilities, energy consultants etc.) have been involved in the energy sector at various times and, in particular, which laws and institutions they have supported. Legislation is seen as crucial to establish niches for the development of socio-technical innovations in the energy sector (Fuchs and Wassermann 2008; Gross and Mautz 2015: 83).

With regard to the question of electric vehicles, it is clear that it will not be possible to achieve a transport transition without changing the legal framework (Canzler and Knie 2016, 2017). Studies are available that explain the complexity of transport regulations, which involve multiple actors at the national, local and supranational levels. The governance instruments available in the sector and the difficulties of implementing political objectives with such instruments are also known (Schwedes et al. 2016). Hope is rather restrained when it comes to the impact of political decisions on the momentum of economic and social developments in transport.

While the impact of the law on areas such as energy and transport has been relatively well investigated, the question of how the law came into being remains under-researched; it has become a 'black box' (see Bauer 2014: 97). In particular, there has not been sufficient research on the role of the addressees of legislation in the creation and further development of legal norms. Legal science is only slowly beginning to investigate this issue, most clearly in Bauer's (2014) administrative and legal monograph. The problem is that the complexity of regulating the energy transition is particularly high. The deregulation of the energy markets in 1998, the increased focus on forms of 'regulated self-regulation' starting in 2005 and the plurality of objectives since 2011, in which deregulation of the markets was combined with the requirement to phase out nuclear energy, have had the effect of making legislative processes hard to comprehend.

We address this research gap and understand the energy transition as a recursive process. In the course of this process, normative expectations are repeatedly revised and re-specified by various instances, each time based on their own dynamics. In this chapter, we focus on the case of e-scooters and examine the legal and commercial re-specifications on the part of companies that operate sharing models as well as users in their – in terms of systems theory – everyday communication.

Theory: Re-specifications and recursiveness

Several actors are involved in legislative processes: not only political actors at supranational, national, regional and local levels, but also those actors intended as the addressees of regulation. There are also opinion-forming actors such as non-governmental organisations, interest groups and the media, which play a role that can hardly be overestimated in today's political mediation processes. To explain legislative processes, we therefore introduce two key concepts: *re-specification* and *recursivity*.

The concept of recursiveness is prominent in Anthony Giddens's theory of structuration. The starting point is the idea of the duality of structure (Giddens 1984: 25–28). It states that social structures in the form of rules and resources are both the medium and the result of interactions. Rules and resources of jurisprudence, for example, enable (and limit) how actors act. However, it is actors who reflexively produce, update and, if necessary, change rules in situational interactions. Individuals and organisations thus (co) form the framework for their own actions (Ortmann 2010).

We adapt this concept to systems theory, and instead of the duality of structure, we focus on the relationships between different systems (Luhmann 2012). From a systems-theory perspective, external suggestions from a system of any kind are never adopted intact, but are handled internally in a specific way each time: external events thus gain resonance in a system, depending on how the system perceives, processes and adapts them (Luhmann 1996). We assume a political and legal system that sets forth norms for collectivity with a high degree of commitment (Luhmann 2009). These are observed by other systems and may be used by them. Such norms are thereby specifically transformed. But the law can, in turn, observe such transformations and subsequently change the laws. This is often done by taking into consideration the mass media observation of the transformations described. To be sure, the mass media observation does not take place objectively either, but is based on specific media dynamics (Besio and Pronzini 2014; Luhmann 2000).

In this chapter, we are particularly interested in the observations and transformations of law on the part of individual actors in their everyday communications as well as commercial organisations (Luhmann 2003). For observations and transformations that are carried out by organisations, Luhmann has used the term 're-specification', which means that organisations put their own unique spin on external expectations and requirements and mold them into a more specific form compatible with their activities. Enterprises, for example, re-specify money in the form of specific investments (Luhmann 1994: 308–313), and schools re-specify the intention to educate into their own curricula (Luhmann 1994: 308–313, 2002: 144). In other words, highly generalised references such as the legal requirement for sustainability are re-specified in a special form by organisations that operate in the economic sector, for instance.

The model can also be used for the adoption of norms in everyday communication by individual addressees or users of those norms. The special thing about the re-specifications that take place at the level of organisations and everyday communication is that they carry out a specification that makes it possible to make norms, laws or other measures manageable for the actors. These re-specifications do not take the form of rational choices by isolated actors. Rather, they are constituted in a field of action that, in our present example, is formed around the topic of the energy transition and mobility.

Recursive norm-building in the case of e-scooters

Initial legal frameworks

First, the legal framework for the use of e-scooters needs to be discussed. It can only be outlined here, as it is very complex due to the combination of road traffic, energy and general regulatory aspects.

On German roads that are dedicated to public traffic, there exists a general freedom of transport derived from the fundamental right of general freedom of action (Art. 2(1) of the German Basic Law; §16(1) of the Road Traffic Licensing Regulations). When it comes to driving motor vehicles on public roads, this principle is breached to the extent that only such vehicles approved by the government may do so (§1(1) of the Road Traffic Act).

There is an exception for slow, small vehicles such as electrically operated wheelchairs. They can be used freely if they do not exceed a speed of 6 km/h (§1(2) of the Road Traffic Act). While special permits were valid for the Segways used in the tourism industry and under instruction, e-scooters, which typically drive faster than 6 km/h, require an approval for road traffic (§§1 and 3 of the Vehicle Registration Regulation), for which, in turn, liability insurance is required. (If the e-scooters reach speeds of more than 20 km/h, riders also need a moped licence.) In order for an e-scooter to be operated, a number plate must be assigned and affixed to the scooter with a stamp, and a registration certificate must be issued. All of this is governed by the Regulation on the Participation of Small Electric Vehicles in Road Traffic (eKFV) of 15 June 2019. From that date, e-scooters were permitted on German roads if they met these requirements.

At that point in time (mid-June 2019), German cities had to develop transport concepts to respond to the use of this new means of transport. Unfortunately, this never took place in the sense of genuine concepts being developed. Most of the preliminary considerations were limited to decisions that e-scooters driving more slowly than 20 km/h could use the bicycle lanes and that faster ones could only be operated on the road, with helmets being required (Koschmieder and Huß 2020).

Above all, possible conflicts in *flowing* traffic, ie, with cyclists or car drivers, were considered, but not in *stationary* traffic, ie, parking on pavements. As mentioned earlier, this is currently proving to be a major problem, since a free-floating model has been opted for, according to which e-scooters can be freely parked in car parks and located by their operators via GPS (Koschmieder and Huß 2020: 81). This is because most e-scooters operate on hire models (those in private ownership do not pose any problems for car-park management, since they are usually recharged in private garages in the evening). Nor was it considered in advance that these means of transport would have to be collected and recharged. The way this is organised can negate the aims of the regulation. For instance, diesel vehicles are sometimes used to transport the e-scooters to a charging point, even though the aim of approving e-scooters was to reduce diesel emissions.

Strategies of users and operators

The strategies of e-scooter users and hire companies lead to various problems and can even result in legislators' environmental objectives being lost in practice.

The first problem concerns competition in the road space, which has increased due to the introduction of e-scooters. Municipalities used the car-sharing model for e-scooters, which turned out to be a somewhat incorrect forecast of user behaviour. The main difference is that car-sharing models for a long time were not designed as free-floating models (although there have recently been such providers as, for instance, DriveNow). At least in Germany, you usually had to park them in specific car parks or specific areas. This is exactly what the German municipalities did not intend, as they wanted to offer incentives to use e-scooters for the 'last mile' (which might be the route from a car-sharing car park to a user's home). This was also linked to the objective of making sharing models more attractive overall. Negative experiences that other countries had had with e-scooters and freely parkable bicycles for hire (eg, France) were largely ignored in Germany.

The re-specification was therefore primarily based on user behaviour in everyday communication. It does not appear that workers and commuters on their way to work tend to use e-scooters; instead, many users are young people and tourists. These two categories of people care little about where they park these vehicles (Jacobs 2019). This means that many e-scooters are parked in the vicinity of tourist attractions such as the Brandenburg Gate. In central locations and in cities such as Berlin, Hamburg and Cologne, e-scooters are 'parked' on the pavements, which among other things means that they become an obstacle for pedestrians, especially those with limited mobility.

Many users see these devices as toys rather than vehicles. In some cases, users ride on the pavement in spite of prohibitions, sometimes even when they are drunk. Administrative offences by riders of e-scooters are increasing, and the number of accidents in which they are involved is rising. According to the police, the most common causes of accidents with e-scooters are driving mistakes, illegal use of pavements and alcohol (Jacobs 2019). Moreover, children often drive these vehicles. The law permits their use from age 14 and up. Some providers stipulate a minimum age of 18, but since the services are paid for via an app, it is not possible to check which age group is actually riding the scooters (Krüger and Waschbüsch 2019).

A second relevant problem is providers' business models, which create a 'digital precariat'. After approval, several companies saw the opportunity to offer hire systems for e-scooters in German cities. Big cities like Berlin are particularly attractive, and large providers such as Lime, Uber Jump, Bird, Tier, Circ and Voi quickly occupied the market. However, e-scooters can only be used when they are charged. As a result, a new source of income has opened up for 'click workers': charging e-scooters. People designated (by some companies) as 'juicers' or 'charging partners'[1] find the locations of e-scooters (mostly in the evening), collect them and re-charge them. The e-scooter operators pay them a fee per unit. In the early morning of the next day, they set up the scooters in the most suitable locations. Juicers are usually self-employed. They are not always provided with a company ve-hicle, and instead use their private car. Sometimes there is no central charging point; the devices are instead charged at home, which can be particularly exhausting (eg, if you live on an upper floor). The pay for this physically demanding work is low. According to newspaper reports, if jui-cers are unable to meet their deadlines, half of their wages are deducted (Krüger and Waschbüsch 2019).

In addition, this group of workers has recently gained publicity for committing a number of illegal acts. According to newspaper reports, some of them supposedly illegally charge the scooters at car charging stations using homemade adapters to make their work easier. In some cases, the devices are reportedly used for personal purposes by having their GPS trackers removed. E-scooters without a GPS tracking system can no longer be found, which makes them easy to resell (Macho 2019). Such cases have received media attention, but it is not clear whether they pertain to in-dividual offenders or if the practice is widespread. However, critically ex-amining these side effects does indicate that the companies' business models put enough pressure on their employees to make them look for other ways to make ends meet.

Another issue is that GPS data makes it possible for both new users and the operators to find the e-scooters based on their geodata coordinates – and the combination of user data and location-based data creates movement profiles. This results in fundamental data protection problems. For example, the Hamburg Data Protection Commissioner has complained that this new form of mobility 'is only made available to users with significant interference to their privacy' and that the 'hire business' unfortunately also includes 'business with customer data'. In addition to contact and account data, he maintains that hire companies have collected a great deal of movement and location information, even though this is not recognisable for the provision of the service. 'Every meter covered is recorded and can be combined to create motion profiles' (Krempl 2019).

These problems can be seen as poorly considered side effects of the free-floating model and arose from commercial re-specification. The relevance of the re-specifications becomes even clearer when one considers that this may counteract legislators' environmental objectives. In order to provide the best possible incentives for switching from cars to more environmentally friendly means of transport, e-scooters should compensate for the fact that you cannot travel directly to a specific address by train (or suburban rail) as you can with a car (not to mention finding a parking space). The young, well-educated, internet-savvy public in particular, who are not great fans of buses once they leave school, should be motivated to think about alternatives to cars. Municipal politicians assumed that this would only be possible if the traffic concept as a whole allowed for a quick 'uninterrupted' journey from door to door. This consideration was not wrong; however, the result of approving e-scooters has not resulted in road users no longer using their cars.

Experience in Germany has so far confirmed what other countries were already aware of: there is no evidence that cars or motorcycles are being replaced. Companies such as Lime claim that e-scooters have replaced around 250,000 car trips in five months, which would be a great success. However, other sources such as the Agora Verkehrswende association believe that there are few reliable figures on a shift of traffic (Hasselmann 2019). According to the German Environment Agency, initial figures on usage behaviour in Berlin confirm that e-scooters are used primarily in the evenings and weekends (Umweltbundesamt 2019), ie, not to commute to work. A recent study from France shows that the use of e-scooters mainly replaces walking. Almost half of the respondents would have walked instead, about a third would have used the bus or train, almost 10% would have taken their bike and only about 8% would have taken a taxi or their own car instead (Koschmieder and Huß 2020: 81; Krohn 2019). These observations suggest that e-scooters are used not so much as a replacement for cars but rather as a replacement for bicycles and walking. As hire vehicles in cities with good public transport networks and where the last few meters can be easily covered on foot or by bike, they therefore tend to be detrimental to the environment (Umweltbundesamt 2019). This is because although e-scooters do have a better eco-balance than cars, of course, they are worse than bicycles (with the exception of electric bikes for hire).

In addition, vans are often used to collect the e-scooters that are by no means electrically operated, but are usually equipped with diesel engines. It is not known how many kilometres of driving result from collecting the devices and re-parking them. However, if – for reasons such as company profitability – the business models for hiring e-scooters include more additional routes with petrol- or diesel-powered vehicles than are saved by using e-scooters, the use of such vehicles is no longer environmentally friendly.

The German Environment Agency has also drawn attention to the fact that the e-scooters' batteries are a problem because they can contain raw materials such as cobalt, nickel, copper and aluminium, and when the batteries are taken apart they may pose risks to the environment and human health. Production and disposal of the devices themselves can also be problematic (Umweltbundesamt 2019). Different sources provide different figures regarding the life span of hire devices, which vary between 28 days and 12 months. The environmental advantages of e-scooters are strongly related to their service life and therefore remain unclear in view of the uncertainty in this regard (Umweltbundesamt 2019).[2] These problems can be reduced if the hire providers use high-quality devices that can be repaired when necessary and are equipped with replaceable batteries. At the same time, as economic actors, companies are bound by profitability needs that can encourage decisions in the opposite direction, especially considering the fact that more and more competitors are entering the market.

In view of the problems and side effects observed, the re-specifications that are currently taking place in the commercial field can be regarded as a free-riding practice, because various actors are attempting to use public goods (in this case, the streets and the parking spaces) in their favour without wanting to cover the costs of the resulting damage for other people and the environment. The free-floating model, which was introduced with a view of protecting the common natural environment and, in particular, the climate, is turning into a free-riding practice in which specific interests take centre stage.

Reaction of regulators

One of the main reasons for the current situation in cities like Berlin is that more and more vehicles have been registered without taking possible side effects into account. The public debates particularly emphasise that legislators gave little thought beforehand to the fact that they would be competing with each other. When, as happened in Kreuzberg's Bergmannstrasse, cities try to convince people to switch to more environmentally friendly means of transport by artificially reducing parking space (by setting up tables and benches, called parklets; Ehlebracht 2018), conflicts are bound to occur. Most of the time, the weakest road users, ie, pedestrians, bear the brunt.

Several associations have raised complaints about this problem. Interest groups that represent people with disabilities or pedestrians, the bicycle lobby and associations advocating for the transport transition have been actively involved. All of them stress that e-scooters cause traffic disruptions and are even dangerous. This is underpinned by the fact that police in various cities are reporting difficulties (Jacobs 2019).

Cities first reacted to these complaints with mere appeals to the providers, reminding them that they have an interest in maintaining a good rapport with those cities. Cities and smaller municipalities publicly stress that they have little influence on where the e-scooters are parked, and demand, among other things, that companies set limits on how many e-scooters are set up in a certain area or that they better inform their customers about the applicable norms (eg, that parking is not permitted in certain green spaces). Complaint management on the part of the providers is also desired, in order to ensure that vehicles that impair or pose obstacles to other road users are removed quickly (Krüger and Waschbüsch 2019).

The fact that the side effects of approving e-scooters have received a large media response also creates strong pressure for the responsible regulatory bodies to act in a regulatory manner rather than simply issuing appeals. Bad publicity can quickly lead to political damage, since the climate and environmental issues are currently very present in Germany. There has therefore been a reaction, albeit a late one. The slowness of the reaction can easily be explained by the time required politically and administratively to formulate regulations according to the correct procedures. The recursive reaction of the law to re-specifications through economic communication is clearly caused by the dynamics of this system (Luhmann 2009).

In their approval – rather late, in a global comparison – of e-scooters as a means of individual transport in German cities, federal legislators ultimately relied on a model of regulated self-regulation (Koschmieder and Huß 2020). As with other local passenger transport, traffic management was to be carried out by the municipalities, which have since signed a memorandum of understanding with the major providers of e-scooters for hire through their municipal umbrella organisations (the Association of German Cities and the German Association of Towns and Municipalities). However, this was only drafted after the fact, once the complaints about haphazardly parked e-scooters for hire had started to pile up. The German Association of Towns and Municipalities has also asked the Federal Ministry of Transport and the Bundestag, as legislators, to ensure that operating licences are issued with the proviso that small electric vehicles be automatically throttled in prohibited areas in order to protect pedestrians and thereby prevent misconduct and serious accidents. However, to strengthen road safety, especially in sensitive pedestrian areas, technological innovations need to be implemented immediately at the federal level as well.

Other stricter regulations are currently being discussed. At the request of the state of Berlin, the Bundesrat is currently discussing whether parking e-scooters and bicycles for hire on pavements should be considered special commercial use of the street in the future. If this question is answered in the affirmative, municipalities would have the option of prohibiting providers from operating if they do not comply with municipal rules. For example, cities could charge special usage fees and set a maximum limit on the number of vehicles that can be parked in certain areas (Latz 2020).

Concluding remarks

As experiences in cities in other countries such as San Francisco, Los Angeles, Paris and Warsaw have already shown, recent events in Germany clearly demonstrate that the problems with e-scooters are not (only) technical in nature: regulation is becoming an explosive issue in a changing transport system. The norms that are drafted and established are crucial with regard to the political goals of a transport or energy transition. The case of the approval of e-scooters in Germany has a limited range, but it has enabled us to demonstrate the extent to which the regulation of complex fields, such as transport, involves ever-increasing recursiveness.

Addressees' re-specifications with regard to the approval of e-scooters have not only caused unexpected side effects but have also turned the actual implementation into a paradox in relation to the legislation's objectives. Downstream regulations do not address all of the problems of e-scooters that have been identified and discussed in the media. A political discussion about the actual role of e-scooters in the energy and transport transition is off to a sluggish start. In the short term, there are no regulations in sight to improve questionable employment conditions, either.

Downstream regulation may be able to solve some problems (in the case we have described: the problem of parking in public spaces). However, it does in turn open up new opportunities for recursive re-specifications in the economic field. New safety requirements may even make additional car trips necessary to collect and re-park vehicles left in prohibited locations. Not only might this be environmentally counterproductive, it may also cause companies to compensate for the resulting costs by reducing quality norms and worsening employment conditions. (This is because there is price competition from above, for instance when it comes to keeping the hiring of e-scooters attractively priced in comparison to taxis). However, this may itself be an issue for interest groups, the media, politicians and various regulatory bodies to react recursively with new solutions.

If the energy transition is not seen as a unilinear process initiated and implemented 'from above', as it were, but rather as a recursive process of transforming relevant infrastructures, business models and values, the expectations directed at legislators may become both more modest and more hopeful – more modest because it is becoming clear that no regulatory body can fully predict or control the consequences of regulations in other contexts; more hopeful because a process such as the energy transition can be viewed as an ongoing project that can be continuously transformed, adapted and perpetuated over time by different parties.

Notes

1 These people are usually not hired as permanent employees of the providers, but instead work with them on a contract basis as 'independent companies'.
2 With privately purchased and used devices, however, wear and tear is significantly less, and the life span of the devices is thus longer.

References

Aigrain, P. (2012) *Sharing: Culture and the Economy in the Internet Age* (Amsterdam, Amsterdam University Press).

Balasescu, A. and Seguin, T. (2018) 'Another economy: towards a cultural dialectics between energy and society' *31*(3) *Eur. J. Soc. Sci.* 251–277.

Bauer, C. (2014) *Die Energieversorgung zwischen Regulierungs- und Gewährleistungsstaat: Die Gasnetzzugangs- und Gasnetzentgeltregulierung durch Bundesnetzagentur und Landesregulierungsbehörden* (Berlin, Duncker & Humblot).

Besio, C. and Pronzini, A. (2014) 'Morality, ethics and values outside and inside organizations: an example of the discourse on climate change' *119*(3) *J. Business Ethics* 1–41.

Bruns, E., Ohlhorst, D., Wenzel, B., and Koppel, J. (2011) *Germany's Electricity Market: A Biography of the Innovation Process* (Dordrecht, Springer).

Bundesministerium für Umwelt, Naturschutz und nukleare Sicherheit (2019) *Klimaschutz in Zahlen: der Sektor Verkehr* (Berlin, German Federal Ministry for the Environment, Nature Conservation and Nuclear Safety).

Canzler, W. (2019) 'Market and technology trends of automotive future in Germany' in Mez L., Okamura L. and Weidner H. (eds), *The Ecological Modernization Capacity of Japan and Germany: Comparing Nuclear Energy, Renewables, Automobility and Rare Earth Policy. Reihe Energiepolitik und Klimaschutz* (Wiesbaden, Springer VS), 155–170.

Canzler, W. and Knie, A. (2016) 'Mobility in the age of digital modernity: why the private car is losing its significance, intermodal transport is winning and why digitalisation is the key' *1*(1) *Appl. Mobilit.* 56–67.

Canzler, W. and Knie, A. (2017) 'Festgefahren: Anleitung zum Wandel der Automobilgesellschaft' *27 Zeitschrift für Politikwissenschaft* 475–481.

Ehlebracht, A (2018) '"Parklets" in der Bergmannstraße: Kreuzbergs neue Begegnungstestzone' *Der Tagesspiegel* 25 March 2018. [online] Available at: https://www.tagesspiegel.de/berlin/parklets-in-der-bergmannstrasse-kreuzbergs-neue-begegnungstestzone/21111328.html (accessed 14.03.20).

Edelmann, H., and Fleischle, F. (2018). *Barometer Digitalisierung der Energiewende. Modernisierungs- und Fortschrittsbarometer zum Grad der Digitalisierung der leitungsgebundenen Energiewirtschaft. Erstellt im Auftrag des Bundesministeriums für Wirtschaft und Energie Berichtsjahr 2018 (Dortmund/Düsseldorf, Ernst & Young GmbH Wirtschaftsprüfungsgesellschaft)*.

Fuchs, G. (2014) 'The governance of innovations in the energy sector: between adaptation and exploration' *27*(1) *Sci. Technol. Stud.* 34–53.

Fuchs, G. and Hinderer, N. (2014) 'Situative governance and energy transitions in a spatial context: case studies from Germany' *4*(16) *Energy Sustain. Soc.* 1–11.

Fuchs, G. and Wassermann, S. (2008) 'Picking a winner? innovation in photovoltaics and the political creation of niche markets' *4*(2) *Sci. Technol. Innovat. Stud.* 93-113.

Giacovelli, S. (ed) (2017) *Die Energiewende aus wirtschaftssoziologischer Sicht: Theoretische Konzepte und empirische Zugänge* (Wiesbaden, Springer VS).

Giddens, A. (1984) *The Constitution of Society: Outline of the Theory of Structuration* (Cambridge, Polity).

Gross, M. and Mautz, R. (2015) *Renewable Energies* (London, Routledge).

Hasselmann, J. (2019) 'Neue Zahlen im Streit um E-Scooter: In Berlin gibt es jetzt 16.000 Leihroller' *Der Tagesspiegel* 23 November 2019 [online] Available at: https://www.tagesspiegel.de/berlin/neue-zahlen-im-streit-um-e-scooter-in-berlin-gibt-es-jetzt-16-000-leihroller/25255730.html (accessed 14.03.20).

Jacobs, S (2019) 'Gespräche mit Vermieterfirmen: Berlin dämmt das E-Roller-Chaos ein' *Der Tagesspiegel* 7 August 2019 [online] Available at: https://www.tagesspiegel.de/berlin/gespraeche-mit-vermieterfirmen-berlin-daemmt-das-e-roller-chaos-ein/24880130.html (accessed 14.03.20).

Koschmieder, N. and Huß, F. (2020) 'E-Scooter – Regulatorische Herausforderungen für die Kommunen' *3*(73) *Die öffentliche Verwaltung* 81–90.

Krempl, S. (2019) 'Datenschützer: Nutzer von E-Scootern hinterlassen lückenlose Bewegungsprofile' *Heise Online*, 16 September 2019 [online] Available at: https://www.heise.de/newsticker/meldung/Datenschuetzer-Nutzer-von-E-Scootern-hinterlassen-lueckenlose-Bewegungsprofile-4525462.html (accessed 14.03.20).

Krüger, A. and Waschbüsch, L. (2019) 'Das Problem mit den E-Rollern: Chaos mit Ansage' *Die Tageszeitung* 6 August 2019 [online] Available at: https://taz.de/Das-Problem-mit-den-E-Rollern/!5611004/ (accessed 14.03.20).

Kungl, G. and Geels, FW (2018) 'Sequence and alignment of external pressures in industry destabilisation: understanding the downfall of incumbent utilities in the German energy transition (1998–2015)' *26 Environ. Innovat. Soc. Transit.* 78–100.

Latz, C. (2020) 'Der Bundesrat diskutiert auf Antrag Berlins über bessere Regulierungsmöglichkeiten von E-Scootern. Bei den Anbietern geht die Angst um' *Berliner Morgenpost* 28 January 2020 [online] Available at: https://www.morgenpost.de/berlin/article228270631/Berlin-will-Obergrenzen-fuer-E-Scooter.html (accessed 14.03.20).

Luhmann, N. (1994) *Die Wirtschaft der Gesellschaft* (Frankfurt am Main, Suhrkamp).

Luhmann, N. (1996) 'Kann die moderne Gesellschaft sich auf ökologische Gefährdungen einstellen?' in Hellmann K-H (ed), *Niklas Luhmann: Protest. Systemtheorie und soziale Bewegungen* (Frankfurt am Main, Suhrkamp), 46–63.

Luhmann, N. (2000, 1995) *The Reality of the Mass Media* (Stanford, Stanford University Press).

Luhmann, N. (2002) *Das Erziehungssystem der Gesellschaft* (Frankfurt am Main, Wissenschaftliche Buchgesellschaft).

Luhmann, N. (2003, 1988) 'Organization' in Bakken T. and Hernes T. (eds), *Autopoietic Organization Theory: Drawing on Niklas Luhmann's Social Systems Perspective* (Oslo, Copenhagen Business School Press).

Luhmann, N. (2009, 1993) *Law as a Social System* (Oxford, Oxford University Press).

Luhmann, N. (2012) *Theory of Society* (Stanford, Stanford University Press).

Macho, A. (2019) 'E-Scooter: wie Lime-Mitarbeiter illegal Strom tanken' *Die Wirtschaftswoche* 17 December 2019 [online] Available at: https://www.wiwo.de/unternehmen/dienstleister/juicer-e-scooter-wie-lime-mitarbeiter-illegal-strom-tanken/25342116.html (accessed 14.03.20).

Ortmann, G. (2010) 'Zur Theorie der Unternehmung: Sozioökonomische Bausteine' in Endreß M. and Matys T. (ed), *Die Ökonomie der Organisation: Die Organisation der Ökonomie* (Wiesbaden, Springer VS), 225–304.

Schwedes, O., Canzler, W. and Knie, A. (ed) (2016) *Handbuch Verkehrspolitik: Zweite, vollständig überarbeitete Auflage* (Wiesbaden, Springer VS).

Umweltbundesamt (2019) *E-Scooter momentan kein Beitrag zur Verkehrswende* (Berlin, German Environment Agency) [online] Available at: https://www. umweltbundesamt.de/e-scooter-momentan-kein-beitrag-zur-verkehrswende# aktuelles-fazit-des-uba (accessed 14.03.20).

Chapter 7

Law and economy without 'law and economics'? From new institutional economics to social systems theory

Lucas Fucci Amato

Introduction

'Law and economics' has drawn its descriptive takes on the consequences of legal decision-making and its normative emphasis on efficiency from considerations imported from the new institutional economics. This expanding approach to economic theory and public policy may not be able to face, however, the opacity of self-referring operations through which law and economy both co-evolve and reproduce their differences. This chapter aims to deploy the fundamentals for subsidising the hypothesis that social systems theory can provide an alternative approach to the interface between law and the economy – this is labelled a constructivist or systemic-institutional approach. The goal is to suggest some hypotheses and conceptual tools for empirical investigation in legal and economic research, using systems theory as a rich map for detailing the institutional forms and alternatives that structure each of these social systems.

This intent implies relocating the scope – or at least the usage – of systems theory, bringing to it an empirical specificity that it generally lacks and a potential normative or directive application that it rejects. This is the price of preventing a sterile repetition of a grand theory and of adjusting its scale to the problems and concerns of a more contextualised and less stylised explanation of contemporary society. That implies on the one hand an increase in scale, in order to observe hypotheses that can be empirically falsified. But on the other hand, the institutional diversity that we then observe in context can feed back into the larger theoretical apparatus and enrich it with a less modular view of historical and present variations in the set-up of social systems, including the legal and the economic systems.

The first step in this direction is given by a parallel between the conceptual architecture of new institutional economics and of social systems theory, the latter especially as developed by Luhmann. The core neo-institutionalist thesis on the function of institutions – ie, to reduce transaction costs – is paralleled to the postulate that systems are self-produced in order to overcome the improbability of communication, or to reduce the complexity of meaning, which leads on the functional level to a differentiation among law, economy, politics and other social systems. This explanation implies a conceptual transition from actors with bounded rationality to systems with codified self-referential communication, structured through generalised expectations. Institutions are conceptualised as the inner structures of social systems, and therefore a hypothesis is advanced: in order to outdifferentiate itself, a system has to build some inner differentiations on the level of institutions such as decisional programmes.

The second step in the argument is to detail the legal system itself. The neo-institutionalist focus on the certainty and clarity in the definition of private rights is contrasted to a systemic-institutional emphasis on procedures, and more widely on the inner differentiation of social systems institutions between organisations and an 'inner environment' that translates the (broadly social) environment into system-specific (legal, economic, scientific) communication. The work points out different modes of legal ordering (legislation, adjudication, arbitration, mediation, contract, management and autonomous legal ordering) which are themselves institutional alternatives for legal decision-making and which each face empirical challenges and institutional boundaries.

Arising then to the third step, the text discusses an exemplary problem of contemporary economy (its hyper-reflexivity by finance) and points out the institutional variability in the setup of property and ownership, emphasising forms that can help to tighten a market linkage between the financial core of economy and its productive periphery.

Convergence and contrast: New institutional economics and social systems theory

The core postulate of new institutional economics is that rational economic activity depends on a calculus not only of production costs (resulting from the use of the factors of production, like capital, work, supplies, technology and specialised knowledge) but also of transaction costs: the costs to perform a transaction in the market. These include the costs of finding investors in a corporation (and the capital market help to reduce these costs), overcoming information asymmetry about some product (eg, by relying on trust in third parties) and formalising a deal. These costs 'prevent many transactions that would be carried out in a world in which the pricing system worked without cost' (Coase 1960: 15). Therefore, institutions are seen as devices to reduce transaction costs. A firm rearranges the factors of production in response to price variations, and according to these it opts to produce some good or service internally (relying on its hierarchical co-ordination of those factors) or to buy that product in the market through contractual arrangements (Coase 1937: 405).

The crucial innovation of new institutional economics is to deploy analytically what was taken for granted by the previous post-marginalist or neo-classical economics: from the market understood as a trivial system of automatic adjustments, through relative prices, of supply to demand and of production to consumption, the focus shifts to organisations (mainly firms), no longer black boxes or blind spots but the crucial variable to define the extension and quality of market transactions (Ménard and Shirley 2014). The fictions of previous economic thought – perfect information, wealth-maximising behaviour, exchange as an instantaneous and cost-free transaction – were challenged. The institutionalisation of economic action could be seen in alternative frameworks: the centralised firm, decentralised contracts and a series of hybrid mechanisms between hierarchical organisation and spot contracts: relational contracts, joint ventures, franchising, strategic alliances, etc (Ménard 2013).

If, in the market, through discrete contracts and transactions, a buyer meets a seller and determines the price, quantity and quality of a product, this implies monitoring and enforcing the deal; an organisation can reduce transaction costs by eliminating exchanges among different owners of the factors of production. Any time that information about some product is difficult to consolidate (given the asset specificity), or many transactions (or transactions with many actors) are required, or some additional uncertainty or risk of opportunism is added to the exchange, an institutional device other than the simple bilateral contract – with the full anticipation of expectations and complete formalisation of the terms – will be called into action (Williamson 1985). Therefore, the understanding that the new institutionalism brought in the face of the classical explanation of economic development centred only on technological change was that 'not only are there a variety of market modes – which is to say that the study of hybrids is pertinent – but there are a variety of ways to organise hierarchies' (Williamson 1992: 344).

Another author of the new institutionalist canon defines institutions as 'the humanly devised constraints that structure political, economic and social interaction' (North 1991: 97). Institutions are the rule of the game and organisations are its players. Microeconomic 'institutional arrangements' rely on a wider 'institutional environment'. That is, individuals and the state need to create institutions that favour, in cost-benefit terms, impersonal exchanges, not ones that incentivise piracy or monopoly. Property rights are seen as the crucial device to structure a sound compensation for economic activity, rewarding saving and investment (North 1994: 361–366). Therefore, economic development can be explained not simply by the levels of capital accumulation (physical, financial or human capital) or by technological changes, but mainly by a structure of incentives (North 1990) – basically, the presence or absence of clearly defined property rights and contract enforcement. The lack of clearly defined and enforced private rights raises transactions costs, ie, expenditures to protect some asset against appropriation or invasion by third parties (Galiani and Schargrodsky 2014). Finally, North explains under-development as a lack of generalised property rights for all social classes: the 'mental models' and values prevalent in some countries generate a path in which only some elites benefit from property rights and the rule of law. These (not yet liberal) social orders of limited access are dominated by corporate and friendship relations, and even disincentivise (through high transaction costs) entrepreneurship and competition on the part of non-elites (North et al. 2009).

Contemporary debate about institutions in economics (eg, Chang and Evans 2005) presents an opposition between the vision of institutions as restraints on human choice and action (a perspective attributed to the new institutional economics) and institutions as enablers and constitutive of human behaviour (a vision presented by the so-called 'political economy institutionalism'). The former focus on efficiency would be linked to instrumental action and a vision of the market as the natural environment for efficiency, institutions (understood as some conventional/informal or legal/state definition) then becoming the eventual minor corrections for market failures (such as externalities). The old institutionalist economists (eg, Veblen 1898) have criticised this underlying view of the rational actor, and even the legal realists (eg, Hale 1935) have presented the market as a coercive order. Relying on analogous criticisms, political economists today conceive of markets not as a natural spontaneous order but as the output of some institutional (ie, political) arrangement.

Indeed, this is a misleading characterisation and contrast. Institutions rely on a paradox: they are enabling constraints – as in the Hobbesian narrative, where the structuring of a civil society (ie, the state) limits natural freedom, identified with the extension of the physical force of each individual in the state of nature. The limitation of freedom (through the alienation of the natural prerogative of self-defence to the sovereign) paradoxically expands freedom (identified with the natural rights granted in exchange by the sovereign state – the right to property included). Limited, civil(ised) freedom expands the plasticity and power available to everyone, organising then a scheme of social cooperation. Smith's metaphor of the 'invisible hand' goes in the same direction: self-interest paradoxically drives the general interest as an unintended consequence of rational action. But what he sees as a natural functioning of the economic system (eg, 'preferring the support of domestic to that of foreign industry') relies indeed on some institutional variables and policy options.

Luhmann's systems theory provide some starting points to 're-describe' (Hesse 1966) these problems under a different conceptual framework. It departs from a challenge to the rationalist-individualist methodology provided by the Enlightenment. The problem of the Enlightenment is seen as apprehending complexity (a dense cloud of unlimited options) and reducing it through structuration, paradoxically making more options discernible, which means more complexity available. Systems create sound from noise and order from chaos. The focus is to guarantee a surplus of non-realised possibilities, a stock of alternatives that can be ever available to new selections of meaning. The differentiation of society into a series of social systems is the concrete vehicle for sustainable complexity growth – which implies fewer (uncontrollable) dangers but more risks (internalised by the systems' operations); less reliance on acquaintances but more generalised trust; less dependence upon tradition and custom and more openness to the contingent future.

What sociology challenged from the 19th century are two basic assumptions of the Enlightenment: 'the equal share of all men in a common reason that they own without any later institutional mediation, and the optimism, sure of its triumph, in relation to the settlement of just situations' (Luhmann 2005a: 21–22). These may apply well to Kant and to the Scottish Enlightenment, Smith included. Sociology explains human action by some incongruent perspective (like its genealogy in the economic organisation of society), distinguishes manifest, proclaimed ends from its latent functions, comes to substitute explanation by factors (such as natural inclinations or psychological impulses) with systemic and self-referential operations (like path-dependent cycles and feedbacks) and finally dismisses causal explanations and advances functional hypotheses: how some problem of system maintenance has come to be solved by the system itself. Functional explanations rely on evolutionary mechanisms (which work out variation, selection and restabilisation), reveal isomorphisms among systems (comparable, functionally equivalent structures) and show equifinality (equivalent results may be produced by different means).

If we depart from the approach of institutions as outputs coming from a routine of transactions between economic agents and come to the inner focus on social systems themselves (society and its functional systems – such as economy, law, politics, education, science, religion, arts, family – as well as organisational and interactional systems), we would need to differentiate the element of these systems (which is communication) from operations in the mind of some human archetype (with its psychological system based on the self-reference of thoughts). We can affirm that the structural coupling between social and psychological systems relies on language, and in this way there is some synchronisation between social and psychological structures. The various ways of friction or confluence between the psychological and the economic social system, for instance, are now opened to exploration by behavioural economics.

A systemic-institutional view would completely dismiss any psychological or intentional bias in the definition of institutions, and so would need to redescribe economic institutionalism and its expectation about law beyond a formalistic understanding of legal interpretation and a sermon praising the certainty and clarity of the definition of private rights in legislation and the courts. The management of legal risks depends upon more complex and detailed systemic mechanisms.

Luhmann's (2013: 87–108) explanation of the emergence of a society based on differentiation among functional systems is as follows: the generalisation of some media – like money, political power and positive law – allowed their wider circulation, beyond the barriers of social strata and personal innate attributes. Therefore, communication came to be specialised around these symbolically generalised media: information was coded as being about the distinction between legal and illegal – and then attributed to the legal system; or being about having or not having (property and money), and then constituting itself as a problem for the economic system.

Social systems – especially functional systems, in modernity – are the crucial device for reducing and enabling complexity in our social formation. By mastering some generalised communication media, each system specialises communication and enhances the chance of acceptance of a communication – having money, you will be admitted to transact; having knowledge, you will be admitted to research. Payments, the elementary economic operation, rely on the acceptance influence given by money. It permits the continuity of communication, its self-reference, and therefore the autopoiesis of economy.

The problem faced by social systems in general is not the reduction of transaction costs, but something more general: the overcoming of the improbability of communication. Luhmann (1981: 123–124) points out three improbabilities: (1) given the separateness of human minds, meaning can only be understood in context; (2) communication in interaction is limited in space and time, so higher-order social systems must emerge and need to command attention; (3) success in communication means that someone understands the other's information, trusts in it and takes it as a premise for enlacing her own communication in self-reference (in agreement or disagreement).

I do not know what you are thinking about what I am thinking. Given the 'double contingency' of psychic systems (Parsons), which are black boxes to each other, the only reliance they can have is on shared expectations. Social systems select, generalise and reinforce these expectations. Functional systems, in particular, command attention and require the continuity of communication by coding it with some symbolic generalised media: money, power, positive law help a communication to be understood and processed. While the first improbability deals with coordination costs, these generalised media are related to the third improbability, as they bring an economy of motivation costs deriving from the incompleteness and asymmetry of information and from the imperfect commitment of parts (Akerlof, 1970; Milgrom and Roberts 1992: 29–33). Social systems beyond interactions deal with the second improbability of communication, and they do this by institutionalising internal structures – an organised public sphere.

From this explanation, we can emphasise that some element (communication) does not simply emerge 'from below', by a routine of interactions or transactions, for instance; in fact, it derives its identity 'from above', emerging as a communication coded by the legal, economic, political or scientific system (Luhmann 1995: 22, 501, n. 23). Indeed, there is a circularity, and the many levels of social systems (interactions, organisations and functional systems) may be explained by a double movement: functional system 'outdifferentiation' (Luhmann 2013: 65–87) relies upon system *inner differentiation*. In other words, to construct its boundaries in the face of society (the general encompassing social system), a partial system has to master some specific symbolically generalised communication medium (power, truth, law, money), and to generalise and manage it the system develops its internal structures – what I will call institutions.[1]

I propose to distinguish three levels of structures, ie, of clustering of communication. The micro-structures of society are the expectations – a continuum between cognitive expectations (which learn from disillusionment – like falsifying a scientific hypothesis) and normative expectations (such as human rights, which are reinforced in the face of their violation). On this level, we can approach the structural coupling between psychic and social systems, observing the co-evolution between mental structures and social structures.

At the level of macro-structures, we can observe the specific merger of a variety of forms of social differentiation in a given social context (Amato 2018a, 2018c). Social 'marks' and references – patron/client, capital/labour, producer/consumer, Brazilian/British, male/female etc – include distinctions proper to functional systems and other references that cut across these systems and are reconstructed by each of them (in terms of purchasing power, educational background, political bases etc.). Indeed, we should understand that modern society redefined previous differences (eg, in nation-states and class hierarchies). Therefore, these differences (other than functional-systemic marks, merged with functional systems programs) are reproduced even in the economic system: in organisational hierarchies, in the technological and organisational asymmetries between vanguards and rearguards (or regional distinctions between centres and peripheries) and in the differences of exchange rates, interest rates and currencies among countries (as segments of a world society).

There is an intermediary level of clustering of social structures, and here I locate institutions. If the prevalent form of system differentiation in contemporary society is functional differentiation, the main institutions that structure communication are structured themselves by functional systems. Institutions are, from below, the clustering of expectations (and a device to generalise, reform and reinforce these expectations). From above, they are slices of the macro-structure, which emerges by the clustering of a given set of institutions.

Following the hypothesis that system 'outdifferentiation' (Luhmann 2013: 65–87) relies upon system inner differentiation, we can understand the emergence of institutions as the internal structures of a social system (at our level of observation, mainly of some functional system). These internal structures are mainly differentiated between an organisational sphere and a public sphere. In the latter, systems develop a kind of inner environment: the irritations coming from the system's environment are translated into systemic-functional communications. Every social or natural problem is phrased as a matter of rights and duties, powers and liabilities. Therefore, structuration in the form of 'legal personality' makes these matters available to be processed by the legal system, using the circulating medium of validity, of valid law. Similarly, the market is the place where supply meets demand, which is indexed through pricing. And politics translates everything to a matter of public opinion.

On the one hand, this internal mirror de-codifies the environment for the system, decrypting the noise coming from outside. On the other, it is the force field of its counterpart: the sphere of organisations. These are social systems based on the self-reference of decisions. They are decision-making systems. Within their own operational boundaries, they can cut across different functional systems and even be apart from any specific functional system. For some functional systems (like law or politics), an organisation may be at the core or on the periphery. Peripheral organisations are more open to other functional systems, and help to bring interface matters to core organisations. In the core of any functional system are the organisations that perform its crucial functional decisions.

This level of structures (institutions) is the counterpart of a level of semantics (programmes), differentiated among a level of pre-programming (in the inner environments), a level of programming decisions (in peripheral organisations) and a level of programmed decisions (in core organisations). Indeed, this understanding brings to the level of social systems Herbert Simon's understanding of 'bounded rationality'.[2] If organisations are the protagonists of a market economy (making the market just the public-sphere counterpart to the organised sphere), they make the most important choices in the economic system. And within a functional system (economy, but also law or politics), there is a circularity of communication among decisions that are more open to learning from environmental irritations and those that are more responsive to the operational closure of a system.

For instance, themes emerge in the mass media as a matter to be solved by politics. They come to visibility in public opinion. Parties, lobbies, interest groups or social movements help to bring new demands to the political system and can translate these demands into programs, declarations, manifestos. They structure these irritations from the economic, educational, religious or natural environment, now translated as a controversy in public opinion. But only the state (ie, the political branches) has the crucial sovereign power to take a decision about any of these matters and impose it on all the polity. Otherwise, in a circular way, public opinion is also managed and shaped by the state and political peripheral organisations.

In economy, markets provide a proxy for necessities, translating into prices the supplies and demands. Firms and families in the 'real economy' – production, trade and consumption – are closer to these environmental irritations but depend on central organisations (banking and financial organisations) to have credit or investment. The force lines of these organisations are reflected in the economic inner environment: markets of goods and services, factors of production and money, ie, financial markets.

Each system is differentiated and identified by its code ('lawful'/'unlawful', 'to have'/'not to have', 'power'/'impotence'). What would be an exclusion is included: the side of unlawfulness is made a question of legality; the side of not having is made a question of social inclusion (ie political, compensation); the side of impotence is re-entered through the distinction between government and opposition, both insiders in the political systems. Through this inclusion of the excluded, systems generalise their operations. Each system can also be identified by its function: generalising normative expectations (binding norms, independent of personal beliefs) is the function of law; making collective binding decisions is the function of politics; assuring the continuity of payments and linking future provisions to current distribution of resources is the function of economy.

Before proceeding with this description, a picture may help us to depict all the differences that Luhmann[3] uses to explain the workings of a functional system. In this case, Figure 7.1 details the institutional morphology of the political, legal and economic systems.

In order to clarify this morphology, we can refer to eight conceptual differences and explanatory postulates. The first one is that between the *organised and public spheres*: the public sphere in part provides the themes for organisations to take decisions about (the medium to which they will give some form); on the other hand, this public sphere is circularly profiled and set up by organisations: rights are the matter of contracts, regulation and legislation (in the legal periphery, performed by lawyers, prosecutors and other legal organisations) and of sentences (the programme produced by courts – the judiciary in state law). By being subjected to these decisions, they are in some sense what these decisions (mainly the sentences) define them as. A noticeable characteristic of the inner environment of functional systems is that they are force fields modelled in a triadic form of competition (Ramos 2019, based on Simmel). It is the competition among suppliers for a buyer that makes a market emerge. It is the competition, among colliding political positions or programmes, for the vote or support of a citizen that makes public opinion run. And it is the opposition between at least two right holders for some legal prerogative (exemption, right, indemnification) that structures legal personality.

The second distinction, also already sketched, concerns the organised sphere itself and differentiates *centre and periphery*. Some organisations that lie at the core of a system may be in the periphery of another: parliaments, which are at

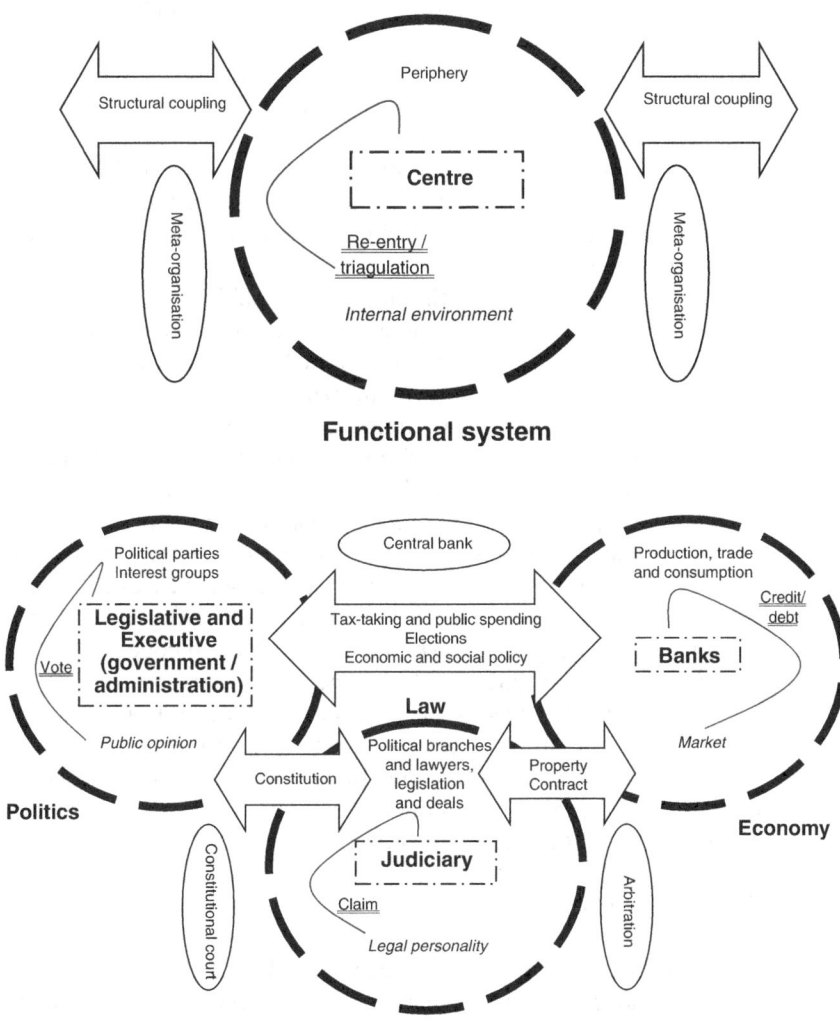

Figure 7.1 The institutions of the political, legal and economic systems
Source: the author (adapted from Amato 2017: 189–190; 2018a: 47).

the core of the political system (besides the executive, including public bu-reaucracy), are in the periphery of the legal system. For politics, the political branches perform the core political function of collective binding decisions. Their programmes are statutes and regulations, the most consolidated political decisions. But for law the congruent generalisation of normative expectations depends ultimately on courts. Their programmes – sentences – are the last word on the valid norm and on the interpretation of statutes and decrees.

The distinction between centre and periphery does not imply any hierarchy. Core organisations simply need to de-paradoxify, to avoid, to reduce to some workable contradiction the foundational paradox of their functional system. Peripheral legal organisations (government, public or private lawyers, mediators, counsellors) do not need to decide legal controversies; only courts are pressured by a core institutional feature: the prohibition of denial of justice (non liquet). Pressured by this imperative, they rely on a paradox: judges transform the duty to decide into the freedom to decide (ie, to justify their decision).

Similarly, banks have to deal with the paradox of liquidity: to incite saving and consumption at the same time, to sell their debts with profits, making earnings both from savers/creditors and from debtors/borrowers. And politics can take every decision in the periphery, but to make it a collective binding decision (eg, programmed as a statute) it relies on the paradox of sovereignty under the rule of law: the ones that make a decision in the name of the state are themselves bound by that decision.

A third pair of concepts is *decentralisation and mechanisms of triangulation or re-entry*. Functional systems assure not distributive justice but decentralisation and expansion of the symbolic media. Decoupled from the demand to attend equally to every concrete individual, and relying only on the positions classified according to its own systemic media and code, a system can control internal consistency and expand its means (eg, money). However, as each system controls its self-reference, a concentration of media may imply systemic integration – restraints on the freedom of a system posed by the operations of another one. Integration reinforces the convertibility of media (eg, power = money), leading to potential systemic corruption, de-differentiation and a positive feedback on social exclusion (Luhmann 1979: 175–179, 2012: 25).

Hence I propose understanding the circulation of communication within a given functional system as a cycle: environmental matters translated by the inner environment (the legal personality, the market, the public opinion) come to central organisations (courts, political branches of the state, banks and finance) by triangulation with some peripheral organisations (prosecutors and lawyers, parties and social movements, firms). This triangulation is proceduralised by vote, judicial claims or mechanisms of credit/debt or saving/investment. They conduct communication to the foundational paradox and to the core decision and organisation of a functional system, touching on the matters of liquidity, sovereignty or the prohibition of non liquet. These are procedural systems, linking interactions to organisations (indeed, they are performed by core organisations, to portray the functional system's inner environment with the mediation of its peripheral organisations). More precisely: within each organisational system, an internal environment (as a proxy for the system's environment) is also built, as Baecker (2006) emphasises. These procedures promote the re-entry of the inner environment into the organised sphere of a system. Access to money, political power and legal forms helps the decentralisation – and therefore disintegration – of systems, amplifying social complexity.

A fourth distinction is that between *operational closure and structural coupling*. Systems reproduce themselves by producing their own elements (payments, collectively binding decisions, valid law) in a chain or network of self-reference. In this sense, they are operationally closed. The cognitive openness they have – to observe a transaction and see it as a payment (economy) or a contract (law) – relies on this closure. But functional systems also develop structural couplings, which are linkage institutions, devices that intensify the irritations between systems, helping to canalise and translate them into communication. For instance, a constitution is an enabling re-straint for both political and legal communication. It is a collective binding decision that structures the core forms of using state power, and it is a programming decision for law, setting a parameter for control of the con-sistency of a legal order. What can be added to this is that structural cou-plings also have or refer to an organised and a public sphere: constitutions organise both the branches of government (the linkage between political branches and the judicial power) and fundamental rights (the linkage be-tween public opinion, state power and legal personality). Between law and economy, property organises hierarchies (organisations as reflected by legal personality) and contracts institutionalise market transactions. Politics, for instance, cannot interfere in economy: it provides economic and social policy, but these selective means will acquire some economic significance that politics itself cannot really control. However, the state, as an organi-sation, has its own systemic boundaries, and in this way can be both a political and an economic agent, dealing with power and money at the same time.

A fifth similar distinction deals with the ideas of *re-differentiation and performance*. Functional systems build their identity and difference from each other by their own functions and cybernetic codes. The code applica-tion is programmed by decisions taken by organisations linked to these systems. In this way, each system also makes hetero-observation, ie, builds programs and organisations to observe other systems (law, for instance, is differentiated among regulatory and business law, educational law, con-stitutional law etc). This is another way by which systems outdifferentiate through inner differentiation. For instance, some organisations in the per-iphery of the legal system (lawyers, registrars and notaries) help to reduce information asymmetries (eg, in the real estate market), understood as a problem of improbability of communication (for the economic system, of payment operations). The imperfect commitment among the parts of a transaction, resulting from the lack of personal trust, is then replaced by a second-order trust or 'reflexive trust': trust in the legal system, and trust that third parties or a judge will trust the documents formalised by some process and by someone occupying a role recognised by the legal system (Campilongo 2014: 105, 115). By performing these operations, law (and its organisational subsystems) is providing a service to the economic system. While the problem some functional system solves for the wider social system (society) refers to its function, the service provided by a functional system to another is called 'performance'.

The sixth pair of concepts is *reflexivity and meta-organisations*. Reflexivity concerns systems' operations applied to themselves, eg, payments referred to payments. In the real economy, payments refer to goods and services; on the level of finance, money is valued by money, payments are referred to expectations about other payments. In law, criminal or private law is reflected on the one hand by procedural norms (norms about how to apply norms) and on the other by principles, policies and purposes (substantive norms that guide the interpretation of formal rules). The constitution itself is a reflexive level for the observation of its legal order. In politics, decisions may deal with a variety of themes: the political system itself, economic policy, religious freedom etc. Representative democracy works out, among other aspects (such as the scission of the state power between government and opposition), by decomposing decisions into second-order decisions (Luhmann 2005b: 28), including the vote to decide who will decide the first-order questions (ie, the representatives). Hyper-reflexivity may threaten the system, as in the excess of participatory decision-making, the excess of financial layers of securities and derivatives and the excess of constitutionalisation, proceduralisation or principlisation of law.

Meta-organisations generally have a relation to reflection and to the backing of the core legal and economic organisations by the state as a specially encompassing organisation (which crosses among various systems through its policies and agencies). A central bank is linked to both the centre of economy (banking and finance) and the centre of politics (the state power). It controls economic reflexivity by a mandate of government. Interest rates control the reflexivity of the real economy by finance, dosing stimuli for saving or consumption, for investment in financial assets or in productive capabilities. Discussions about the autonomy of central banks deals with the correlation between political reflexivity (representativeness, legitimacy) and economic reflexivity (monetary policy, efficiency). Development banks perform a similar role in relation to industrial policy – helping to improve the economic periphery (production, trade, consumption).

Supreme courts (especially when performing judicial review) are at the top of the core legal organisation (the judiciary, in state law) and decide cases with a collectively binding prerogative, akin to the core of politics. Constitutional courts perform a similar role, even if not hierarchically on the top of the judicial branch. Decisions about constitutional interpretation are controls on the reflexivity of law and also pose questions concerning the representativeness of judges as the decision-makers.

Finally, arbitration is a partial substitute for judicial performance, and applies mainly for economic disputes. The linkage to the core of law is related to the eventual need to use state courts to coercively enforce arbitral awards. But here there is not a linear correlation with legal or economic reflexivity.

The seventh difference to understand the isomorphisms and equivalences among functional systems is that between *upward insulation (organised sphere) and downward insulation (organised centre plus public sphere, without organised periphery)*: procedural devices of triangulation (inner environment → peripheral organisations → core organisations) help to decentralise systems and also to prevent some systemic crises. These crises, one can hypothesise, may come from an insulation of the system, ie, a failure of this triangulation, which leads to problems of reflexivity. A failure of political representation comes when party competition, social mobilisation and dispute about political programmes (the political periphery) fail but there is some form of control of this periphery (corporatism or authoritarianism) closely linking it to the state (the system's core) and delinking it from the general, anonymous, universalising reference to public opinion. This is upward insulation, and includes the insulation promoted by lobbies as a kind of private corporatism. Downward insulation occurs when the centre of a system tries a link with its inner environment without reference to the peripheral organisations: in politics, a charismatic leader of government calls its people directly, dismissing mass media, party competition or protest movements. This characterises populism.

The same tendencies can be detected in law and economy. In all cases, they deal with inflation or deflation of the symbolically generalised media (Luhmann 2012: 227–232). Populism inflates some politician (or the state in general), devaluing power. A crisis of pessimism comes when the promises are broken and power suffers a deflation. Deflationary politics underestimates power and so wastes the chances for taking risky decisions.

Through upward insulation, legal argumentation and judicial decision remain formalistic, deferential to legislators and private deals. This is legal deflation. By downward insulation it turns into activism, and courts then recognise as rights prerogatives coming from the public sphere without previous support by legislation, for instance. This is legal inflation – the use of legal validity beyond the capacity of the legal system to generalise normative expectations.

For the economy, upward insulation leads to deflation through lack of financial reflexivity (eg, no speculation generating information about investment alternatives). Downward insulation is the direct calling of banks and financial institutions by the financial market, without attention to production, trade and consumption. This leads to inflation or financial bubbles, with the overvaluation of assets.

By inflating and devaluing the generalised communication media (money, power, law), a crisis in one system tends to infect other systems. The generalisation of uncertainty calls for system integration, and then differentiation and the decentralisation of their media are jeopardised.

The eighth difference is that between *basal self-reference and (theoretical) reflection*. The basal self-reference of social systems consists in the linkage among their communication, identified by the binary codes ('legal'/'illegal', 'having'/'not having', 'power'/'impotence' or 'government'/'opposition'); these codes mobilise the usage of some communication media (like positive law, or democratic power, or money) to solve some identified problem in a technical sphere of competence. This autopoiesis is reinforced when the system elaborates its own identity on a theoretical level, which supplies criteria for judging the consistency and adequacy of the practical operations. Luhmann observes that systems can reflect themselves by inner theories (like legal doctrine, or dogmatics, focused on solving localised conflicts within a given body of positive law) or by scientific, external theories (like sociology). He admits, however, that some theories (like jurisprudence) are built through a structural coupling between some system self-description and a hetero-observation, a philosophical or scientific view (Luhmann 2004: ch. 11).

In this sense, one may add that theoretical reflection mimics the institutional morphology of a system. In this sense, if there is a core legal doctrine (ie, dogmatics) concerned with legal interpretation *de lege lata* and with grasping precedents, there may also be peripheral doctrines[4] – concerned with legal reform or creation (by politics or by private deals, private ordering and arbitration) – which are primarily directed to legal innovation (placed in the periphery) rather than to the legal control of consistency (this being carried out mainly by courts, ie, the legal centre). However, of course, a legal innovation may lead to a new legal order, and then we may have new organisations (a different core and a different periphery). Concerned as it is with legal decisions that need to be taken (constrained by the prohibition of non liquet), a reflection will be again a (core) dogmatics (for the new legal order of reference), not a peripheral anti-dogmatics.

The most demanding 'law and economics' pretensions to explain legal evolution and justify judicial decision-making by reference to 'efficiency' proved to be a dead end. In opposition to this, a peripheral legal doctrine, consisting of *de lege ferenda* enquiries, may be more open to sociological, economic and political considerations – in the line of a 'sociological jurisprudence' (Pound 1907) – because it is not constrained by the duty to decide a case according to today's valid law.

Here one can think also of a coupling between comparative law and comparative political economy. This differentiation between legal dogmatics (directed in some way to the core question of deciding according to current law) and legal anti-dogmatics (or peripheral doctrine) is not a strict difference between normal and revolutionary science: routine problems and solutions, and disruptive changes of paradigm. Indeed, an important part of legal reflection may be routinely concerned with legal innovation or reform. This chapter's proposal is to follow this path.

The division of legal labour: Programmes, orders and institutions

Risk is the contingency self-produced by a system; 'we can speak of risk only if we can identify a decision without which the loss could not have occurred' (Luhmann 1993: 16). Insecurity is the uncertainty that a system cannot control, predict, calculate (Knight 1921: ch. 7). To the extent that a functional system masters some symbolic medium and then overcomes the improbability of communication, it generalises trust as a solution to problems of risk (Luhmann 1988: 95). Trust is a reduction of complexity that allows communication under the presupposition that there is some convergence of expectations (Luhmann 1979: pt. 1). The instability of this rests upon the power to institutionalise some of these expectations – counting on social support to generalise them and punish their violation. Conflicts are the parasites of society, and law provides the immunological function of containing and managing these risks (Luhmann 2004: 475–477).

The legal system has the function of congruently generalising normative expectations in the temporal, material and social dimensions of meaning (Luhmann 2014: 73–74). In other words, if morality (and its code: 'good'/ 'bad') cannot provide structured programs for ethical reflection, and if religion becomes a differentiated system (unable to generalise a specific set of beliefs to everyone), the law must impose some counterfactual expectations that resist violation. These expectations are made to last by being the matter of lasting norms backed by sanctions, premiums or punishments (the temporal dimension of meaning).

Second (in the material dimension), these normative expectations may be formulated in decisional programmes as conditional or finalistic programs. The former define some hypothesis of incidence and prescribe some legal consequence. The latter only set up a goal, leaving the means indeterminate. To overcome this indeterminacy of finalistic programs and comply with the prohibition of the denial of justice, judges need to rely first upon their lack of political responsibility (and the guaranties of the judicial carrier). This political immunity differentiates judges from politicians and even from policy makers. Second, to 'conditionalise' a finalistic program (Luhmann 1983: chs. 4–5, 2004: 196–203, 2014: 174–185), judges will not consider the generality of means available to comply with the state of affairs programed by a principle or policy. They will need to decide while limiting the analysis of means and ends to the arbitrarily constrained discussion evoked in the concrete case under judgment. They decide under the law (including under the legal definitions about their competence, roles and division of powers), not only about the law.

One could agree with economists' concerns about legal certainty, and even consider that finalistic programmes cannot be definite justifications for sentencing, always requiring the formulation of a conditional programme (rule) as an immediate reason to decide. Otherwise, we can have principle bubbles, a problem of hyper-reflexivity in the legal system (Neves 2013) comparable to the over-financialisation of economy without reference to the capitalisation of productive firms.

However, the certainty of rights is not just a matter of text interpretation and theoretical abstraction, generalisation and categorisation. In this sense, it is important to recall Luhmann's (1980: 32) critique of Weber's appraisal of legal formalism as a basis for predictability in a legal system. The social mechanism of trust generalisation is the legal process. Therefore, in the social dimension of meaning a legal decision is presumed to have generalised support from third parties because it is a result of a procedure: by accepting this (pre-defined) procedure, everybody is presumed to accept the (contingent) decision coming from it. We could generalise to all inner structures of law (procedures, but also organisations and the inner environment), ie, to all legal institutions, the learning capability that Luhmann attributed to the procedural systems. And in some sense every formalised procedure is a service that the legal system performs to other social systems (like in electoral procedures, or in the formalisation of economic deals or disputes).

Legal programs help to generalise the references of meaning beyond concrete persons and abstract values. Legal and political procedures select the valid norms, coming from the periphery of law (eg, in legislation and contract) to its core (recognition in a sentence). As the doctrine of stare decisis emphasises, enforced expectations restabilise the system as presuppositions for the following interpretations and applications of law, and even for legal change in the centre (eg, in case law, by distinguishing or overruling).

Legal innovation can be sustained only with support from the legal periphery (political branches), if not with mobilisation of the political periphery itself. Indeed, here the focus is a prior question: what can be considered a legal innovation? Indeed, law generalises some norms, and legal interpretation deals with following rules – including second-order rules, about how to interpret a given legal norm, how to take a programmed decision and what sense to give to the programming decisions that are being applied. In a free parallel with Wittgenstein's understanding of rules (Hershovitz 2002), one may say that a hard case emerges when interpretation (rule-following) is impossible without creation: 'Once I have exhausted the justifications, I have reached bedrock, and my spade is turned. Then I am inclined to say: "This is simply what I do"' (Wittgenstein 2009: §217).

In other words, a hard case is the one that puts into question the institutional framework of judgment: requiring some change in the institutions under judgement (eg, a change in tort law) but also facing the institutional limitations of the role of the decision-maker (does the judge or the court have the power to carry out this change?). Of course, these institutional constraints are a matter of interpretation and include the ideals and interests of organisations and their members: 'when such ideal pictures have acquired a certain fixity in the judicial and professional tradition they are part of "the law" quite as much as legal precepts' (Pound 1923: 654).

Hence, the hypotheses advanced on this topic are:

i. Legal interpretation (indeterminacy in the level of programs) may require a solution at the level of legal institutions, requiring a different legal arrangement or organisation.

ii. To advance empirical studies in law we may depart from some distinctions between legal institutions, which will widen our vision of the means to structure an economic transaction beyond the possibilities commonly envisaged by economics.

iii. Even when we approach the level of institutions, detailing the basic distinctions about internal legal structures, there are some boundary problems which require legal innovations in this demanding sense: new legal setups of rights, duties, powers and liabilities (in the inner environment) or new organisations (at the legal centre or periphery), novelties that challenge the basic current institutional setup of the legal system and some legal order; this view of some possible boundaries for legal institutional innovation completes the grasping of institutional alternatives.

Both the organised and public spheres can be set up in a variety of institutional forms. Here I focus on the organised sphere of law, and the relation between centres and peripheries (concerning both organisations and their respective ways of legal programming). In the next topic, I provide an example of the setup of the 'legal personality' in parallel with the setup of economy, through a discussion of property rights.

Interpreted strictly, new institutional economics presupposes as a limiting condition that maximising behaviour (economic action) occurs under some institutional setting and that this context can be re-framed as a matter itself of a deal and a bargain (Unger 1996: 24). What a view of the institutional morphology of the legal system would deploy is that the legal performances directed to economic communication can in fact occur by a variety of forms. We can deal with profiling of the legal institutional alternatives concerning legal organisations and programming (ie, legal decision-making) starting with Fuller's (2001) analysis and comparison of different forms of social ordering through law.[5]

The basic legal operation – interpretation concerned with the code 'legal'/ 'illegal' – is programmed through a variety of decisional programmes, each produced by different organisations. In this sense, a hard case for some organisation may require not only that it interpret law with a wider openness to the environment (eg, through consequentialist argument) but that the battleground change. The centre of law, jurisdiction, is characterised by the settlement of disputes through a procedure that emphasises the presentation of reasoned arguments and proofs and the impartial adjudication of rights or wrongs by a third party.

As Luhmann (2004: ch. 7) points out, the prohibition of the denial of justice implodes the vision of law as a chain of commands from a representative legislator (or the political organisations in the legal periphery) to some bureaucratic and rational-formalistic judges. While even in routine cases finalistic and analogical judgements require finding of law, in undecidable cases judges draw a distinction between what law requires (unavoidably, a decision) and what law provides (no substantial orientation to program their decision). The gap may be filled only by resort to economic consequences, moral principles or other political considerations. Courts will then perform a role of compensating the incompetence of the periphery in legal programming, and will have to take programming decisions (not sufficiently programed). The constitutional interface between law and politics and the programming decisions that constitutional or supreme courts need to interpret or take are a limiting case for deciding controversial matters still *under* the law.

In some sense, this self-defining competence works to correct the faults in legislative programmes, such as failures to comply with the conditions that Fuller (1969: ch. 2) considers inner to the aspirations of legality: general programmes (rules) in place of mere ad hoc decisions, publicity of these programs, non-retroactivity, clarity, non-contradiction among decisional programs, non-impossibility of demanded conducts, constancy of law through time and congruence between official action and declared rule.

Law's hyper-correction by organisations performing incongruous roles (such as judge-made law in areas first regulated by statutes) may result in amplifying divergences, generalising an infection of the legal system, raising risks and uncertainties and leading to some epidemic state of incongruous expectations. The question 'who decides' at the core of a division of the legal labour – evokes then the paradox of *Kompetenz Kompetenz*, the self-referred competence of judges to decide about their own competence.

Someone may then move to the periphery of the legal system itself or, in a limiting case, to another legal order or to some organisational settlement parallel to state adjudication. Basically, arbitration arises here as expertise-based judgment that mimics the role of the judge as an impartial third-party decision-maker but builds only selective linkages to state power (such as for the coercive enforcement of an arbitral award).

Before that, within a state-law order, someone may recur to mediation as a barrier to the escalation of a conflict to courts. Mediation works by scattering conflicts in dyadic relationships, fostering dialogue and face-to-face communication (ie, interaction) among parties with conflicting but somewhat complementary interests.

It is just among all these options, in fact, that we find the polar opposites of contract versus organisation. Contracts work by reciprocal self-determination and presuppose some condition of fairness in bargains. Organisations work through managerial direction, by the issuing of commands that are given to order communications towards a shared end.

A hypothesis one may investigate concerning this variety of ways of legal settlement deals with the empirical question about how and in what measure the congruent generalisation of normative expectations is violated or reinforced by the structural couplings with other systems, merging with expectations structured by economy, politics, science etc. Another path to take is enquiry about the limiting institutional conditions of these forms of legal ordering in the centre or the periphery of law. The single case really focused on by new institutional economics – by contrast to the classic contract with fully articulated promise and acceptance – is incomplete, relational contracts, which structure not discrete exchanges but long-term transactions. However, this is only one innovation that legal sociology has brought to economic analysis. Socio-legal studies reveals more institutional alternatives.

At the outward limits of cognitive openness and operational capacity of legal programing through sentencing and courts lies the problem of structural injunctions, demanding discretionary choice among alternative means and bureaucratic coordination for the implementation of localised reforms in routines and organisations at odds with law (a version of this scenario is a firm's reorganisation under bankruptcy law). The scenario pushing the limits for mediation involves triadic or more complex relationships without civil inter-dependence, as exemplified by problems of restorative justice. The boundaries of managerial direction lie in experimentalist governance, which replaces command-and-control delegation (through a chain from planners to frontline executors) by some kind of decentred discretion with compliance to metrics, monitoring and self-correction of policies and results. Finally, a limiting condition for legislation is legal pluralism, because it may violate the integrity of law, which is possible in some measure within a legal order (with its own hierarchies and criteria for interpreting and building consistence).

The 'legal'/'illegal' code can be programmed not only by different kinds of norms (conditional or finalistic legal programs) and different organisations within a national legal order, but also by alternative legal orders.[6] As systems theory recognises legal unity by the single difference 'legal'/'illegal', it also acknowledges legal plurality, based on the different norms and orders that can programme the attribution of that guiding difference (Neves 2003: 146–148). This leads us to a problem (and possibility) rarely envisaged by new institutional economics (apart from Ostrom's works on the governance of commons; eg, Ostrom 2014): the question of legal pluralism. Indeed, the (empirical or methodological) reduction of the legal system to state law is a rarely disputed bias in American social sciences. Legal realists, for example, contest a vision of law as a coherent and complete system, technically applied through deductive logic. In its place they point to the interpretive indeterminacy of law and the necessity of political and ethical choices among colliding interpretation of norms, in light of their proclaimed ends (a trend concerned with the real consequences of different legal choices could then be developed, opening space for 'law and economics' analyses). Contrary to their European contemporaries in the beginnings of the 20th century, American critics of legal formalism did not give centrality to the non-state legal orders taking place in society. In Anglophone legal anthropology, in turn, classic authors could borrow a realist (Roscoe Pound's) definition of law as a form of 'social control' differentiated by 'the systematic application of the force of a politically organised society' (Radcliffe-Brown 1952: 212). A decade before this focus on institutionalised sanctions, Malinowski (1926: pt. I) proposed understanding law with an emphasis on reciprocity and interaction, not on coercion; law would be revealed mainly by processes and institutions, and conflicts would be seen as opportunities of negotiation.

Back to the foundations of new institutional economics. Coase's (1960) work on the problem of 'social cost' deals with the role of property rights in internalising externalities (like noise or other kinds of environmental pollution) and points to three alternatives: free bargaining among the right holders involved, judicial claiming and administrative (governmental) arbitration – transaction costs versus litigation costs versus taxation costs.

Komesar (1996), in turn, works on a distinction between rational action within some institutional framework and decisions about what institution to work in, in which setup to perform a choice: markets, politics or courts. His proposal of this comparative institutional analysis is a participation-centred approach: performance variation of some institution is relative to the participation of the main institutional actors common to all institutions (such as consumers, producers, voters, lobbyists and claimants); official actors, like legislators and judges, are taken to be secondary. Information and organisation costs are then compared by reference to transaction costs, claiming costs and participation costs. Besides these three institutional environments, there may be other alternatives, such as firms and unions in labour and business law. These may equally be actors in a decision-making process taken in the market, in politics or in the judiciary, or the institutions themselves within which choices are made and conflicts are solved.

The coincidence of legal orders – ie, legal pluralism and respective 'ordering costs' – is to be posited then as an evolutionary acquisition akin to solving some problems of complexity structuration or communication facilitation through the structuring of a second-level choice: not only inside some legal order but among competing legal orders. Indeed, the institutional morphology sketched in the previous topic represents the basic features of nation-state legal, political and economic systems. But all these systems can be reprogramed by different legal, political or economic orders. In this sense, human-rights courts perform work comparable to the constitutional courts and national judicial review; the International Monetary Fund and the World Bank work as central banks or development agencies for the international order; and the United Nations reproduces the distinction of the national political system between a parliament (UN assembly) and the executive (the Security Council). Self-regulated private orders – transnational arbitration, codes of conduct of multinational enterprises, modular contractual clauses – indeed mimic the national legal system, with their own programmes, doctrines and organisations. In this way, these orders may either immunise themselves from national laws or build selective reference and openness to them. Therefore, any given legal order may emulate similar or different legal orders, and the pluralism of legal ordering turns itself itno a second level of institutional multiplicity (besides the choice among different organisations and forms of programing within a given order).

Economic institutions and reflexivity

Arising then to the third step of this chapter, we detail the internal structures of the economic system and ask about the role of law in linking finance to production, through the mechanisms of debt and credit, saving and investment. Those alternative setups of the institutional linkages between law and economy provide the empirical illustration for a new legal approach to economic questions.

The centre of the economic system is based on the generalisation of trust: to sell their debts (in the face of savers, holders of deposit accounts) as credits (to their borrowers), banks need to avoid having all (or a large proportion of) their deposit account holders decide to demand their money back at the same time. The convergence of expectations built upon a generalised trust is the sole basis for preventing a bank run and sustaining the continuity of this paradoxical cycle of turning debt into credit. The same can be said of preventing a crash in stock exchanges.

In fact, this paradoxical working can only continue because it is externalised and reproduced through different operational levels: banks in relation to firms and families as depositors and borrowers; banks borrowing from and lending to each other, selling and buying financial products among themselves; banks sustaining their liquidity through government bonds. Here we find a structural coupling between politics and economy: monetary policy operationalised through the central bank. This is a meta-organisation in the sense that it is connected to or derived from the centres of both social systems: just as it is a Trojan horse inside economy, it relies on the state monopoly of power, and then of taxation and money printing, so that beside prudential regulation, the government can lend money to solve a bank liquidity crisis, bailt out a bank in a solvency crisis, or even as a matter of routine reinforce depositor confidence through deposit insurances. In this way, government provides a kind of second-order expectation based on its own economic robustness. This second-order expectation fills the gaps in the level of first-order trust in the private financial system itself.

Hyper-reflexivity of a system may inflate its communications and therefore devalue its symbolic medium. As when political power is inflated by some form of populism or over-participation, or positive law is inflated by arguments loosely based on considerations of principles and consequences, there are financial bubbles pressured by the proliferation of self-referring levels of economic reflexivity – as in the financial markets and investment banks workings on securitised debt and derivatives. A level of financial reflexivity arises which has a loose connection to the economic periphery – specifically to the funding of production. Corporations finance themselves through retained and re-invested earnings, but promising start-up companies may not find channels for their capitalisation.

We can exemplify the workings of the institutional interface between law and economy through property rights and ownership regimes, and then see how institutional variety in this area may help not only to constrain or prevent hyper-reflexivity (as in a kind of normative limiting of economic 'turbo-autopoiesis') but mainly to channel finance to production, narrowing the triangulation among markets, firms and the financial core of economy. If property rights and contract are the institutional interface between law and economy, we may include corporate arrangements and then envisage how the legal setups of these institutions (as a question of the definition of private rights, of the shape of legal personality and the market order) answer to the fundamental economic problem of reflexivity and to the linking of finance to production (preventing inflationary hyper-reflexivity as much as deflationary under-reflexivity, ie, the scarcity of financial mechanisms).

Authors working on 'law and economics' approaches emphasise that we should understand transactions not simply as exchanges of goods and services but as the trade of bundles of rights that one party attributes to the other (Demsetz 1967). Property rights would be the expectations of consuming a good or service provided by an asset, directly or through exchange (Barzel 1997: 3). Coase (1960) mentions property rights as devices to internalise costs and understands that a firm may inflict damages on third parties (such as noise or pollution), pointing to some cases in which a neighbour must support damages if these disturbances are inseparable from a utility that exceeds them. 'What has to be decided is whether the gain from preventing the harm is greater than the loss which would be suffered elsewhere as a result of stopping the action which produces the harm' (Coase 1960: 27). Indeed, the problem of internalising externalities has been approached before by a precursor of the legal realists: Hohfeld. While 19th-century formalism observed property rights as mutually exclusive spheres of liberty, Hohfeld (1917) observes them as bundles of faculties, an 'aggregate of privileges of use, rights of exclusion, powers of conveyance, and immunities from extinguishing or changing those other faculties or creating new ones' (Rodriguez 1998: 13, n. 22). This implies on the one hand that there may be freedom to cause damage to others without liability or immunity – Coase's problem. On the other hand, however, this implies a tool for remodelling the legal inner environment (the setup of rights) in relation to its coupling with the economic system.

Publicly listed companies have evaded the rigidities imposed by property rights for joining capital and achieving economies of scale. However, stock markets may yet be under-developed to fund emerging companies, either by debt or by equity securities. Compared to assuming debt, the position of holding shares gives the investor only the expectation of receiving (variable) dividends, not a credit (with fixed interest rates) to be demanded. For businesses with innovative potential (companies or projects), however, stocks can guarantee greater return to the investor (compared to bonds) while requiring less in terms of already established profitability and equity to serve as collateral. If the risk is shared, the variable return may be more advantageous than the loan interest. Although transaction costs are higher (in shareholding as compared to bonds), there are comparative advantages in terms of financing ventures in more uncertain market niches and earlier organisational phases.

But shareholding also has varieties, Schapiro (2010) says, especially in a continuum from the distribution of bonded securities (the atomisation and dispersion of investor shareholding) to concentration in controlling blocks. There will be, therefore, greater or lesser investor influence in corporate governance. Strategic investors (such as banks and state agencies or private companies with some special expertise in the field) organised through private equity funds are important for monitoring the early stages of an emerging business, providing advice until its maturation. Therefore, relational governance can supply to some degree the lack of a capital market able to channel investment to not-yet-consolidated firms. Some relational investors may induce the self-organisation of over-the-counter markets that help to make usable the instruments of investor pressure on entrepreneurs, such as put options (the entrepreneur's duty to buy the investor's stake in his business) or tag-along rights (the right to sell shares to a third party for the same conditions given to the entrepreneur who wants to dispose of the company).

The point is that these schemes of funding, which densify the links between financial reflexivity and economic periphery (on the supply side, ie, production), can include a variety of shareholders such as public banks and agents, private investors (in private equity funds) and cooperatives (Amato 2018b). If each of these parts can own different rights – usually merged in property ownership – 'disaggregated property' becomes an instrument of expansion for entrepreneurship, and can be the conceptual basis for thinking of multiple investment funds with different powers, privileges and immunities. This is the case of public rotating funds that work as funds of funds, investing in (private, first-order) funds directed to provide venture capital (Unger 2001: 491–506). This is only an example of detecting a functional problem coming from self-reference (eg, hyper-reflexivity) and mapping empirical alternatives of systemic-institutional setups answering to the diagnosed flaw (eg, financial channels besides the stock exchanges).

Final remarks and a research agenda

This work has provided some guidelines for an institutional detailing of the structures, deciding programmes and organisations within social systems, especially the legal and economic systems. The thesis is that this systemic-institutional approach can deal with problems akin to the new institutional economics, providing a comparable approach and organising some insights to widen the range of vision of the institutional alternatives, both within the legal system itself and in its performances for structuring economic communication (ie, transactions).

Starting with the parallel between transaction costs and the improbability of communication that social systems help to overcome (by structuring complexity of meaning), the work focuses on the view of functional systems and their inner structures. These institutions include a sphere to 'pre-programme' decisions and systems for decision-making. The centre and the periphery of the legal system, for instance, work in a division of labour among programming and programmed decisions, and the variety of forms of legal ordering expand the view of institutions beyond the contrast between contract and organisation.

Finally, the text focuses on the economic system and a contemporary failing of that system: hyper-reflexivity and the lack of channels to link finance to production. By understanding property rights widely enough to cover the diverse forms of corporate ownership, one can explore the corporate and financial legal arrangements that tighten the linkages between the economic periphery (especially production) and its financial core. The exemplary case discussed was the problem of funding start-up companies, which involves high transaction costs and uncertainties in the financial markets. Disaggregated property schemes that help to structure relational governance for these firms would be an interesting tool for dealing with this problem.

Notes

1 Luhmann (2010: 86) defines institutions in an early work as 'expectations of behavior that are temporally, objectually and socially generalised, and as such form the structure of social systems'. Later (Luhmann, 2012: 191), he admits that the symbolically generalised communication media (power, positive law, money) can be understood as institutions, as they set a frame of reference that reduces complexity and absorbs uncertainty – they work like rules to follow, in the sense of Wittgenstein (2009: 184–242). They symbolise the probable acceptance of communication by the generalised others, ie, support, institutionalisation. And we

might call culture, Luhmann (2012: 248) adds, the 'combined effect of all com-munication media – language, dissemination media [printing, internet etc.], and the symbolically generalised media'.

2 Luhmann (1990: 125–129, 2014: 179–185) uses the difference between programming and programmed decisions developed by Simon (1955, 1977: ch. 2) and recognises that this is a continuum (Luhmann, 2014: 353, n. 73).

3 On the centre and periphery of the political, legal and economic systems, see Luhmann (1993: 180–184, 2004: ch. 7, 2009: 272–279). On the structural couplings among politics, economy, law, science and education, see Luhmann (2004: ch. 10, 2009: ch. 10, 2013: 108–115). On the internal environments or public spheres of the economic, political and scientific systems, see Luhmann (2009: ch. 8, 2013: 102, 2017: ch. 3). The concept of the public sphere as the inner environment of a system is due to a suggestion by Dirk Baecker, as recognised by Luhmann (2000: 104). The difference between the public sphere and the organised sphere is emphasised by Teubner (2012: 88–96), who does not, however, clearly differentiate between the legal and political public spheres.

4 Ramos (2017) speaks in a similar sense of a 'peripheral dogmatics'.

5 See also Winston (2001: 48) and Rodriguez (2016: ch. 7). Strictly speaking, 'managerial command' is contrasted by Fuller (1969: 215–216, n. 29) to law itself, and Fuller's theory is not clearly receptive of legal pluralism (see Waldron 2010). Therefore, I am deliberately re-describing Fuller's original vision.

6 Indeed, what Willke (1986) calls 'relational programs' are in fact programs by which state law opens space for other legal orders and remits questions to these private or public-private legal orders (which would be better coupled to other functional systems, such as economy and science). In other words, 'reflexive law' (Teubner, 1986) is just the boundary norms of state law that programmes self-regulation in a neo-corporatist fashion.

References

Akerlof, G.A. (1970) 'The market for "lemons": quality uncertainty and the market mechanism' *84*(3) *Quart. J. Econ.* 488–500.

Amato, L.F. (2017) *Construtivismo jurídico: Teoria no direito* (Curitiba, Juruá).

Amato, L.F. (2018a) *Inovações constitucionais: Direitos e poderes* (Belo Horizonte, Casa do Direito).

Amato, L.F. (2018b) 'Legal forms for market democratization' *Paper presented at the 13th Research Workshop on Institutions and Organizations* (São Paulo, Center for Organization Studies).

Amato, L.F. (2018c) 'Luhmann e Mangabeira Unger: da crítica social ao construtivismo jurídico' in Amato L.F. and Barros M.A.L.L. (eds), *Teoria crítica dos sistemas? Crítica, teoria social e direito* (Porto Alegre, Fi), 243–277.

Baecker, D. (2006) 'The form of the firm' *13*(1) *Organization* 109–142.

Barzel, Y. (1997) *Economic Analysis of Property Rights,* 2nd ed. (Cambridge, Cambridge University Press).

Campilongo, C.F. (2014) *Função social do notariado* (São Paulo, Saraiva).

Chang, H.-J. and Evans P. (2005) 'The role of institutions in economic change' in Dymski G. and Da Paula S. (eds), *Reimagining Growth* (London, Zed Press), 99–129.

Coase, R. (1937) 'The nature of the firm' *4*(16) *Economica* 386–405.

Coase, R. (1960) 'The problem of the social cost' *3 J. Law Econ.* 1–44.

Demsetz, H. (1967) 'Toward a theory of property rights' *57*(2) *Am. Econ. Rev.* 347–359.

Fuller, L.L. (1969) *The Morality of Law*, 2nd ed. (New Haven, Yale University Press).

Fuller, L.L. (2001) *The Principles of Social Order* (Oxford, Hart).

Galiani, S. and Schargrodsky, E. (2014) 'Land property rights' in Galiani S. and Sened I. (eds), *Institutions, Property Rights, and Economic Growth* (Cambridge, Cambridge University Press), 107–120.

Hale, R.L. (1935) 'Force and the state: a comparison of "political" and "economic" compulsion' *35*(2) *Columbia Law Rev.* 149–201.

Hershovitz, S. (2002) 'Wittgenstein on rules: the phantom menace' *22*(4) *Oxford J. Legal Stud.* 619–640.

Hesse, M. (1966) *Models and Analogies in Science* (Notre Dame, University of Notre Dame Press).

Hohfeld, W.N. (1917) 'Fundamental legal conceptions as applied in judicial reasoning' *26*(8) *Yale Law J.* 710–770.

Knight, F.H. (1921) *Risk, Uncertainty and Profit* (Boston, Houghton Mifflin)

Komesar, N. (1996) *Imperfect Alternatives: Choosing Institutions in Law, Economics, and Public Policy* (Chicago, Chicago University Press).

Luhmann, N. (1979) *Trust and Power* (Chichester, Wiley&Sons).

Luhmann, N. (1980) *Legitimação pelo procedimento* (Brasília, UnB).

Luhmann, N. (1981) 'The improbability of communication' *33*(1) *Int. Soc. Sci. J.*, 122–132.

Luhmann, N. (1983) *Fin y racionalidad en los sistemas* (Madrid, Nacional).

Luhmann, N. (1988) 'Familiarity, confidence and trust: problems and alternatives' in Gambetta D. (ed), *Trust: Making and Breaking Cooperative Relations* (Oxford, Blackwell), 94–107.

Luhmann, N. (1990) *La differenziazione del diritto* (Bologna, Il Mulino).

Luhmann, N. (1993) *Risk: A Sociological Theory* (Berlin, Gruyter).

Luhmann, N. (1995) *Social Systems* (Stanford, Stanford University Press).

Luhmann, N. (2000) *The Reality of the Mass Media* (Stanford, Stanford University Press).

Luhmann, N. (2004) *Law as a Social System* (Oxford, Oxford University Press).

Luhmann, N. (2005a) 'Iluminismo sociológico' in Santos J.M. (ed), *O pensamento de Niklas Luhmann* (Corvilhã, Universidade da Beira Interior), 19–70.

Luhmann, N. (2005b) *Organización y decisión: Autopoiesis, acción y entendimiento comunicativo* (Barcelona, Anthropos).

Luhmann, N. (2009) *La política como sistema* (México, Universidad Iberoamericana).

Luhmann, N. (2010) *Los derechos fundamentales como institución* (México, Universidad Iberoamericana).

Luhmann, N. (2012) *Theory of Society I* (Stanford, Stanford University Press).

Luhmann, N. (2013) *Theory of Society II* (Stanford, Stanford University Press).

Luhmann, N. (2014) *A Sociological Theory of Law*, 2nd ed. (New York, Routledge).

Luhmann, N. (2017) *La economía de la sociedade* (México, Herder).

Malinowski, B. (1926) *Crime and Custom in Savage Society* (New York, Harcourt).

Ménard, C. (2013) 'Hybrid modes of organization: alliances, joint ventures, networks, and other "strange" animals' in Gibbons R. and Roberts J. (eds), *Handbook of Organizational Economics* (Princeton, Princeton University Press), 1066–1105.

Ménard, C. and Shirley, M. (2014) 'The contribution of Douglass North to new institutional economics' in Gagliani S and Sened I (eds), *Institutions, Property Rights, and Economic Growth* (Cambridge, Cambridge University Press), 11–29.

Milgrom, P. and Roberts, J. (1992) *Economics, Organization and Management* (Englewood Cliffs, Prentice Hall).

Neves, M. (2003) 'From legal pluralism to social miscellany' *26 Beyond Law* 125–154.

Neves, M (2013). *Entre Hidra e Hércules* (São Paulo, WMF Martins Fontes).

North, D.C. (1990) *Institutions, Institutional Change and Economic Performance* (Cambridge, Cambridge University Press).

North, D.C. (1991) 'Institutions' *5*(1) *J. Econ. Perspect.* 97–112.

North, D.C. (1994) 'Economic performance through time' *84*(3) *Am. Econ. Rev.* 359–368.

North, D.C., Wallis, J.J. and Weingast, B.R. (2009) *Violence and Social Orders: A Conceptual Framework for Interpreting Recorded Human History* (Cambridge, Cambridge University Press).

Ostrom, E. (2014) 'Institutions and sustainability of ecological systems' in Galiani S. and Sened I. (eds), *Institutions, Property Rights, and Economic Growth* (Cambridge, Cambridge University Press), 84–106.

Pound, R. (1907) 'The need of a sociological jurisprudence' *19*(10) *Green Bag* 607–615.

Pound, R. (1923) 'The theory of judicial decision I' *36*(6) *Harvard Law Rev.*, 641–662.

Radcliffe-Brown, A.R. (1952) 'Primitive law' in Radcliffe-Brown (ed) A.R., *Structure and Function in Primitive Society* (Glencoe, Free Press), 212–219.

Ramos, L.F.R. (2017) *Por trás dos casos difíceis* (Curitiba, Juruá).

Ramos, L.F.R. (2019) *Antitrust and Competition* (Dissertation, Universidade de São Paulo, São Paulo).

Rodriguez, C.F. (1998) *Disaggregation with a Purpose* (Thesis, Harvard Law School, Cambridge).

Rodriguez, C.F. (2016) *Juízo e imaginação* (São Paulo, Malheiros).

Schapiro, M.G. (2010) *Novos parâmetros para a intervenção do Estado na economia* (São Paulo, Saraiva).

Simon, H.A. (1955) 'Recent advances in organization theory' in Bailey, S.K. Simon H.A., Dahl R.A., Snyder R.C., Grazia A., Moos M., David P.T., and Truman D.B., *Research Frontiers in Politics and Government* (Washington, Brookings Institution), 23–44.

Simon, H.A. (1977) *The New Science of Management Decision,* 3rd ed. (Englewood Cliffs, Prentice-Hall).

Teubner, G. (1986) 'After legal instrumentalism? strategic models of post-regulatory law' in Teubner G. (ed), *Dilemmas of Law in the Welfare State* (Berlin, Gruyter), 299–325.

Teubner, G. (2012) *Constitutional Fragments* (Oxford, Oxford University Press).

Unger, R.M. (1996) *What Should Legal Analysis Become?* (London, Verso).

Unger, R.M. (2001) *False Necessity*, 2nd ed (London, Verso).

Veblen, T. (1898) 'Why is economics not an evolutionary science?' *12*(4) *Quart. J. Econ.* 373–397.

Waldron, J. (2010) 'Legal pluralism and the contrast between Hart's jurisprudence and Fuller's' in Cane P. (ed), *The Hart-Fuller Debate in the Twenty-First Century* (Oxford, Hart), 135–155.

Williamson, O.E. (1985) *The Economic Institutions of Capitalism: Firms, Markets, Relational Contracting* (New York, Free Press).

Williamson, O.E. (1992) 'Markets, hierarchies, and the modern corporation: an unfolding perspective' *17*(3) *J. Econ. Behav. Org.* 335–352.

Willke, H. (1986) 'Three types of legal structure: the conditional, the purposive and the relational program' in Teubner G. (ed), *Dilemmas of Law in the Welfare State* (Berlin, Gruyter), 280–298.

Winston, K.I. (2001) 'Introduction' in Fuller (ed), L.L. *The Principles of Social Order* (Oxford, Hart), 25–58.

Wittgenstein, L. (2009) *Philosophical Investigations* (Chichester, Wiley-Blackwell).

Part III

Analysing law through systemic approaches

The political interface

Chapter 8

Observing courts

An organisational sociology for socio-legal research

Marco Antonio Loschiavo Leme de Barros

Introduction

Courts[1] are an important organisation in the operation of modern society. This was observed historically based on their differentiation as a distinct partial decision-making system, responsible for controlling counterfactual normative expectations by decisions. In order to observe courts in the legal system, it is important to consider the internal observation in which law observes itself at the level of second-order observation, distinguishing legislation and jurisdiction as a cybernetic circle (Luhmann 2004: 278).

When the modern legal system was formally established, courts began to play an prominent role in society, with the legal experience revealing its interpretive character and its main function of settling disputes[2] by the force of a decision and its justifications (see MacCormick 2005). In a functionalist perspective (Becker 1970; Luhmann 2004; Ziegert 1992; see also Bredemeier 1962), law is not only about valid claims, statutes and contracts but also about how decision-making processes operate with a double pressure: to decide each case and to guarantee the decision beyond the particularity of the case (Luhmann 2004: 287). Many expectations have to be filtered through decision-making processes before acquiring a legal form. This can be understood due to the fact that everything that is legal is now determined based on its own operations, or that courts should take legal communication seriously (Ziegert 1992: 210).

Whereas on the one hand this gave greater autonomy and superiority to the performance of courts within the legal system, on the other hand it confirmed an open crisis of the legal dogma produced at the end of the 19th century, ie, its progressive distance from society.[3] During the beginning of the 20th century, two distinct positions arose as possible solutions for the dogmatic crisis: either an improvement of Pandectism, a view derived from legal positivism, or an approach to reality as portrayed in Eugen Ehrlich's idea of living law, a law beyond the legal text, ie, a law that is practiced by society in various customs, independent from any state power (Ehrlich 2009). Hence, no existing theory of law adequately accounts for the complexities of court operations, since they channel different roles, expectations and socialisations,[4] not only as a process of settlement of disputes.

Moreover, courts are criticised either as excessively formalistic or as psychologised.[5] If courts are originally organisations of society – and not necessarily of a power of the state – they could also justify their decisions based on decision-making rules that come from any social practice. There is no doubt that courts still deal with an open crisis involving uncertainty about their operations. Also, courts are being criticised for managerial proceedings that are reducing workload and keeping cases from being resolved (Tamanaha 2017: 144).

Are courts, after all, only means to process conflicts, aiming to reduce social disorder as much as possible – instances of controlling decisions – or also planning instruments, a factor that modifies society – instances of programmatic decision-making? This is a question regarding the court's observations, an inquiry about the observer and the observation.[6] In addition to the criticisms, it is possible to understand the difficulties of operations of courts as a result of a certain insufficiency of the legal system. This observation focuses on the insufficiencies of judicial communications that are not able to filter the external pressures on the decision-making processes (Luhmann 2004: 283). Courts and judges are not able to acquire immunity from political pressures. Judicial independence and neutrality are placed under suspicion when judges perform a new function, sometimes blurred with the administrative or legislative.[7]

Considering the complexity that has been presented, how should these organisations be observed? This chapter recalls the history of sociology of organisations to present an exploratory and alternative sociological framework to study courts in society. Many relevant sociological works have been focused either in a legal-centralist fashion on dispute resolution, judicial hierarchies or means of law-making and law-finding; or in a judicial behaviouristic manner – yet few studies deal with a comprehensive sociological theory that discusses the court's communication.

Exploring some ideas from Niklas Luhmann's social systems theory, I argue the importance of observing how courts construct their own meaning about society while deciding cases. This unveils a peculiar form of observation of courts as social courts. The interest is to preserve the presupposed complexity of their operations – not reducing the observation to a legal-centralistic approach or to a behavioural one, but emphasising the specificity of courts' communication. Besides this introduction, this chapter is divided into three sections. The first section presents a brief overview of a sociological tradition that deals with the observations of organisations; the point is to highlight the observation of courts as an organisational form and the consequences for socio-legal research. The second section offers an account of the idea of social courts by applying an exploratory typology. The typology reveals different dynamics of courts' communication in society.

The final section underscores a methodological achievement of observing social courts as a form to contribute to the debate about the empirical implications for socio-legal research based on social systems theory.

Sociology of organisations and courts

Ever since Max Weber's 'The essentials of bureaucratic organisation: An ideal-type construction' (Weber 1976), sociologists have observed how organisation contributes to the development of world society. Organisations have their specific purposes and rules, setting a regime of authorities via bureaucracies. The literature related to the topic has been attentive to the application of Weberian concepts in different contexts, trying to understand empirically some of the characteristics of bureaucracies (eg, hierarchy, pre-established rules, top-down decisions, membership and formal rationalisation). The common assumption is that organisations control individual actions according to pre-established purposes. Another Weberian approach focuses on the democratic deficits of organisations, mainly considering informal operations and adjustments, as well as the dysfunctions of bureaucracy themselves. The study of informal relations or of organisations' environments is an important example of the sociological contribution to understanding the complexities of organisations.[8]

In addition, it is important to remember the claim of Burns and Stalker (1966) about organic organisations, since it is possible to observe a looser structure, considering the flows of organisational communication. A major element in organic organisations is flexibility, which allows a quick adjustment of structures to transformations in the environment. These distinctions are important to underscore the different roles of organisations in society. There are several kinds of organisations, not only mechanistic (based on formal structures and pre-established rules and purposes) – many other organisations are established upon lesser divisions and substantive rationalisation processes.

There is still a common ground that integrates the different studies of the sociology of organisations: organisations can be observed based on their own elements and communications. Regarding this perspective, a functionalist approach can contribute to this debate, since organisations are observers as autonomous bodies. I explore some ideas of organisational systems presented by Luhmann in order to promote a holistic theoretical framework to observe courts in society.

Organisational systems

Organisations are not the equivalent of functional systems. In the work *Organisation and Decision*, originally published in 1978, Luhmann discusses the rise of organisations in a more general context previous to world society, insofar as they constitute systems of decision and are related based on an organisational network (Luhmann 2005: 59), enabling reciprocal stimuli and the appearance of new organisations. Stichweh (2015: 29) clearly points out Luhmann's insight: the orthogonal use of organisational communications for functional differentiation.

For social systems theory, there is a presupposition of a certain ortho-gonality of organisations in relation to the functional systems of world society. Organisational communications can circulate in several functional systems and may be part of the processes that are followed in the same organisation; they ensure and operate with complexities.[9] Hence, organisations can be multi-systemic and multi-referential. Functional systems can even operate as attractions for organisations, since they can induce self-simplifications that make organisations prefer to connect to a specific system considering the logic of their future evolution (Stichweh 2015: 29–33).

Organisations appeared as evolutionary acquisitions oriented toward the absorption of social uncertainties. When an organisation appears, a network of recursive decisions emerges, and every social transformation occurs as a communication of decisions, or at least is guided toward it. It is undeniable in understanding the origin and dependence of a society of organisations (Perrow 1991) that the social growth and consolidation of different functional systems was part and parcel of the growth of organisations within society: a strong connection of the functional systems with organisations was observed, especially following a bureaucratic logic.

According to Luhmann's observation (2004: 77), this is the result of the capacity of organisations to generate redundancy, avoiding surprises and absorbing insecurity. It is not by chance that in every social system there are a series of organisations that produce the redundancy needed to maintain the functional systems: governments, private corporations, courts, churches, hospitals and many others.

Moreover, organisations are endowed with an internal selectivity which can mark their difference from the environment (eg, internal environment of the system) and at the same time ensure their unity. Any organisational decision serves as a point of departure for future decisions, since the decision belongs to the organisational unit and is fixed at temporary points that secure the continuity of new decisions. In a systemic view, organisational decisions are mutually conditioned in the sense that without other decisions, there would be no base to decide (Luhmann 2005: 43). Different from functional systems, which have an invariable and encoded structure – even if it is programable and non-hierarchised – and a structure for re-entry of the environment into the system (or internal environment), organisations are more permeable to the internal environment of the systems and of society.

Organisational communication is also ensured by a hierarchical structure of its own, which produces an autonomous internal complexity. Hierarchy can be understood as a chain of command that assures that decisions are formally taken (not necessarily that there is a concentration of power at the top) based on any information outside the organisation. Hierarchy must be perceived as an internal distinction of the organisations that determines their operation – yet there is no hierarchy between different organisations or between functional systems and organisations. In this way, the decision-making premises and organisational culture are also consolidated as structures. For an unorthodox systemic perspective, organisational culture can be shaped as premises of undecidable decisions (unmarked side).

Two clarifications should be highlighted. First, hierarchy promotes communication among organisations, besides ensuring their internal selectivity. This is why organisations do not need to connect all the time to a single functional system, because they are autopoietic systems per se and produce their own operational frontiers based on decisions. Second, from the standpoint of the organisations, the functional differentiation of society has endorsed a new organisational treatment: decisions may or not meet the functions of systems, operating based on the code and on the specific programmes – organisations increase the complexity of world society (Luhmann 2004: 422).

The delimitations of an organisation's decision-making possibilities are not necessarily connected to the functions and codes; rather, they are established by the organisation, which constantly reconsiders its frontiers, since innovations are guaranteed by the possibility of establishing new relations with the decisions. In this sense it is also possible to think about the distinction between formal and informal structures of organisations that marks the relations between functional systems and organisations in world society (Holzer 2015: 38).

In a nutshell, organisations can observe and reflect different information regarding the environment, but they are limited by their hierarchical structure, which enables inclusions and exclusions, especially when promoting the distinction between members and non-members (Luhmann 2005: 8–13). For Luhmann (2005), organisational communication is comprehend based on and only among its members, and therefore it is worth underscoring that organisations are based on formalised expectations among their members to define the basic parameters of organisational communication.

In the case of law, courts arise as an internal differentiation of the legal system. These organisations are connected not solely to functional legal limits but to the communication produced by their operations (ie, legal decisions). Considering this framework, I argue that in a complex society, it is possible to observe courts outside the legal system. Courts are increasingly related to other organisations that do not belong to the legal system – eg, banks, parliaments, regulating agencies, hospitals, universities and so many others. In addition, there is an internal examination about the plurality of argumentation methods based theoretically on non-legal techniques and criteria for the decision-making of courts – eg, econometrics, statistics, theory of rational choice, game theory and so many others. Courts thus have a significant issue to confront: how to decide cases that are substantially justified by non-legal arguments, or that were not satisfactorily filtered through legal programs? These situations indicate that the courts' communication is not simply the same as legal communication.

There is a debate about techniques and criteria to solve the problems of adjudication of consequences, which are treated and developed through legal argumentation above all by means of judicial communication. These arguments generally question the social effects of decisions and are therefore selected and decided by law. In this sense, adjudication should be observed as a communication produced by the courts. Even without adequate legal programs, decisions are made by the courts. The difficulty then lies in ensuring the quality of decisions (Luhmann 2004: 202), above all because consequentialist decisions accept a future present – not a present future. Consequentialist decisions thus approach the future in a utopian manner in law, since they reduce complexities imagining and assuming certain events.[10]

From the organisational standpoint, this utopian operation actually indicates that courts do not necessarily operate based only on law codes and programmes. Different from other legal organisations, they go more easily beyond the frontier of the functional system and communicate with society in another way. There is thus communication of the courts outside the law, which on the one hand can represent, according to Luhmann's view, another kind of irritation of the legal system, or a development as an 'internal environment' of law; on the other hand, it allows an understanding that the courts do not communicate exclusively in the legal system but also participate in other social systems.

Courts as organisations

Different structures – limited by the internal operations of each system – contribute to adjusting the expansion of the communication of courts in the social subsystems. These structural factors may be organised based on the encoding/programming relation, and it is important to remember that only in the structural form of its code is the system invariant and unchanging, although always available to be adapted or transformed via programmes (Luhmann 2004: 195).

Regarding programming, as underlined before, courts also communicate outside the legal system, even if bound by the demands of other codes. It should be recalled that when Luhmann discusses programming, he interprets the values of the codes as possibilities or means that accept different forms for organisations (2004: 195). In this way, beyond the structural couplings, the connections between other systems may occur via organisations, especially at the level of programming. As an illustration, courts often prevent the political system from applying public force illegally, mainly by exerting control of the legality of administrative acts or interpreting the rule of jurisdiction to decide an impeachment case. Simultaneously, this communication is only possible if the political system assures the self-determination of the courts, providing them with financial and administrative autonomy and enabling them the necessary resources to enforce their decisions (Luhmann 2004: 371–375).

Under some circumstances the expansion involves the mobilisation of the consequences of decisions by the courts. In the case of politics, for example, it is questioned how the decisions of courts are expressed as forms of political pressure, or to what extent they influence the legislative process.[11] Without a doubt, courts can operate as a political organisation when their decisions are communicated by means of power, evoking the consequences of the decisions in the political system, and also when they contribute to the legal delimitation of politics, resulting in the production of statutes or undermining administrative acts.

As regards the economic system, it is found that legal decisions also interfere in economic processes by creating mechanisms for the execution of credits or by securitising risks by means of judicial deposits and guarantees – and more generally by adjudicating economic rights. The courts ultimately administrate scarcity by means of their decisions, communicating with the economy and putting under debate the impacts of their decisions on public and private budgets (see Bora 2010).

In all these situations there is a contingent situation of reciprocity between these functional systems, in which communication is connected by means of organisations. This asymmetrical correspondence marks the co-evolution of systems (Luhmann 1995: 26–41), and it takes place inconstantly and at different times – temporal disharmony – by reducing the complexity of the environment based on the communication produced by the organisations themselves. Paradoxically, organisational communication is also a condition to increase the internal complexity in other circulating systems. It is important to clarify that this co-evolution is not finalistic or linear, but a differentiation that implies successive additions of complexity to the system and therefore the design of new operational limits. It should also be emphasised that the view of this increase of complexity through reduction of the system's complexity via organisation is not causal, since it depends on a determination established not only by the system – and here one should consider the distinction between encoding and programming as internal structures of selection.

Moreover, this situation can be understood as a movement of adjustments and balances of the temporality of world society as a whole, motivated by accelerations and decelerations as a function of the time of each functional and organisational system. The dilemma in systemic observation refers to the future of modern society, which is 'de-futurised' through utopias and technologies (Luhmann 1976). However, this point is structurally developed with the accumulation of knowledge and the acceleration of the new operational limits in each system: the transformation of politics into law, the legal delimitation of politics and others. The treatment of the future produces environmental pressures that in turn have repercussions on the systems. Organisations play an important role because in many situations decisions represent a future present that triggers transformations in the system.

In brief, organisations connect with the environment based on a communication and function of their own and the way in which they connect to the codes and programs of the social systems. Considering the sociology of organisations, it is possible to agree with the view of the multi-centre processes of management and the multiplicity of injunctions, in one and the same organisation, that reinforce the possibility of the different connections that can be established by organisations. The Brazilian sociologists Dutra and Campos (2013) discuss this idea considering the problem of coordination and control of organisational performance – ie, under the systemic reference, management must privilege a functional orientation when selecting the organisational objectives – which produces operational tensions.

Nobody would deny that courts concern themselves more with ensuring normative expectations than with solving the problems of payments proper, just as in hospitals what prevails is a focus on producing diagnoses and treatments rather than on dealing with the management of the scarcity of medicines. However, it is also not possible to deny the variety of management in these organisations. As already seen, courts concern themselves with the extra-legal repercussions of their decisions, just as hospitals demand that medicines be supplied to their patients. In this sense, the functional variety of organisations implies forms of management that are also distinct, so that we can talk about religious management, scientific management, political management, management of medicine etc.

The variety of forms of organisational management actually reveals the conflicts of management. It is possible to question, so to say, over which functional reference the operations of the courts will prevail, and what the consequences of this are in relation to the other operations. The same could be asked about the state, banks, schools, universities, hospitals etc. The impossibility of establishing a single functional referential centre or monopoly for each organisation in a poly-contextural society reveals the complexity of the point.

When privileging a functional reference, the organisation does not exclude the others and does not even isolate itself, but generates irritations and tensions in other operations and even other organisations. It is possible to consider as an example the political and economic management of the courts. Similarly, Dutra and Campos (2013: 39) discuss the management of the health system in Brazil and affirm that this organisation is disputed by different forms of management, such as medical, scientific, economic and political management. The problem is a result of the attempt to politically change the mode of operation of the functional system of medicine, since this system, centred on the identification of diseases, operates precisely in the reverse direction of the policies that seek to prioritise prevention to the detriment of the clinical activity of diagnosing and offering treatment. This is not a problem of lack of management, it is a problem of organisational conflict of management: the conflict between political management and medical management in the organisational arrangement of health.

In light of these observations, it can be argued that organisations are also forms and that there is a vast agenda of systemic study about organisational operations and their dynamics in society. Indeed, it is necessary to reflect increasingly on organisations based on organisational variables. The interesting fact is that the systemic reference offers precisely these variables based on concepts such as programmes, structural couplings and communication. This point is discussed next.

Form of organisations

Organisations can be observed as a form marked by two sides. Assuming the marked side, for Dirk Baecker (2006), while understanding the form of the firm, it is possible to distinguish the organisation by its history, by its culture, by the systemic reference and by organisational communication.

History is an essential part of any organisation. According to Baecker (2006: 112), the history of the organisation is embodied in several structures and operates in line with its trajectory and memory – just as is pointed out by the Weberian tradition, the history is present in the organisation's procedures, its written and unwritten rules, its technologies, its members and networks. This is relative knowledge, produced by the organisation, and it is essential to understand this process in order to apprehend its operations.

The idea of culture is also relevant, since it defines the organisation's identity based on a comparison. Baecker (2006: 114–115) approaches organisational culture also as a form, so that the concept points to a difference. On the one hand, a culture consists of the memory of certain beliefs and values, considered to be valid since they have proven to be successful. So the identity of an organisation is the product of the culture it chooses in a selective manner and in relation to other organisations. The other side – unmarked – includes possibilities that have not been selected; in this way, culture as a memory is both the reproduction of particular values and the constant memory of alternative options which make these values appear as questionable contingent selections. The differential approach to the culture of organisations enables a critical analysis of the operations based on memorisation, which is continuously active in social communication. The culture of an organisation marks at the same time the ideas of its preservation and of its transformation.

Another important aspect is to know what systemic reference should be considered when observing an organisation, because it is that which explains the way the organisation produces and reproduces itself, distinguishing itself from its environment. Even if organisations are not limited by functional systems, it is necessary to situate, at the time of observation, the functional system to which they are connected. In other words, at the level of analysis one must render explicit which specific system is being observed. It is possible to adopt different perspectives of observation, thus accepting a scenario with multiple environments and different systems compatible with an organisation that operates in these environments.

A model of a court, for example, is proposed that corresponds to a differentiated organisation of society which, even if it has arisen for an internal differentiation of the legal system, does not belong exclusively to it. The court is not an equivalent to the legal system itself, but a central organisation of the system that can operate peripherally in other systems.[12] If one takes an ecological perspective of the systems, there is no 'super-system' that coordinates all the others. Thus, it is not necessary to neglect consideration of the operation of the other systems when studying an organisation, since the latter remains functionally connected to the other systems.

Finally, Baecker's analysis elucidates the fact that the firm's distinction also occurs in terms of communication. This is the most relevant element to analyses, since it corresponds recursively to the idea of an organisation as a difference in relation to the other – functional and interactional – systems. Thus, the court distinguishes itself from society – including the various subsystems – and from all those who do not participate in it and who consider this distinction. Only a communicational model of an organisation is able to meet the requirement of this distinction (Baecker 2006: 127).

In this view, organisations produce their own meaning, according to their respective dynamics – after all, they refer to each other.[13] For example, the firm's communication only makes sense for the members or for its participants, and is determined by successive internal decisions and structures, which are generally hierarchical. There is thus a distinction between corporate and non-corporate communication. It is not exactly a matter of an immediate superposition between different communications of social systems, but actually of the production of a communication peculiar to the firm that contains a history (memory), a culture, and also refers to different functional systems simultaneously. One should recognise that there is an evolution by means of the decisions, which confers a certain thickness on the trajectory and distinction of the organisations in relation to the functional systems.

Hence, I argue the importance of studying the communicational model of courts as a social organisation just like Baecker's insights about the firm. The comparison of the organisational forms of a firm and of a court does not mean that firms are operationally equivalent to courts, nor that there is an economistic orientation or a privatistic model dominant in the courts. On the contrary, the characterisation of the form of the firm is discussed to indicate the variety of other types of organisation, each with a specificity and characteristics of its own. Courts ensure connections between systems based on their own operation. Next, this communicational view of the courts is presented based on a contextualisation of their expansion in world society.

Social courts

The end of the 20th century marked the rise of the communication of courts in world society, coinciding with a wave of constitutionalisation after World War II (see, eg, Gardbaum 2013; Hirschl 2007). Many reasons triggered this expansion. Preponderant among them is the constitutionalisation of fundamental rights – eg, the third and fourth generations – and of mechanisms to allow and facilitate direct access of the population to the courts.[14]

On the one hand, it is possible to observe an expansion of the political power of judges and courts, who participate more actively in political communication, causing a new rearrangement of the representative bodies. On the other hand, the capacity of judges and courts to decide complex cases and to represent the aspirations of society is problematised. Hence, there is a discussion about the legitimacy of court decisions on sensitive areas of public policy, mainly in countries where judges are not elected (see, eg, Tushnet 2006; Waldron 2006). Courts as a counter-majoritarian power may operate as true political opposition via controlling and restricting certain government decisions (Taylor 2007: 227).

Although the foundations of the counter-majoritarian role of courts in society are discussed and criticised, there is no substantial change in the majority principle when political decisions are transferred to judges, only an instrumental reason that authorises a deficient substitution of a legislative majority by a judicial majority in light of a democratic regime. This said, it is possible to establish a typology of the observations of courts in society based on their communications – for this text, this position marks an exploratory view of social courts.

Typologies of observations regarding courts in society

The dynamic in courts' communications not only emphasises the performance of the judicial function in the legal system, it also reveals that some courts can be seen as peripheral in other systems.[15] For this study, we characterise these observations as the operation of a social court.

According to observation of the legal system, the judiciary is the power of the state that operates both to control the other powers and to solve conflicts in society. However, understanding the argument of social courts allows expansion and perception of other of their operations, especially the way in which their communication affects the political system by influencing the trust of state institutions, forming public opinion or exerting political pressure on the other powers; forbidding, restricting or applying public policies; or even controlling the legality of the action of political authorities.

Also from the standpoint of the economic system, courts can influence the functioning of the markets through their decisions. The main argument indicates that in a market economy it is essential for judges to ensure a certain predictability of decisions for businesses, investments and transactions to be successful. For this, judges must ensure the maximum protection of individual rights, especially the right to property, and compliance with contracts (Arida et al. 2005).

In this scenario, a slow-paced court with unpredictable decisions interferes in the expectations of the markets and generates impacts on the economy, even if one acknowledges the independence of this matter as regards the existence of a structural uncertainty of the decision-making process of law – ie, a decision is always risky, since it selects among mutually exclusive options (Falcão et al. 2006). This structural uncertainty is often anticipated and priced into contracts and businesses, or even by judges themselves when they set requirements as the security of the judgment.

Therefore, it is possible to refer to different selections of information available in the memory of the courts, which can be evoked in various ways. It should be recalled that from a systemic perspective, communication is not only the transmission of some content but the synthesis of a distinction between information, communicating and understanding. In this sense, it is possible to argue for the existence of a spectrum of courts' communication which selects information concerning several social systems. As an illustration, the courts may refer to the economy (and it is then possible to analyse their informative content), but they may also ask why and how to talk about the economy (a situation in which the act of communicating is explored).[16]

The communication process is, therefore, variable and depends on choices, while the court itself elaborates its understanding and lack of comprehension based on these choices that can be connected to different codes of society (Luhmann 2010: 298). Likewise, these communications generate redundancy, which allows an expansion to new selections on this colour spectrum. Equally, the communication of the courts is doubly contingent: nothing ensures that by producing a communication about economic, political or legal content, the court will establish an immanent and invariable meaning, nor that the judge (ego) will understand the meaning of the legislator (alter) when interpreting a given legal norm. There is always a need for a new communication, and this in fact proves to be a highly risky situation.

It should be recalled also that Luhmann analyses organisational communication based on the idea of superposition of risks on the decision. This is not mere risk management, but a matter of critically monitoring all the

decisions by means of second-order observation. Many strategies are mobilised for organisations to reduce risk, such as delegation of powers and
responsibilities, imposition or prohibition in written form and even fragmentation and reordering of decisions, ensuring the obligation of decision-
making. These organisational solutions intend to eliminate risk and solve
the problem of double contingency; even so, they do not eliminate risk, but
ensure consistency (Luhmann 2006: 191).

Thus, the spectrum of communication of the courts can be made compatible
with greater or lesser consistency of decisions – ie, obviously it is presumed that
the communication of the court is superposed on the legal one, but this does
not eliminate the possibility of other communications, other superpositions
and interferences. It is also possible to underscore this discussion by means of
structures, especially considering that the self-determination of courts depends
on the hierarchy and successive past decisions – ie, on the courts' memory.

In order to elaborate on this issue, we refer here to the classification of
Guarnieri and Pederzoli (2002) – also discussed by Campilongo (2002) –
concerned with judges' behaviour. The authors relate the different positions
on the spectrum to the structures of the courts, generally summarised in two
variables: political autonomy and judicial creativity. The judicial role would
then be inter-connected to the organisation and to the traits of the group of
judges; this concept examines the influence of judges' behaviour on decision-
making. The judicial role is seen as a set of values and attitudes of the judges
that determine the decision.

As regards the evaluation criteria, they are divided into judicial creativity,
which implies that decisions may or may not be taken based on pre-existing
laws, and degree of judicial autonomy of the political institutions (executive
and legislative power), which is presumed based on the functional and administrative guarantees of judges.

Thus, a table with the ideal types is elaborated in Figure 8.1.

		Political autonomy	
		Low	High
Judicial creativity	Low	Executor	Guardian
	High	Delegate	Politician

Figure 8.1 Typology of judicial roles.
Source: the author, based on Guarnieri and Pederzoli (2002).

These four types can be summarised as follows. The *executor-judge* is a characterisation of the mouth-of-the-law judge. This figure allows low judicial creativity, since there is no space for legal argumentation and interpretation in decision-making. It also establishes the court as the executing agency of the legislator's will. In this model, there is a precise distinction between legislation and case law. The *delegate-judge* is a characterisation of a judge who is subordinated to executive agencies, although in cases of legislative omission there is space for exercising judicial creativity (discretionary power). It should be noted that in these cases the supervenience of legal norms always ultimately binds and diminishes judicial creativity. The *guardian-judge* is a characterisation of the judge as the last bulwark of the legal system. In this model, the judge has all prerogatives to implement rights that are enshrined in legal texts, independent of considerations regarding the impact on the other bodies of the executive power. This characterisation is generally related to the performance of the counter-majoritarian function of courts and also to the idea of constitutionality control. Finally, the *politician-judge* is a characterisation of a realistic judge who does not obnubilate the political choices that exist in the lawsuit. These figures openly exert political power and do not suffer any kind of constraint, due to the solid functional and administrative guarantees they enjoy.

I claim that Guarnieri and Pederzoli's types can be expanded – with a functionalist focus – and transposed for consideration of the communicational model of the courts mentioned previously. Thus, it is not actually the behaviours of judges that define the scope of the courts' communication, but the interactions that are bound to the communicational structure itself that operates the information. It should also be clarified that 'the court' always refers to a given functional system,[17] even if it is not limited by these frontiers.[18]

Generally, because these are cases that require maintaining a normative expectation, the courts operate at the centre of law. There are situations, however, in which courts can and do ultimately communicate at the periphery of other systems, even if from the standpoint of the law they may be illegal.[19] At this point, the communicational model reveals that courts must deal with the problem of double contingency based on the relationship between legislation and case law; therefore, every decision is creatively risky and provisional in the entire model, and does not refer only to law.

Thus, a functional model is suggested to observe the operations of courts in society. An alternative typology Figure 8.2) is offered to debate how a court describes itself as an organisation of society. These types, however, represent distortions, reductions and simplifications, and have blind spots, precisely because they are ideal types. In practice, the different operations are superposed because of the complexity of communication, which is

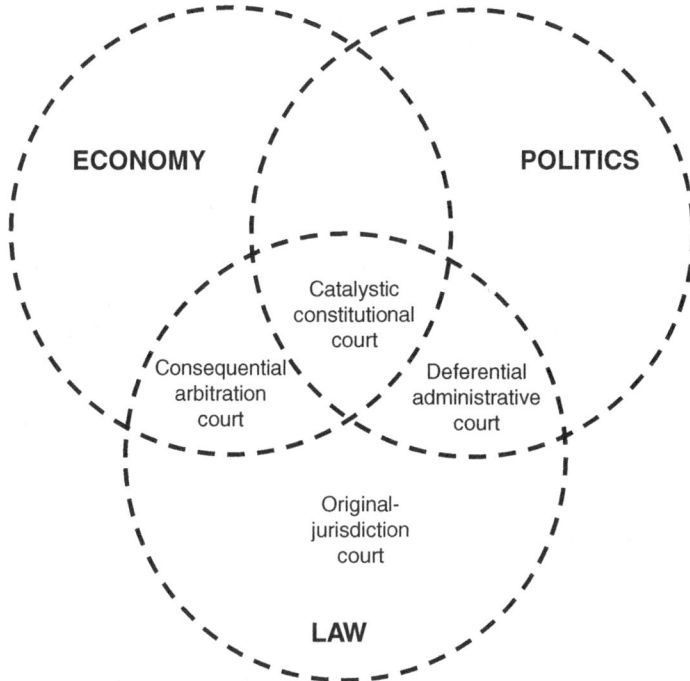

Figure 8.2 Typology of the courts.
Source: the author.

expressed in the fact that a decision in the legal system may extend to other organisational positions in different systems.

Without accepting any normative-corrective attribution, this typology presents a holistic position to understand the multiplicity of positions in relation to the communication of the courts in society.[20]

Some initial remarks should be underlined regarding the typology. First, it should be realised that courts are organisations that refer to law, although other types at the same time refer to other functional systems. In this sense, every court originates in the problem of decision-making by law. Second, the difference between courts is related more to the position in law than to behaviours proper; therefore, it can be assumed that some organisations are at the centre and others on the periphery. Central courts – ie, the original-jurisdiction court – make the final decision to unfold the paradox of law (adjudication of the code); peripheral courts decide provisionally about programs with reference to information from other systems, sometimes connected to contractual and corporate arrangements or outlines of public policies.[21] Third, and as already mentioned, courts do not have to obey functional limits.

From the organisational perspective, it is not a problem to indicate that in some communications there is a crystal-clear transposition of irritations from the economy and from law to arbitration courts, from law and politics to administrative courts or from the three systems to constitutional courts.

There is a true organisational communication, limited only by organisation. The representation of the intersections does not indicate a corruption of codes, a colonisation of systems or a non-differentiation; it only emphasises that there is organisational communication beyond the functional systems and that, for the systems, organisations are a form of connection to the environments. The circles should be literally understood as the circulation of a specific communication, always open to future selections.

Finally, each of these courts selects information in different ways. That is, courts of arbitration communicate differently from administrative courts, just like judicial and constitutional courts do. Next, each observed type will be presented: the original-jurisdiction court, deferential administrative court, consequential arbitration court and catalytic constitutional court.

Original-jurisdiction court

Regarding legal operations, courts have the task of supervising the consistency of legal decisions. They observe other programs, including decisions that already observed the law previously – in this case proceeding to a second-order observation in law, used for the consistency of the legal system that can be reputed as new information (Luhmann 2004: 297).

The court thus occupies an originalist and peremptory position at the centre of the legal system and represents the paradox concerning the adjudication of the 'legal'/'illegal' code. Generally in this space there is a canonical interpretation of conditional programs and also a strong tradition of respect for precedent, acknowledging in this case a presumption of extreme force to avoid extra-legal materials and arguments (expert reports, opinions, borrowed evidence etc) despite any evaluation of the impact of the decision on society, or of any consideration outside them, so that the court of original jurisdiction is similar to the representation of Guarnieri and Pederzoli's guardian-judge.

This perspective is justified in a line focusing on the functioning of the courts within the legal system and concerning itself with issues of self-reference, stability of normative expectations and predictability of court decisions. These courts, specifically, are associated with the function of law and operate exclusively with legal communication, respecting its codes and conditioned programs.

Deferential administrative court

The deferential court model refers to a weak concept of constitutionalism and even a dialogical current of the connection between organisations.

Judges must be analysed with regard to the other powers, since they sometimes decide in favour of government and sometimes in favour of the opposition. This perspective is related to the debate about the operation of courts on the periphery of the political system (Taylor 2007: 248) and the balance between powers, with special thought to the fact that particular centres of decision influence the results of public policies, whether by allowing the initial discussion of certain topics, implementing an affirmative measure or even delaying a decision about sensitive issues.

Administrative courts began to appear with reforms in public management over the past decades, defending the instance of decision with the presence of experts (not necessarily court judges). As has been seen, this attempt at modernisation was sustained on the premise that in some cases involving technical knowledge it was better to allocate the decision to specialists, to the detriment of the judicial route, and sectorise the regulation of areas. Therefore, regulating agencies, councils, and decision-making committees were created.

It should be emphasised that the communication of these courts is different from the judicial one and is ensured by the delegation of powers and by flexible legal norms – ie, indeterminate legal concepts and general clauses or legal principles. In certain situations, open or legally indeterminate cases depend explicitly on the complementation of technical knowledge to supply solutions in the concrete case of what is presumed to be noise from the political system. Administrative judges have judicial creativity and do not so solidly connect the decision-making process to a given substantive rule. However, they do not enjoy the same guarantees as the judicial courts, above all because they can be submitted to judicial review. Actually, these courts are ultimately constricted by state authorities and refer to the different finalistic programs of politics, subject to a 'route correction' at any time, besides being submitted to constant government pressures.

It should also be recalled that the political character of these courts is bound by factors such as the authorities' trajectory: method of selection, repercussion of public opinion, judicialisation of certain non-programmed demands and coverage of the decisions.

Consequential arbitration court

The third position observes the courts as consequentialist, since they take into account non-legal arguments, especially those related to the possible extra-legal effects of the decision.[22] A consequentialist court can therefore render canonical interpretations more flexible, and prefers to evaluate and discuss prognoses that emphasise economic issues and problems of substantive justice. Examples of these courts are arbitration chambers and alternative means of resolution based on operations of an arbitrator.

In consequentialist courts, judges operate on the periphery of the economic system, above all when dealing with problems regarding scarcity and discussing contracts and when they influence budgetary issues. Here we have a model that meets the requirements of economic communication, such as more power for negotiated solutions, law and economics, speedy decisions and a broad opening of information and review of positions. On the other hand, law ratifies and acknowledges the validity of these decisions, giving them executive force.[23]

Actually, it is important to underscore the problem of the lack of information in decision-making – be it because of poor institutional capacity to collect and ponder circumstantial or other evidence or because of the complexity of the problem challenged – which makes it difficult for judges to assess consequences as in the model of the court of original jurisdiction. Luhmann (2004: 193–197) points out that this difficulty of assessment is frequently renewed, since the calculation is never neutral in relation to reality, so that the assessment is reviewed retrospectively even if probability theory seems to be adjusted to this practice, and therefore does not present stability in the temporal dimension – a situation feared by practically all organisations.

In this sense, since arbitration courts theoretically operate in a more adjusted form regarding the problems of assessment, the boom of these organisations and the optimistic effect generated by their consolidation in different jurisdictions beginning in the 21st century are justified. Again, this boom must be observed in connection with the society of experts. These descriptions bet on the idea of control by consequences that is increasingly present in the operations of arbitration courts.

Catalytic constitutional court

The fourth position reveals the figure of a catalysing court, which can act on the margins of the systems and without being restricted by operational functional limits from triggering certain changes. As pointed out by Young (2012: 172–174), this is a useful metaphor to represent the multiplicity of court communications, presupposing a range of communications in other systems. The catalytic court allows a certain degree of pragmatic self-knowledge by the court in order to balance the social systems; thus, the court has a wisdom capable of acting at the right time to exert more or less interventionist measures.

A catalysing court thus reflects the excessive overload on organisations – with the proviso that courts are not responsible for the separation of the functional systems and can thus work with finalistic programs even if they need to reach a final decision. In this way, for law, catalytic courts prevent systemic blocks, since they resolve inter-systemic conflicts, which generally have repercussions on the communication of constitutional courts. These courts bind centres of politics and economy, generating noise for law when, for instance, they assimilate the risks of scarcity or of collectively binding decisions, determine the need to establish limits on public expenditures, ensure the autonomy of the central bank or even enable access of other organisations to justice, such as social movements, non-governmental organisations, political parties and government, aiming to protect *interna corporis* interests.[24]

Catalytic courts actually communicate in a calculating and strategic manner, approaching the figure of the politician-judge. These judges, like consequentialist ones, know that compliance with the law is not always the determining factor of decision-making – and Luhmann (2004: 302) also upholds this point when he questions the existence of a science of legislation whose laws are the base of the rationality of all legal decisions.

However, different from the consequentialist court, this model bargains, bluffs and creates obstacles with interests that are not evident, at the same time as it has ample guarantees of protection. In history it is strongly marked in welfare societies which excessively politicise law, burdening it with expectations produced by the constitutionalisation of public policies and expanding the powers of the courts.

Obviously, these organisations vary according to society and context. Judges can operate as originalists, deferentialists, consequentialists or catalysts for various reasons, including the flexibility conferred on them by the constitution's text and case law, so that they can interpret and decide on a specific case; their political and philosophical trajectories; the political and economic system's capacity to deal with undesired judicial decisions; the degree of political and economic support received by courts from other public or private organisations; the culture of judicial independence; the rule of law; and even judicial creativity.

Beyond these types, the classification allows combinations between a consequentialist and a deferential position as a situation of experimentalism, between a consequentialist and an original-jurisdiction position as a managerial position, and finally between a deferential and an original-jurisdiction position as a dialogical situation. It is not surprising that administrative courts mimic the structures of judicial courts, or that arbitration courts influence the opening of other courts; these are intermediary and dynamic situations that support the holistic character of this typology.

There is no predominant or more appropriate observation. The focus is to trace and indicate observations underlining the functional aspect of courts in society. Therefore, it is worth mentioning that here we are not prescribing a given position of the court, nor referring back to theoretical debates structured as polarised arguments and sometimes marked by strong ideological content. It should also be recalled that this text presents a second-order observation about courts in society.

Final remarks

This text offers a typology that allows reflection on social courts. This typology does not claim to perform an exhaustive mapping but rather to observe different communications of courts that unfold in world society. Nevertheless, it is also important to stress a methodological contribution of this study regarding a possible empirical use of social systems theory, mostly focusing on organisations.

For Luhmann, empirical research is not about unveiling and discovering an objective reality and offering explanations of necessary causes. Systems theory excludes any possibility of the ontological existence of reality, since the world society is actually a possibility of semantic construction by the observer – just like a construction of an organisation. There is a plurality of possibilities of observations that opens up with systems theory, and its radical constructivism promotes several observations about society. What is an empirical observation? Observation of the contingency, mainly the partial communications of each functional system, organisation and interaction.

Sociology makes a second-order observation in relation to the observations produced in other systems, yet sociological observation makes not a simple copy of the other observations but rather a production of theories, which assume a distance from everyday obviousness to achieve a level of consistency (Luhmann 2007: 883–898). Although Luhmann himself did not produce empirical research or emphasise empirical applications, due to the abstraction presupposed in his theory, there is a vast research agenda proposed – just like the observation of social courts discussed in this chapter, mainly via observation of less-complex systems such as organisations or via interactions.

There could be sceptics who would reject this possibility. However, it is important to take the legacy of social systems theory seriously. Luhmann's legacy was to offer a comprehensive theory compatible with the degree of complexity of modern society. More than 20 years after his death, countless and relevant social transformations operate in society and require new observation by sociology, especially in the face of technological changes. This finding reinforces the need to rethink Luhmann's work and subsequent developments, including strategies for controlling the level of abstraction of this theoretical framework. In this sense, to reject the viability of an empirical research agenda is to drop the importance of systems theory into disuse today.

Another kind of scepticism could reject the viability of the empirical character of systems theory, because it mistakes the epistemological ground for the methodological aspect of the theory. Empirical research in systems theory does not have the same meaning as in empiricism or rationalism traditions – otherwise this scepticism would surely fall into the straw man fallacy. This kind of sceptic usually makes no distinction between the sociological and philosophical features of Luhmann's work. Confusion arises when the methodological consistency of systems theory is confronted with assumption-based methods such as the subject/object distinction which aim to establish a correspondence between scientific claims and a given reality. As long as the refutations remain based on the subject/object distinction, world society is considered an object separated from the observer.

Different from this perspective, I have argued that empirical research based on systems theory admits the epistemological foundations of radical constructivism and the methodological partialities of the observer-observation. The main distinction becomes 'system'/'environment'. This conceptual change has far-reaching methodological consequences and must be considered by sociologists, who are largely concerned with the observation of organisations in a complex society.

Notes

1 The term 'court' is used to designate indifferently any and all instances or levels of decision-making within the legal system based on conditioned programmes – the process of decision-making based on the implementation of conditions. No hierarchical distinction is made between courts. In this sense, a court may refer to the traditional organisation that performs the judicial function, but it may also imply other extra-legal organisations, such as arbitration courts or administrative courts.

2 An emphasis on the central function of courts as a process of disputes can been understood as a legal-centralist observation (see Ziegert 1992). For a classical approach regarding the legal-centralist observation of courts, see Shapiro (1981).

3 The Brazilian legal theorist Tércio Sampaio Ferraz Jr (2001: 81), discussing the development of legal dogma from the 19th century onward, argues that a price is paid for this, ie, the risk of progressively becoming distant from reality – since dogmatic science, as it is an abstraction of an abstraction, will concern itself increasingly and preponderantly with the function of its own classifications, with the legal nature of its own concepts.

4 Tamanaha (2017: 127) distinguishes two orientations of law that legal organisations account for, ie, law as fundamental rules of social intercourse and law in connection with government objectives.

5 See the iconoclastic perspective from the American legal realists, or even the debate regarding the ideological functions of courts, like Brigham (1987).

6 This can also be observed as a matter of understanding the passage from the centrality of a code-based culture to that of decision-making, which means a move from the social importance given to the figure of the legislator to that of the judge – which implies understanding the programmatic changes within the legal system and strengthening the power of judges in society. Evidence is taken from different experiences of transition from the liberal state to the welfare state, marking the plurality of sources of production and of types of legal rules, which do not completely fit formal hierarchical models of legal systems. See, eg, Ost (1991).

7 In this sense, considering administrative problems, the rise of other decision-making structures competing with the judiciary has also been observed, like private ordering (see Galanter 1981).

8 For example, Burns and Stalker (1966) argue that bureaucratic organisations may stifle and hinder technological innovation, and that it is preferable to distinguish mechanical organisations from organic ones. Mechanical organisations are the Weberian bureaucratic systems.

9 An important research agenda has been inaugurated by systems theory on the sociology of organisations. The main idea of this agenda is the observation of organisations based on the chaining of processes that lead to decisions. Thus, the organisation operates first regarding its own history of decision-making. Second, although the decision-making processes may refer to the external environment, decisions are always internal products and become relevant only if they are communicated and understood as decisions (as communicated decisions, not as individual acts). See, eg, Holzer (2015).

10 Utopia next to technology is a form of 'de-futurisation', which is related to the future present. Luhmann (1976:143) argues the following about utopia: '[utopia] remains a present future, and at least an infallible sign of the presence of critics. It moves away if we try to approach it. It does not vanish, however, as long as the structural conditions of the present society endure, but it may resettle with new symbols and meanings, if the old ones are worn-out by disappointments and new experiences. Our recent experiences seem to show that these utopian futures speed up their change and may change so quickly that they never will have a chance to be tested and get confirmation in a present'.

11 In Brazilian constitutional law, for example, effects on the legislative power are exerted regarding court injunctions or actions to control constitutionality by omission, both the binding ones of higher courts – eg, binding precedents or general repercussion – and those resulting from writs of mandamus, cases of misconduct in public office or claims concerning social and economic rights, because they interfere directly in the operations of the executive power or legislative power – and, more importantly, because they have a latent capacity to affect budgetary provisions.

12 The reference to the legal system does not answer all questions regarding the reproduction of the court. In other words, law does not determine the court directly, just as law is not the only one to comprise the judicial form. In the systematic view, it should be recalled, courts take on a central role in law because they unfold the paradox of the code's application – two opposite values that are simultaneously relevant but cannot be used at the same time at the moment of adjudication. Thus, any and all doubts about applying conditioned programs that come from the periphery are spelled out in this paradox, which is momentarily overcome by the judicial decision. It can be perceived, therefore, first of all that courts do not solve the paradox (they only unfold it), and second, their operations are not always relevant and necessary to operate law, unless there is a doubt or conflict about programs. Besides, many other alternative structures can be considered by law for decision-making, which is not restricted to the communication of courts. See, for example, Luhmann (2004: 274–304).

13 It is important to recover the idea of communication in social systems theory, which conserves a first aspect identified as redundancy, a selection of information based on the possibility of other information that should be considered simultaneously, oscillating, so to say, between the information selected and not selected. Its second important aspect concerns a paradox: only what is new is accepted as information, ie, what presents some element of surprise. However, it is only possible to accept a piece of information by transforming it into an already-known message, fitting the communication into pre-established patterns. There is a complex – an inherently connected and networked form – in the

balance between variety and redundancy whenever communication occurs. In brief, communication deals with information by means of the variety/ redundancy.

14 In the Brazilian case, the expansion of the judiciary power occurred especially at the end of the 1980s, and resulted from (beside the context of redemocratisation) the new system of control of constitutionality and from the expansion of the powers of the Brazilian Federal Supreme Court established in the 1988 constitution. See, eg, Taylor (2007) and Arguelhes and Ribeiro (2016).

15 New semantics is presented to deal with the description of the courts, including the concepts of networks, operative circularity, efficacy and legitimacy as a result of the integration between law, politics and economics. Furthermore, a double paradox is indicated: politics and economics may fail to observe law for political or economic reasons, and conversely, law may fail to observe politics and economics for legal reasons. Courts deal at the same time with this paradox in every consequentialist decision, since what prevails is a dependency between political power or money and efficacy of court decisions, which escapes law, at the same time that there is a demand for legitimacy or for administration of scarcity observed in court decisions, which escape politics and economics.

16 On heterogeneity and organisations, see Besio and Meyer (2015: 241).

17 It can be suggested that this reference is rendered explicit in practice based on the legal rule challenged, and the problem presented to the judiciary marks the alternation between one behavior and another – eg, it is the claim that defines the contours of the dispute.

18 One should observe a paradox, since the courts need to unfold, when deciding a case, which are the limits and how they observe the limits of the systems in their operations.

19 It should be recalled that from the systemic perspective, operations on the illicit side are also located within law, so this communication is also a legal operation.

20 The typology is also inspired by classifications by Young (2012), Guarnieri and Pederzoli (2002), Campilongo (2002), and, above all, by Luhmann's reflections.

21 In the systemic view, it is therefore acknowledged that differences between these courts mark a difference in relation to their cognitive isolation or their perviousness to more open and indeterminate topics.

22 It is important to distinguish between consequentialist courts and the means of operation of the consequentialist argument by law, which presupposes a filtering and an observation regarding the functioning of law.

23 The case of economic plans in Brazil supports this point. Over three decades ago, the judiciary took a long time to decide on cases of the judicialisation of economic plans (*Cruzado, Bresser, Verão, Collor I* and *II*) which were designed through extra-judicial agreement. It is not for nothing that the Brazilian Federal Supreme Court found it difficult to decide on the cases, which to some extent justified searching for an extra-judicial alternative via the provisioning of resources. This can be understood based on the institutional fragility of the court for selecting and assessing the economic consequences of its decisions vis-à-vis other more peripheral organisations that have the capacity of solving problems like this one of the plans – such as arbitration courts.

24 It should be recalled that political parties often strategically appeal to constitutional courts in order to change majority decisions in which they were defeated.

References

Arguelhes, D.W. and Ribeiro, L.M. (2016) 'Criatura e/ou criador: transformações do Supremo Tribunal Federal sob a Constituição de 1988' *12*(2) *Revista Direito GV* 405–440.

Arida, P., Bacha, E.L. and Resende, A.L. (2005) 'Credit, interest, and jurisdictional uncertainty: conjectures on the case of Brazil' in Giavazzi F., Goldfajn I. and Herrera S. (eds), *Inflation Targeting, Debt, and the Brazilian Experience, 1999 to 2003* (Cambridge, MA, MIT Press), 265–294.

Baecker, D. (2006) 'The form of the firm' *13 Org. Crit. J. Org. Theory Soc.* 109–142.

Becker, T.L. (1970) *Comparative Judicial Politics: The Political Functionings of Courts* (Chicago, Rand MacNally).

Brigham, J. (1987). *The Cult of the Court* (Philadelphia, Temple University Press).

Besio, C. and Meyer, U. (2015) 'Heterogeneity in world society: how organizations handle contradicting logics' in Holzer B., Werron T., Kastner F. (eds), *From Globalization to World Society: Neo Institutional and Systems-Theoretical Perspectives* (New York, Routledge), 237–257.

Bora, A. (2010) 'Technoscientific normativity and the "iron cage" of law' *35*(1) *Sci. Technol. Human Values* 3–28.

Bredemeier, H. (1962) 'Law as an integrative mechanism' in Evan WM (ed), *Law and Sociology* (New York: The Free Press), 73–90.

Burns, T. and Stalker, G.M. (1966) *The Management of Innovation* (London, Tavistock).

Campilongo, C.F. (2002) *Política, sistema jurídico e decisão judicial* (São Paulo, Max Limonad).

Dutra, R.T. and Campos, M. (2013) 'Por uma sociologia sistêmica da gestão de políticas públicas' *2 Conexão Política* 11–47.

Ehrlich, E. (2009) *Fundamental Principles of the Sociology of Law* (New Jersey, New Brunswick).

Falcão, J., Schuartz, L.F. and Arguelhes, D.W. (2006) 'Jurisdição, incerteza e estado de direito' *243*(1) *Revista de Direito Administrativo* 79–112.

Ferraz Jr, T.S. (2001) *Introdução ao estudo do direito: Técnica, decisão, dominação* (São Paulo, Atlas).

Galanter, M. (1981). 'Justice in many rooms: courts, private ordering and in-digineous law' *13*(19) *J. Legal Plural.* 1–47.

Gardbaum, S. (2013) *The New Commonwealth Model of Constitutionalism: Theory and Practice* (Cambridge, Cambridge University Press).

Guarnieri, C. and Pederzoli, P. (2002) *The Power of Judges: A Comparative Study of Courts and Democracy* (Oxford, Oxford University Press).

Hirschl, R. (2007) *Towards Juristocracy: The Origins and Consequences of the New Constitutionalism* (Cambridge, MA, Harvard University Press).

Holzer, B. (2015) 'Two Faces of World Society: Formal Structures and Institutionalized Informality' in Holzer B., T. Werron., Kastner F. (eds) *From Globalization to World Society: Neo Institutional and Systems-Theoretical Perspectives* (New York, Routledge) 37–60.

Luhmann, N. (1976) 'The future cannot begin: temporal structures in modern society' *43*(1) *Soc. Res.* 130–152.

Luhmann, N. (1995) *Social Systems* (Stanford, Stanford University Press).

Luhmann, N. (2004) *Law as a Social System* (Oxford, Oxford University Press).

Luhmann, N. (2005) 'Organización y decisión' in Luhmann N, *Organización y decisión: Autopoiesis, acción y entendimento comunicativo* (México, Anthropos), 1–98.

Luhmann, N. (2006) *Risk: A Sociological Theory* (New York, Gruyter).

Luhmann, N. (2007) *La sociedad de la sociedad* (México, Herder).

Luhmann, N. (2010) *Introdução à teoria dos sistemas* (Petrópolis, Vozes).

MacCormick, N. (2005) *Rhetoric and the Rule of Law: A Theory of Legal Reasoning* (Oxford, Oxford University Press).

Ost, F. (1991) 'Jupiter, Hercule, Hermès: trois modèles du juge' in Bouretz P. (ed), *La force du droit: Panorama des débats contemporains* (Paris, Esprit), 241–272.

Perrow, C. (1991) 'A society of organizations' *20 Theory Soc.* 725–762.

Shapiro, M. (1981) *Courts: A Comparative and Political Analysis* (Chicago: University of Chicago Press).

Stichweh, R. (2015) 'Comparing systems theory and sociologial neo-institutionalism: explaining functional differentiation' in Holzer B., Werron T., Kastner F. (eds), *From Globalization to World Society: Neo Institutional and Systems-Theoretical Perspectives* (New York, Routledge) 23–36.

Tamanaha, B. (2017) *A Realistic Theory of Law* (Cambridge: Cambridge University Press).

Taylor, M. (2007) 'O Judiciário e as políticas públicas no Brasil' *50 Dados* 229–257.

Tushnet, M. (2006). 'Weak-form judicial review and "core" civil liberties' *41*(1) *Harvard Civil Rights-Civil Libert. Law Rev.* 1–22.

Waldron, J. (2006) 'The core of the case against judicial review' *115 Yale Law J.* 1346–1406.

Weber, M. (1976) 'Os fundamentos da organização burocrática: uma construção do tipo ideal' in Campos E. (ed), *Sociologia da Burocracia* (Rio de Janeiro, Zahar) 15–28.

Young, K. (2012) *Constituting Economic and Social Rights* (Oxford, Oxford University Press).

Ziegert, K.A. (1992) 'Courts and the self-concept of law: the mapping of the environment by courts of first instance' *14*(2) *Sydney Law Rev.* 196–229.

Chapter 9

Casting off from the rock of uncertainty

Observations on the empirical application of Luhmann's sociological theory and a case study on the concept of normative expectations

Mark Hanna

Introduction

Several years ago, a handful of scholars met every month on Baker Street in London to discuss Niklas Luhmann's sociological theory. Although the participants came mostly from a legal background, and were therefore principally interested in using Luhmann's theory in the study of law, over the course of years that the meetings were held the group explored a wide range of the various aspects of Luhmann's sociology. However, the subject of an empirical agenda for Luhmann's sociological theory never came up. It may be supposed that this was a result of the predominantly legal background of the participants. Legal scholarship, based as it is on argument and interpretation of the legal code, is notorious for its failure to reflect on its methodology in general, and even more so for its failure to engage empirical research methodology (Epstein and King 2002). But that was not the primary reason that the topic of an empirical approach never figured in the otherwise wide-ranging discussion of Luhmann's oeuvre in the group's meetings. Rather, the subject was never broached because it appeared to contradict Luhmann's 'radical constructivism'. This radical constructivism was valued not just by the group but at a more general level by those in the UK academy who were interested in Luhmann's theory and sought to use it to develop sociology, law and other fields (Moeller 2011: 79). 'Constructivist epistemology', 'paradox', 'self-reference' and 'blind spot' had become 'eigenvalues' of the research group, as they had of the wider system. This had become the 'rock of uncertainty' that provided some sure footing and comfort against beleaguered claims to objectivity, and casting off from the rock in an empirical direction appeared altogether too risky – ie, risking achieving nothing but self-validation and selective construction or, worse, risking, as Luhmann himself may have put it, being 'made to see, more or less tactfully, in front of everyone's eyes, that he is trying to lay anchor on hostile shores' (Luhmann 1985: 53).

Admittedly, Luhmann himself contributed to this dissociation of his theory from empirical research. His focus on self-referential systems necessitated a more radical epistemology, as the shift from the subject/object distinction to system/environment revealed the problems of observing the world as a separate and independent object from the observer – for science as much as for any observer (Luhmann 1995: 13). 'How is it possible', he asked, 'to think of science as capable of observation without itself being a system: namely, a system with a network of communication, a system with certain institutional arrangements, a system with certain value preferences, a system with individual careers, and a system that depends on society?' (Luhmann 2013a: 42). Much empirical research, he concluded, is concerned with 'validating its own constructions' (Luhmann 2012: 16). If a century of empirical research in sociology had achieved anything, he argued, it was limited to the measurement of 'macro-sociological' phenomena such as divorce rates, the rise and fall of crime etc. (Luhmann 2012: 16). Such bare facts of social life obviously do not amount to a sociology, and by themselves offered little in his quest for a theory of society (Luhmann 2012: 16).

However, there needs to be a distinction made here between 'hard' and 'soft' empiricism. It is clear that Luhmann's theory and method are at odds with a hard empiricism that claims any objective truth or that 'data alone could be a sufficient condition for knowledge about society' (Bulmer 1984: 39). But the utility of a soft empirical application to Luhmann's theory and method has been noted before by others, including Luhmann himself.[1] Knudsen, in particular, has directly addressed the empirical application of Luhmann's theory and method, and offers excellent insights into the role of Luhmann's functional method of analysis and theory of observations in this regard.

In this chapter, I want to build on Knudsen's observations on the role of the functional method and observation theory in a soft empirical programme for Luhmann's theory and method. But I also want to present a practical example of the use of such an empirical programme in the concept of normative expectations. This concept will be presented as a model for the 'observation of facts' and the circular relationship it has with 'theory'.

Why do we need this soft empiricism? There are two primary reasons. First and foremost, it develops the theory. The insights that are gained through the observation of facts can be uploaded to refine the theory. Second, it expands Luhmann's theory. It branches out its relevance in accordance with the complexity of facts. When Herbert Blumer criticised social theory in the 1950s for its shortcomings in comparison to empirical science, he suggested that its 'divorcement from the empirical world' only led to theory becoming 'compartmentalised into a world of its own, inside of which it feeds on itself' (Blumer 1954: 3). Feeding off itself is fine, the systems theorist may say, but we must also acknowledge that communication on certain themes, even where they have achieved a sticky recursivity, can easily run into culs-de-sac and peter out. Web searches for 'Niklas

Luhmann' can be seen to reach their zenith in the early 2000s[2] (Google Books 2020). Such quantitative data can hardly offer a comprehensive analysis of the continued relevance of Luhmann's sociology, but one can detect some correlation of this diminishing currency on a more qualitative basis in many parts of the world.

It is surprising how those who remain convinced of the utility of Luhmann's sociology neglect the important question as to how it is sustained in communication. Will it still be used in 100 years? Will it even still be talked about in 100 years? Those are ultimately methodological questions, and it will be argued that a soft empirical application of Luhmann's sociological theory is a way of stimulating its use and communication, and a way of refining and developing it and expanding it in new dimensions.

In the next section I will detail the functional method of analysis and its empirical application. The third section will turn to Luhmann's theory of observation and detail the use of second-order concepts in empirical observation. The final section will then provide a practical example of how this empirical application of Luhmann's theory through the use of functional method and second-order observation may work. It will present the use of normative expectations as a *concept* for the accumulation of facts through empirical observation, and how this helps refine Luhmann's theory not simply in relation to law, conflict and society's immune system but in revising theoretical insights into the integration of different forms of societal differentiation.

The functional method of analysis

Luhmann did not often pause to consider his own methodology, and in fact there are only two occasions when he systematically addressed the issue. The first was early in his career (Luhmann 1964: 31–53), but he addressed it once again when his theory was more developed and he had already made the 'autopoietic turn'. In the book which definitively announced the shift in focus to self-referential systems and set out to establish a 'unified theory' for sociology (Luhmann 1995: xlv), he identifies the method that he uses 'throughout' as the 'method of functional analysis' (52).

To begin with, it is worth noting that the functional method that Luhmann (2012: 3) outlines in this respect is very different from the 'structural-functionalism' of Parsons and Durkheim, for example.[3] As Knudsen (2010: 1–2) points out, Luhmann's functional method may have received limited attention because it has been conflated with 'out-of-date Parsonian functionalism or some kind of social instrumentalism', which has been widely critiqued on a methodological basis.[4] However, Luhmann's recommended functional method is altogether different, because rather than starting from given system structures and then attempting to identify conditions for their persistence, it begins by problematising existing systemic structures and then uses the problem to compare equivalent solutions. This proves to be an important methodological shift, and as will be seen, it offers more opportunity for development of empirical research.

The primary application of the functional method lies in the construction of the problem, and it is most definitely a *construction* of the observer (ie, using the distinction between problem and solution). There is no need for an empirical approach at this juncture. The problem is just a device to bring into view various potential solutions – although, as will be seen, factual analysis does help to refine the understanding of the problem. But the construction of the problem is always first and foremost a task for theory. The functional method presupposes a thorough preceding theoretical analysis of the problem (Luhmann 1970: 25). It is only through such theoretical analysis of the problem that a clear point of reference or criterion can be established under which a range of potential solutions can be brought into view. The construction of the problem is not, therefore, completely contingent, but is instead rooted in the rigor of Luhmann's unified theory of society. And indeed, as Luhmann utilises the functional method throughout the construction of that unified theory of society, basic societal problems already figure heavily in the theory. Knudsen catalogues these basic problems as 'double contingency', 'contact', 'motivation or connectivity' and 'paradox' (2010: 24). The problem of double contingency relates to social complexity and the contingency of selections between ego and alter (leading to questions such as 'Why do almost all possible actions and interactions *not* take place?', 'How does society manage to sort out what is possible?' etc. – see Luhmann 2012: 15), and provides the basis of emergence of the full range of social systems which mediate expectations through communication (Luhmann 1995: 103ff.). The problem of contact relates to communication with individuals who are not present, and is resolved through diffusion media (Knudsen 2010: 24). The problem of motivation relates to the need for improbable communication to be accepted and used as the basis of further communication. Finally, the problem of paradox relates to the contingency of all communication, and is resolved by invisibilisations and displacements.

However, the basic problems established by Luhmann are only 'archetypes' (Knudsen 2010: 31). Other problems can be constructed within the framework of the theory, and, as will be seen, the great benefit of an empirical approach lies in the refinement and development of the theoretical construction of problems. Moreover, the functional method, especially in its empirical application, can reveal the coupling of different functional systems that serve primarily as solutions to different problems (eg, law and mass media), and thus the co-evolution of problem-solutions.

Once the problem has been properly theorised, it is then used as a 'connecting thread to questions about other possibilities, as a connecting thread in the search for functional equivalents' (Luhmann 1995: 53). If the constructed problem is, for example, the distribution of material needs over time, it can be used then as a connecting thread in this search: how do established solutions such as legally secured financial structures compare in this respect to forms of neighbourly help? If the problem is the improbability of communication, how does television compare to social media, or how does theatre compare to the news? The problem is therefore used to bring into view and compare a range of alternative solutions. The functional method is primarily one of comparing solutions. Through it we come to 'recognise the existence of structural dynamics, adaptation, development and, one of Luhmann's key concepts, the functional equivalence of different kinds of structures' (Hornung 2006: 191).

The purpose here is not to solve the problem. The method of functional analysis 'can (but does not have to) result in the possibility of substitution'; indeed, in most cases the problem will have already been solved (Luhmann 2013a: 82). Moreover, it is important to note that the functional method itself is not concerned with establishing causalities. That is, in constructing a problem and then using it as a 'connecting thread in the search for functional equivalents', the method is not concerned with explaining the problem-solution relation as one of cause and effect. According to Luhmann, the insight of the functional method 'lies athwart causalities' (Luhmann 1995: 53). The method is about comparing problem-solution relations, and for that one can posit causalities as hypotheticals, 'for the moment', as Luhmann says – and, I would argue, one can even posit them as hypotheticals indefinitely if one wishes to remain at that level.

For even without any claim to causality, what this method achieves is insight and information. By broadening the perspective and bringing into view outlying and irregular solutions, the functional method admits more complexity than is accessible to the observed system, and often more than what has so far been admitted to established scientific perspectives. At the same time, the possibilities brought into view are not completely contingent. Potential solutions are always bound by the constructed problem. The functional analysis opens a 'limited field of comparisons' (Knudsen 2010: 13). It is this limiting and broadening which makes the functional method so fruitful. The functional method of analysis serves as a way of interrupting or gaining distance from existing social structures, and through this it generates further analyses and questions about structural relationships between the problem, established solutions and other possibilities. Bound by problem construction and system reference, this constitutes *information* – and invariably 'surprising' information,[4] for by shifting what is 'known and trusted' into the context of other possibilities, the functional method breaks frames and undermines 'intuitive evidences' (Luhmann 1995: 56). As a 'technique for scientific observation', it 'irritates, unsettles, disturbs and possibly destroys' (Luhmann 1995: 56).[6] Now we arrive at a sound juncture for empirical research. It is on the basis of the information and insight generated by the functional method that the opportunity presents itself for empirical research. As Luhmann puts it:

Then one comes to statements like: if (it is really the case that) inflation solves problems of distribution in a relatively conflict-free way (with whatever side effects), inflation is a functional equivalent for a national planning that is politically riskier, because it is richer in conflict. *Only on the underpinnings of a scaffolding composed of such statements does it seem worthwhile to investigate underlying causalities empirically.* (1995: 54, emphasis added)

The functional method of analysis, in other words, provides a suitable scaffolding for embarking upon empirical research. What can be investigated empirically, and indeed what is worth investigating empirically, are the operational relationships between the problem and the functional equivalents that have been revealed through the functional method of analysis, as well as the operational relations between the functional equivalents and the established and taken-for-granted solution system. If, for example, the problem is the improbability of political communication on global themes – or more pointedly the problem of such political communication running into a cul-de-sac – how does the mise-en-scène of protest movements provide a solution to the problem? How does it compare to news media, for example, or political institutionalism? Opportunities for empirical research into such questions present themselves in myriad ways. The operational recursivity of the systems involved can be analysed, for example, through documentary interviews or content analysis. Or the distinctions employed by the observers involved can be analysed, for example, through content analysis of documents or participant observation. Structural couplings can be analysed, for example, through content analysis or interviews on 'decision intersections' etc. (see Besio and Pronzini 2010). The functional method is therefore very effective in general for generating insights and pointing out lines of enquiry for empirical observation.

In the next section I will discuss using the 'problem'/'solution' distinction as a programme for observation of such structural relations, but first let me say something about the apparent dissonance between such empirical investigation and the radical constructivism of Luhmann's sociological theory. How can one reconcile this recommendation of empirical research in relation to a sociological theory that fundamentally excludes any observation of 'the world as it really is'?

At points, Luhmann suggests the 'greater epistemic value' of insights generated by the functional method, that functioning in spite of heterogeneity is 'itself a kind of proof', its potential as a 'valid indicator of truth', or at the very least that the insights generated by the functional method cannot be put down to 'error or pure imagination'. This is immediately qualified, however, with the disclaimer that 'this is in no way to say that the semantic form in which the results are presented "corresponds" to reality' (Luhmann 1995: 58). Rather, it is a claim only that the functional method, and any empirical derivative thereof, merely 'grasps' at a reality – that is to say, it 'proves itself to be a form of ordering vis-à-vis a reality that is also ordered' (Luhmann 1995: 58). Ultimately, the empirical application of the functional method must be a modest one. It is no basis for a hard empiricism. The knowledge about society acquired through such method does not aspire to truth, or a description of the world as it really is.

The full epistemological implications of the Luhmann's theory and method can only be appreciated after discussing his theory of observation in the next section, but at this stage it can be said that what is offered by an empirical application to Luhmann's functional method of analysis is a way to develop and refine the theory. It constitutes a continuous move between the conceptual and the factual, in such a way as to test the theoretical construction of the problem and sharpen it up in reflection with social reality. This is what is meant by a sociology that is both 'factual and conceptual'.[7] The relationship between theory and method is, as Knudsen says, a 'circular' one (2010: 12). The theory 'steers' method, not only by specifying the problems that can be traced to varying solutions but more broadly by sensitising it to 'tendencies that it regards as relevant and for which it can offer meaningful interpretation' (Besio and Pronzini 2010: 10). The method, and particularly empirical investigation, generates information that can then be ploughed back into the development of the theory.

If such an empirical approach is so constructive to theory building, one may ask, why did Luhmann himself not employ it more extensively? Though he admits an empirical application to the functional method of analysis, the extent of Luhmann's empiricism is mostly limited to the use of trivialities (eg, since no interaction system can realise all possible communications within itself, there is a necessary difference between interaction and society). But if Luhmann did not engage in a more empirical application of the functional method, it was because he was more devoted instead to the primary task of fleshing out an adequate unified theory of society. He was embarked, as he put it, on a flight 'above the clouds' (Luhmann 1995: 1). At such a high level of abstraction, we could only expect to 'catch glimpses below of a land with roads, towns, rivers, and coastlines that remind us of something familiar', which would be insufficient 'to guide our flight'. That was undoubtedly the correct approach. To conduct empirical research on the ground takes up a significant amount of time gathering data relating primarily to a single theoretical issue. Luhmann could never have covered the vast expanse that he did if he had engaged in such groundwork. But what he did provide us with is a global positioning system, not only providing for global navigation of a unified theory of society but highlighting places of interest. This is to be refined now by the groundwork of those interested in the task of accumulating facts from empirical observation and 'uploading' them for the development of Luhmann's theory. This not only promises further refinement of the theoretical construction of particular problems studied, but because Luhmann provided such a unified theory of society, once these empirical findings are uploaded to the theoretical level they may find refraction across the great expanse of his theory.

Even a rudimentary design for a more empirical approach to Luhmann's theory is not complete, however, until we consider and integrate another more complex aspect of that theory and method, ie, the theory of observation. The next section will therefore turn its attention to that, and the design of a concept for second-order observation.

Second-order observation concepts

Whereas the functional method is relatively simple, Luhmann's theory of observation is complex, paradoxical. This is where the rock of uncertainty is *really* located, and to cast off in the direction of an empirical approach requires an even greater leap of faith. It is necessary, though, to enter the labyrinth, find some navigation within it and chart a course out. For as Knudsen (2010: 41) points out, there is a significant relationship between the functional method, as a 'way to generate potentially surprising observations', and Luhmann's theory of observations. The theory of observations indeed 'has consequences for how scientific research is carried out' (Knudsen 2010: 43).

Owing much to the influence of Spencer-Brown's calculus of form, the theory of observations is central to Luhmann's systems theory. Observation is defined as the 'handling of a distinction in order to indicate one side and not the other' (Luhmann 2017: 102). Nothing can be observed without a distinction.[8] To observe something in the world, a difference has to be made between this thing and everything else. Such distinctions are always asymmetric, in that they identify one thing and not everything else. Yet the nature of this asymmetry can vary, with important consequences. A distinction can be made by indicating something as distinct from everything else, without specifying the other side of the distinction. For example, the indication of a chair does not rely on a contrast with everything that is not a chair. Luhmann classifies what is indicated by such a mode of distinction as 'objects' (Åkerstrøm Andersen 2003: 67; Luhmann 1993: 15). But something can also be observed by using a two-sided form, indicating in a way that restricts what constitutes the other side of the distinction. These are binary and totalising distinctions, 'cutting the world in two parts', so that 'there are only these two sides of the world and no third thing' (Luhmann 2017: 108) – eg, 'paid'/'not paid', 'citizen'/'foreigner', 'legal'/'illegal'. The 'condensates' of such a mode of distinction are referred to as 'concepts' (Åkerstrøm Andersen 2003: 67; Luhmann 1993: 16). I will return to this conceptual mode of distinction shortly, as it proves important to any empirical application to Luhmann's sociological theory.

Regardless of whether the distinction is objective or conceptual in this sense, though, it always carries along another side that is not indicated in the moment of indication and therefore has no operational significance. This is referred to as the 'blind spot' of observing (Luhmann 2017: 103). The observer must concentrate on one side only, and anyone who wishes to observe must figure on such a blind spot. The observer, that is, cannot observe herself as the one who handles the distinction. The unity of the distinction must be made 'invisible' in order to observe (Luhmann 2017: 104). This is not to say that one cannot observe that observation always operates with a blind spot, for that is what we are doing now. But observation of the blind spot only arrives at the paradox of the unity of the distinction. As Luhmann says, one is then 'stuck', and can only move forward by making a 'creative jump by offering a substitute distinction' (2017: 104). Only then can one escape the 'clutches' of the paradox and leap to the 'level of autological observation of observation', with all its attendant risk and reward (Luhmann 1993: 76).

Both of these aspects of the theory of observation – the blind spot and the creative jump to other distinctions – prove instrumental to any empirical application to Luhmann's sociological theory. However, before this can be fully appreciated, it is first necessary to make further observations by way of the distinction between first-order and second-order observation. First-order observation is the plain indication of something in the world. Second order-observation is an observation of an observer in this operation. It is an observation of how the observer observes – an observation, that is, of the distinctions the observer uses to observe. As an observation itself, second-order observation uses a distinction in order to observe how the actor sees what he sees as well as what he does not see, ie, the blind spot of the first-order observation. But as an observation itself, second-order observation also suffers from its own blind spot. The second-order observer may fixate on her own blind spot and the paradox of observation, and thereby adopt a third-order perspective reflecting 'on the conditions of the possibility of second-order observation and its consequences for what can then still be a common world or a society that makes description possible' (Luhmann 2013b: 328). This is necessary to some degree in any methodological design, but pursued in isolation is largely a philosophical pursuit. Faced with the paradox of observation, the second-order observer can also make the creative jump to other distinctions and thereby engage in further observation of the observer. As Luhmann (2017: 112) states, 'there are many possibilities' in this respect. However, only some of the distinctions used are suitable for further observation of society along empirical lines. I will return to this point.

Despite the fact that both first-order and second-order observation employ distinctions, and both suffer from a blind spot because of that, the quality of observations is very different at each level. For the first-order observer the world is 'ontically given' (Luhmann 1993: 68, 2017: 330). His observations appear necessary because the world is 'ordered' and 'unambiguous' (Luhmann 2013b: 332). He will observe that eating meat is 'wrong', for example, not as an actualisation of one side of the distinction ('wrong'/'right') in communication but because he is moved through observation of the suffering of animals in the production of meat.[9] The first-order observer, therefore, 'observes on the basis of values. His values give him the distinction that guides his knowing and acting' (Luhmann 2013b: 331). Second-order observation, on the other hand, 'has to do without these logico-ontological assumptions' (Luhmann 2013b: 332). For the second-order observer the observations of the first-order observer are determined by distinctions, and it is clear that 'distinctions can vary' (Luhmann 2013b: 330) – and not simply the distinctions used by the first-order observer, but also the distinctions that justify observing this observer. In other words, the second-order observer does not simply see what she sees; rather, she sees what others see as well as what they do not see, and she must therefore orientate herself to the contingency of the world. Furthermore, for the second-order observer – and this is especially true of second-order observation through the use of concepts as a mode of distinction that restricts what can constitute the other side – values do not determine observation in the way they do for the first-order observer. For the second-order observer, the values of the first-order observer appear contingent (they could be different), and the indisputability of values is only produced in communication (as the actualisation of the value as one side of a distinction).[10] Thus, what second-order observation achieves is an analytical 'distance' from the 'value commitments' of first-order observers (Luhmann 2013b: 332).

It is this facility for distance in observing the 'eigenvalues of the system' (Luhmann 2013b: 332) that marks out second-order observation as a sociological method. Sociology, it is said, 'assumes the position of a second-order observer. It is concerned with the observation of observers' (Luhmann 2013b: 329). This is the proper domain for sociology (qua Durkheim's 'social fact'), because the observed observer need not be a psychic system but can be a social system, or more abstractly communication. The communication system, as Luhmann says, has the 'ability to observe' (2017: 105). And this is not simply to say that functional systems like law, politics or the economy observe, but that even 'interaction' observes (Luhmann 2017: 105).[11] Admittedly, there is a price to pay for this recognition of society as the object of second-order observation. Sociology must be part of what it observes. As Luhmann states, 'when we create theories of society, we cannot avoid being internal observers' (2017: 108). Thus, once again, we must relinquish any claim to the rigorously objective viewpoint traditionally associated with empirical methodology. But sociologists as second-order observers can still engage in external observation by, for example, 'talking about the economy or politics without intending to earn money or acting politically in the process', even if by communicating they are already taking part in society (Luhmann 2017: 108). Moreover, there is still the distance achieved by concepts and the separation of first-order and second-order observation (Luhmann 1993: 16), and even if second-order observation is also first-order observation and therefore must be somewhat solipsistic and value-laden in the selection of observers to observe, this can be attenuated (though not obliterated) through the use what Åkerstrøm Andersen calls 'second-order concepts' – that is, through the copying and re-entering of a conceptual distinction into itself (2003: 67). Such conceptual self-observation can operate as a methodological design to limit the effect of solipsism and values on second-order observation, for example, by questioning how or why it selects the observers it observes.

Of course, even with that attenuation and a flight from the paradox of the blind spot and self-observation, the sociological method of second-order observation still cannot make claims to hard empiricism. Ultimately, the theory of observation must dispense with ontological certainty and renounce any claim to 'scientific elucidation of the world as the totality of things' (Luhmann 2017: 105). Indeed, it is this program that 'inevitably leads to a "constructivist" understanding of science' (Luhmann 2013b: 330). But much like Luhmann's qualification of this constructivism in relation to the functional method (as 'grasping' at reality as a 'form of ordering vis-à-vis a reality that is also ordered'), the constructivism of sociology as second-order observation is also qualified. For although the knowledge it gains 'is and remains societal knowledge', the sociological method of second-order observation nonetheless 'knows more than a society without sociology would know' (Luhmann 2013b: 330).[12] Through second-order observation sociology achieves the 'distance from direct value commitment in society' which allows it to be 'guided within its operationally closed system by the network of its own communication' (Luhmann 2013b: 332). Within its own boundaries sociology can 'reconstruct society through the distinction between self-reference and other-reference in relation to itself' (Luhmann 2013b: 332).

Thus, despite its ultimate constructivism, the theory of observation does not dictate that sociologists cling to the rock of uncertainty and wither on the paradox of observation. Instead it offers the basis for a move from the conceptual to the factual. Taking stock of the theory of observations, we find that distinctions offer a programme for observation of the world; that second-order observation concepts achieve a distance from value commitments and gain perspective on the operational latency of society on this basis; that as a sociological method, such concepts can gain more knowledge about society than would be possible without them. Observing the observation of others on a factual basis must therefore, once again, be recognised as a potential way for developing the theory. Furthermore, we must also at this point consider the (functional) relation between the functional method of analysis and second-order observation concepts in this respect. As Knudsen points out, 'the functional method can be characterized as a program for observation characterised by the guiding distinction problem/solution' (2010: 45). As a concept, the distinction of 'problem'/'solution' acts as a 'kind of dynamo' that drives analyses further (Knudsen 2010: 38). It provides a programme for observation, yet is sufficiently empty in that it does not specify the content of the problem. But once the problem is constructed by theory, the concept becomes 'dynamic', allowing the 'analysis to transgress its own boundaries, and running together with other distinctions and thus opening up new questions' (Knudsen 2010: 50). This is what is meant by the statement that the functional method 'is suitable for both practical and theoretical purposes'; that 'in the form of a question about latent functions, it is particularly suitable for observing what others cannot observe' (Luhmann 2013b: 333).

Finally, it is worth once again relating these observations on the potential empirical application of second-order observation to Blumer's influential critique of the methodology of social theory. In his article 'What is wrong with social theory?', Blumer argues that social theory 'shows grave shortcomings' in comparison with empirical science (1954). The factors presented as underlying this deficiency include social theory being 'conspicuously defective in its guidance of research inquiry' and 'rarely couched in such form as to facilitate' empirical investigation. Furthermore, it is charged that social theory 'benefits little from the vast and ever growing accumulation of "facts" that come from empirical observation'. Blumer argues that these deficiencies can only be addressed through the use of 'concepts'. Thus, he complains that the concepts typically employed by social theory (such as attitudes, class, norms, social control etc.) are 'vague' and 'ambiguous'. The uncertainty as to what they are referring to, he argues, obstructs 'asking pertinent questions and setting relevant problems for research'. The obvious answer is to make concepts clearer and more definitive, but for Blumer the balance between the conceptual and the factual is not easily achieved for social theory. This is because more definitive concepts lose the necessary 'abstract character of a class with specific attributes', because theoretical concepts are constituted by 'something beyond the definitive empirical content' and because the relevance of isolated empirical content to theory is easy to presume but difficult to establish. In constructing these problems, Blumer appears to pose the 'heretical' question as to whether social theory can ever develop more definitive concepts to overcome its perceived problems. But he sees a way to cut the Gordian knot by recommending that social theory employ 'sensitising concepts' that can be 'refined' through instances of empirical research. Thus, on the basis of the sensitising concepts of social theory (ie, concepts that 'suggest directions along which to look'), he suggests that we 'infer that any given substance in our natural world and its content are covered by one of our concepts', and that on that basis, the sensitising concepts can then be 'tested, improved, and refined', 'assayed through careful study of empirical instances which they are presumed to cover'.

Of course, Luhmann's theory, method and epistemology must be recognised to be at odds with Blumer's. Observation theory does not make the same claim to 'direct study of the natural world', and it is focused on 'operations' rather than 'substance' (Blumer 1954: 9). However, it must be recognised that much of what Blumer recommends as sensitising concepts that can be improved and refined through careful study of empirical instances and that are capable of asking 'pertinent questions and setting relevant problems for research' is satisfied by Luhmann's use of concepts as second-order observations. These binary distinctions that 'cut the world in half' are highly sensitising, because they offer a guiding distinction for identifying the facts of value commitments in communication. They are in this sense open. At the same time they are also closed in restricting the other side of the indication and their totalisation. They are a perfect balance between what Blumer recommends as definitive and sensitising concepts.

The theory of observations and its symbiosis with the functional method of analysis are complex, and may appear a little too abstract for those who prefer a more empirical or grounded approach. But it is necessary to give at least this brief picture of the relationship between the functional method of analysis and second-order observation before we consider any empirical application of Luhmann's theory. In keeping, though, with the programme for the circularity of theory and method, the next section can now present a practical example of the use of the functional method of analysis and second-order observation as a basis of a more empirical approach using the concept of normative expectations.

Case study: Use of the concept of normative expectations

Expectations provide an excellent concept for an empirical investigation. To begin with, they can be distinguished, as both Galtung (1959) and Luhmann (1985: 32) have done, as either normative or cognitive. Expectations are cognitive when they are 'adapted to reality in the case of disappointment'. They *learn* from disappointment. For normative expectations, 'the opposite holds' (Luhmann 1985: 33). Normative expectations are not given up when they are disappointed by reality. They signify a determination *not to learn* from disappointment, and thus are 'adhered to, even when frustrated' (Luhmann 2008: 20).[13] This 'cognitive'/'normative' distinction is a two-sided form, an indication that restricts what constitutes the other side of the distinction. It reduces expectation to two things, either cognitive or normative. There is no third type of expectation. Either one learns to adapt expectations in the face of a disappointing reality or one does not learn, one holds on to expectations despite the disappointing reality. The distinction 'cognitive'/'normative' is, in other words, a concept. On the one hand it is definite and concrete (ie, it is closed), through its totalisation and its exclusion of third possibilities. On the other hand it is a sensitising concept (ie, open) because it offers a guiding distinction and programme for observing expectations as either cognitive or normative.

The distinction between normative and cognitive expectations must also be recognised as a programme for second-order observation. That is, it is concerned with observing the observations of others. Of course, the first-order observer in this context does not use the distinction 'cognitive'/ 'normative'. For the expectant individual, expectations are either disappointed or fulfilled. But we replace that distinction with the distinction between cognitive and normative. Now we are running it together with other distinctions ('disappointment'/'fulfilment', 'cognitive'/'normative', 'problem'/'solution'). Apart from the general reflexivity of the concept, this achieves two things. First, it means we can see things the first-order observer cannot see. That includes seeing the unity of the distinction 'fulfilment'/ 'disappointment'. Replacing the distinction – or more precisely, using the reflexivity of applying the 'cognitive'/'normative' distinction to the 'fulfilment'/'disappointment' distinction – achieves a distance from value commitments. That is, one does not co-expect what one observes as normative expectations, just as one does not adapt expectations in line with observed cognitive expectations.

Secondly, where the observations of first-order observers do generate value commitments – in other words, when first-order observers normatively expect – the concept allows for observation of the institutionalisation of those normative expectations in communication. Normative expectations are 'social facts' par excellence. Durkheim's (1982: 52) definition of social facts may have been 'ambiguous' in some ways (Lukes 1973: 3), but he had a solid basis in locating social facts in 'resistance' and the 'representations and actions' of individuals who 'fight against' and 'struggle free' from disappointment.[14] Expectations were an important object of inquiry for Weber, Mead and Parsons too, but they figure most prominently in Luhmann's sociology. For Luhmann (1995: 292), the concept of expectations occupies a 'central theoretical position'.[15] Expectations in general are 'not necessarily subjective' and do 'not necessarily apply only to psychic structures'.[16] That is, expectations register as prominently in society as they do in psychic systems. They mark the inter-dependence of the psychic and the social, and manifest themselves in different ways in each sphere. Vis-à-vis the environment of the psychic systems they register as consciousness, and 'vis-à-vis the social structure, as *communication*' (Luhmann 1995: 267, emphasis added).

This is especially the case for normative expectations. It is in the possibility of disappointment, 'not in the regularity of its fulfilment, that the reality reference of expectation proves itself' (Luhmann 1985: 32). Disappointment, as Luhmann says, takes on an 'emotional character' and 'stimulates activities' (41). This is also where the functional method comes into play. Expectations are a 'life necessity' (40), in that meaningful communication can only be sustained if alter can anticipate the expectations of ego in social interaction. Yet these 'expectations of expectations' are prone to 'error' and a rich 'source of conflict and discrepancy' (22, 13).

This is the basic problem of double contingency. But we can problematise this further in the case of normative expectations. If a normative expectation is communicated – ie, where an expectation is retained and projected against a disappointing reality, and it does not register as merely foolish or deviant but rather finds a more general level of support – then it can be traced to various solutions that supervise, channel or cool out the disappointment. Of course, not all normative expectations are communicated or projected against disappointment. Some otherwise legitimate expectations may go unarticulated and may not stimulate communication. I may expect that students will not sleep in class while I am teaching. If I am confronted with a disappointing experience in this regard, I do not give up the expectation, even if I decide it is the student's responsibility to pay attention and therefore say nothing. But some normative expectations (because they are contentious or have more at stake) find greater articulation and conflict. Society may even select them as important conflicts, and they may find institutionalisation and stabilisation at a much more general societal level beyond the interaction context that they arose in. This is indeed Luhmann's theory of the function of law in providing 'social support for contra-factual expectations' (Luhmann 2004: 270). Law stabilises normative expectations in a social dimension when anonymous third parties removed from the interaction context communicate that they also share the normative expectation. Law stabilises normative expectations in the factual dimension when the normative expectation can be 'imbued with meaning' and abstracted to a more systemic level of communication. Law stabilises normative expectations in a temporal dimension when it provides the social structure to back up those expectations over time, ie, tomorrow, next month, next year and so on (Luhmann 1985: 73).

We are not concerned here with any functional specification of the legal system or a concept of law. Rather, we are using this as an invitation in the search for functional equivalents.[17] Now we arrive at the point of presenting a practical model for the use of the functional method of analysis and second-order observation in the accumulation of 'facts' from empirical observation. Although there is insufficient space to engage in a full theoretical construction of the problem here (as would be necessary in any empirical application of the functional method), the preceding discussion is hopefully enough to at least posit the problem of the stabilisation of normative expectations in society, and the possibility of using the problem as a connecting thread to various solutions that can be then compared with the legal system or other taken-for-granted solutions in this regard. Furthermore, in the distinction 'cognitive'/'normative' we have a concept for observation, a concept that is both definite and sensitising – definite because it provides a concrete definition of normative expectations (they are not cognitive expectations and they are no third thing), sensitising because it suggests directions along which to look (through the reduction, normative expectations can be searched for in the complexity of the communication they stimulate and the various solutions that they can be traced to). Moreover, it is a concept that can facilitate empirical enquiry, as expectations, particularly normative ones, register in social structure. That is, they can be investigated at the factual level. Finally, it is a concept for second-order observation, ie, for observing the observation of others. Unlike the ontological concept of 'is'/'ought' that continues to dominate legal theory and to limit perception of the complexity of law in society, the concept of normative expectations avoids logico-ontological considerations and provides instead a programme for observing the normative expectations of first-order observers at a distance from those value commitments, and does so across the full spectrum of social systems, from interaction systems to functional systems.

I have previously employed this as a basis for more factually orientated research into Luhmann's sociological theory (Hanna 2017). This includes research into functional equivalents to international law in relation to normative expectations of nuclear disarmament. After proper construction of the problem of such normative expectations in world society and the limits of law in this respect (literally, a non liquet), the research was able to use the problem as a connecting thread to search out functional equivalents, which in turn highlighted the work of social movements and social movement organisations in this respect. To investigate this further, the research engaged in methods that are typically considered to be more suited to empirical research. This included content analysis, looking, for example, at constitutional instruments of social movement organisations or minutes of the meetings of their internal steering organs. It also included interviews with key members of the organisations for data about organisational decisions. The objective in such factual research was to identify anti-nuclear normative expectations, to test how well the social movement organisations stabilised these expectations in the social, factual and temporal dimensions. This developed the theory of the emergence of anti-nuclear social movement organisations as functional equivalents to law. It revealed how social movement organisations stabilise expectations through social institutionalisation at the global level; how they abstract anti-nuclear norms from their interactional contexts around the world and imbue them with a more general meaning; and how they carry normative expectations through time through the recursivity of their decision-making, an insight which dovetailed with Luhmann's theory of organisations (2000, 2003). But in keeping with the basic premise of this methodology – that theory and method have a circular relationship – it also invited further factual research, amongst other things, into the structural relations between these functional equivalents and the established solution of law and politics.

The more empirical approach has also been employed in research into the relationship between normative expectations at the interactional level and the development of law in society (on file with the author). Rather than problematising law and searching for and comparing solutions, though, this approach identifies the communication of normative expectations in personal protests against racial segregation on public transport that took place in the United States in 1955, and it traces this normative communication through a range of social structures to a decision of the Unites States Supreme Court in 1956. The research has benefitted from a wealth of factual records of the communication of the normative expectations in question, including police arrest records (of those who were prosecuted for violation of city and state segregation laws), documentary records, film and audio recordings of interviews with participants, court documents (based on the varied and complex litigation such normative expectations generated), media reports and of course the communicated decisions of social movement organisations, from the local to the national level. Starting as it did from the interactional level, the research had to be careful not to venture into the psychic realm (eg, what moved participants to communicate their normative expectations in protest at segregation on public transport), but its execution proved the relative ease of avoiding this, as normative expectations could be identified at the interactional level purely as communication.

The insight that this empirical approach gives birth to, and the various ways it can be ploughed back into developing Luhmann's sociological theory, is too vast and complex to be unpacked here. The obvious gains of these particular studies on normative expectations are in relation to development of Luhmann's (1995: 387ff.) theory about conflict and society's immune system, as well as a correction of the excessive focus on legal code in the general application of Luhmann's theory to legal research. But I will reserve my last comment to underline one other important insight that arose from the studies, in the hope that it will provide a brief illustration of how Luhmann's theory can benefit at a more general level from the accumulation of 'facts' from empirical observation and how it can, as Knudsen says, be 'surprised by method'.

In the final presentation of his unified theory of society, Luhmann attempts to address criticisms of those who question the primary domination of functional differentiation – based on contrary experience of law, politics etc – in other regions around the world (2013b: 128, referring to Neves's 2001 critique about the allopoiesis of law in Brazil). In doing so, he admits that the 'major societal subsystems float on a sea of constantly dissolving minor systems', and acknowledges the 'interface' relations between interaction systems, organisations, protest movements and functional systems (132). Presenting the first three forms of societal system differentiation in quick succession, he outlines the way in which interaction systems 'realise society' and 'involve communication in the societal system' (132); how organisations can reproduce themselves and absorb uncertainty through their decisions, their opportunities for structural coupling, and how they are the 'only social systems that can communicate with systems in their environment' (151); how protest movements 'mobilise society against society' and stimulate communication (154); and their capacity for structural couplings when they are 'complemented by the innumerable constructions of functional systems' (163, 165). However, there is a need to develop the theoretical understanding of this interface of the different forms of societal system differentiation. For example, in the study of normative expectations of racial equality on public transport in the United States in the 1950s, important (ie, stimulating) normative expectations can be clearly traced through the full range of the different forms of societal system differentiation. For example, a 'no' voiced by a black passenger refuting segregation on public transport can be 'empirically' traced to protest movement communications, to myriad organisations, then not just to law but to mass media (from local to global), religion (eg, in church gatherings), the economy (eg, in bus boycotts), and in dense structural couplings between the different functional subsystems. What appears is a rich and complex picture of law that reveals limitations of the excessive focus on code and legal autopoiesis in the predominant use of Luhmann's sociological theory in legal study. Some may be wary of the admission of such societal complexity as blurring the conceptual purity of legal theory, but it must be recognised that even if Luhmann himself did not fully connect the different forms of societal system differentiation, his theory provides the basis for development along these lines. Somewhat ironically, this is the programme that may deliver the original goal of charting the 'immense and structured complexity' of law (Luhmann 1985: 5).[18]

Conclusion

Luhmann's sociological theory is vast and complex. Within its global scheme there are a multitude of different aspects that can be usefully subject to empirical observation. Moreover, already located within the theoretical framework are a multitude of concepts, or models for concepts, that provide the programmes for such empirical observation. When the complexity generated from this reduction of complexity is applied to the complexity of a constellation of diverse factual patterns, the theory sharpens up and acquires 'flexibility', 'a greater range of application', 'a growth of selection achievement' and a 'better capacity to adapt' and 'control itself'.[19] From the lens of Luhmann's theory and method, these diverse factual patterns are bound within the framework of self-referential communication throughout interaction systems, organisations, protest movements and functional subsystems. But when empirical observation through this lens is adopted by researchers around the world, an infinite variety of factual patterns will come into view, and offer unique possibilities for developing the theory.

This chapter has tried to show that the risks of casting off the rock of uncertainty in the direction of a more empirical approach to Luhmann's theory will be modest if it involves a soft empiricism based on Luhmann's functional method and theory of observations. Moreover, it has tried to show the benefits of adopting such an empirical approach in refining and developing Luhmann's theory and method. If we consider these potential benefits as a whole, together with the potential risks posed to Luhmann's sociological theory by remaining stuck on the rock of uncertainty, we must ask: how can we not admit the complexity and cast off in such experimental directions?

Notes

1 Luhmann addresses this question only a few times. For more recent developments, see Knudsen (2010), Besio and Pronzini (2008, 2010), Vogd (2009), and Nassehi and Saake (2002).
2 Search for Luhmann' at Google Ngram Viewer. Available at: https://books. google.com/ngrams/graph?content=Niklas+Luhmann&year_start=1800& year_end=2008&corpus=15&smoothing=3&share=&direct_url=t1%3B %2CNiklas%20Luhmann%3B%2Cc0#t1%3B%2CNiklas%20Luhmann%3B %2Cc0 [Accessed 14 Mar. 2020].
3 Merton (1967: 88) also criticises structural-functionalism on this basis, arguing that the approach treats cultural forms as 'specialised and irreplaceable', and suggesting instead alternative functions – some latent, some manifest. See also Merton (1957: 86ff.). Luhmann, too, shared this aversion to structural-functionalism and may have drawn some inspiration here from Merton's notion of alternative functions, but whereas for Merton the issue is one of exposing latent functions, for Luhmann it is about comparing functional equivalents (and of course, with the later shift from structural to operational latency). Luhmann's early ideas were also influenced, though, by the idea of 'equifinality' advanced in Bertalanffy's open systems theory (see Bertalanffy 1968: 40).
4 The excesses of Parsonian functionalism are evidently what Blumer (1954) had in mind in his influential paper.
5 Luhmann 2012 'The function of methodology [...] is more likely to be concerned with refined forms of intrasystemic information generation and processing. Methods can thus enable scientific research to surprise itself' (Luhmann 2012: 13). See also Knudsen (2010).
6 In this sense, Luhmann's functional method of analysis takes up to some extent Feyerabend's infamous methodological command that 'anything goes', not to 'postpone alternatives' and to admit the 'principle of proliferation': 'invent and elaborate theories which are inconsistent with the accepted point of view, even if the latter should happen to be highly confirmed and generally accepted' (1970: 26). (Although Luhmann certainly gives more primacy to theory than Feyerabend.)
7 'If we are guided by the alternative between critical and positive (methodologically "empirical") sociology, we shall not get very far. We need not reject it (that would not help). We must complement it. Suggestions can be made in both factual and conceptual respects' (Luhmann (2012: 16).
8 'Observation without drawing distinctions is impossible' (Luhmann 1993: 76).
9 As Luhmann (2013: 331–332) says: 'One does not announce that one is in favor

of justice, peace, health, conservation of the environment, and the like; to provide opportunity for reacting by accepting or rejecting this utterance one says merely what one considers to be just and unjust'.

10 Or, as Luhmann (2013: 331–332) puts it: 'The second-order observer relates the semantics of values to their use in communication.'

11 See also Åkerstrøm Andersen (2003: 64). Interesting in the latter sense – though undoubtedly at the boundaries of sociology – is the interchange of the observations of psychic and social systems – eg, the social system observes psychic systems, psychic systems observe social systems (see Luhmann 2017: 105).

12 Luhmann refers in this respect to Lazarsfeld's concept of latent structure analysis and its relation to 'the methodology of empirical social research.' However, according to Luhmann (2013b: 330), the radically constructivist revision means that the 'condition of structural latency has to be replaced by the condition of operational latency. For second-order observation, this means that necessary latency becomes contingent, namely, selectable and always possible in different ways – depending on which distinction is taken as the basis for observation.'

13 See also Luhmann (1985: 33, 2004: 149).

14 See also Lukes (2019). It should be noted in this context that Durkheim's concept is limited by his classical subject/object-orientated approach, which leads to a focus on constraint and structures of legal rules, moral maxims and social conventions, etc, rather than the communication of normative expectations, and thus even the expectations of a persecuted individual constitute social facts.

15 The full scale of this cannot be stated here.

16 This is especially clear through second-order observation: 'Some time ago, there was a discussion with Johannes Berger in Bielefeld, in which he criticised the concept of expectation as subjective and therefore in principle useless for sociologists. [...] But the design of the present systems theory makes it apparent that I want to try to escape this subject-object distinction and to replace it with the distinction [between] the operation and [...] the observation of this operation. [...] Under such conditions, the concept of expectation no longer contains any subjective component' (Luhmann 2017: 72).

17 In accordance with Luhmann's recommendation for his functional theory of law (2004: 93).

18 Ironic because Luhmann set out in 1972 to establish such a sociological theory of law in response to 'empirical' approaches that he felt missed this complexity of law. He was quite right, but now we see a role for more empirical approaches to investigate and develop the complex theory of law that Luhmann eventually went on to construct.

19 Just like any reflexivity (see Luhmann 1985: 452–454).

References

Åkerstrøm Andersen, N. (2003) *Discursive Analytical Strategies: Understanding Foucault, Koselleck, Laclau, Luhmann* (London, Policy Press).

Bertalanffy, L. (1968) *General System Theory* (New York, George Braziller).

Besio, C. and Pronzini, A. (2008): 'Niklas Luhmann as an empirical sociologist: methodological implications of the system theory of society' *15*(2) *Cybernet. Human Knowing* 9–31.

Besio, C. and Pronzini, A. (2010): 'Inside organizations and out: methodological tenets for empirical research inspired by systems theory' *11*(3) *Qualit. Soc. Res.* 1–22.

Blumer, H. (1954) 'What is wrong with social theory?' *19*(1) *Am. Sociol. Rev.* 3–10.

Bulmer, M. (1984) *Sociological Research Methods: An Introduction* (London, MacMillan).

Durkheim, E. (1982) *The Rules of Sociological Method: And Selected Texts on Sociology and Its Method* (New York, Palgrave MacMillan).

Epstein, L., and King, G. (2002). 'The Rules of Inference' *69*(1) *University of Chicago Law Review* 1–133.

Feyerabend, P. (1970) 'Against method: outline of an anarchistic theory of knowledge' *4 Minnesota Stud. Philos. Sci.* 17–130.

Galtung, J. (1959) 'Expectations and interaction processes' *2*(1–4) *Inquiry* 213–234.

Hanna, M. (2017) 'Between law and transnational social movement organizations: stabilizing expectations of global public goods' *44*(3) *J. Law Soc.* 345–373.

Hornung, B.R. (2006) 'The theoretical context and foundations of Luhmann's legal and political sociology' in King M., Thornhill C. (eds), *Luhmann on Law and Politics: Critical Appraisals and Applications* (Oxford, Hart) 187–216.

Knudsen, M. (2010) 'Surprised by method—functional method and systems theory' *11 Qualit. Soc. Res.* 1–18.

Luhmann, N. (1964) *Funktionen und Folgen formaler Organisation* (Berlin, Duncker & Humblot).

Luhmann, N. (1970) 'Reflexive Mechanismen' in Luhmann N. (ed) *Soziologische Aufklärung I: Aufsätze zur theorie sozialer systeme* (Opladen, Westdeutscher) 92–112.

Luhmann, N. (1985) *A Sociological Theory of Law* (London, Routledge).

Luhmann, N. (1993) *Risk: A Sociological Theory* (New York, de Gruyter).

Luhmann, N. (1995) *Social Systems* (Stanford, Stanford University Press).

Luhmann, N. (2000) *Organisation und Entscheidung* (Opladen, Westdeutscher Verlag).

Luhmann, N. (2003) 'Organization' in Bakken T. and Hernes T. (eds), *Autopoietic Organization Theory: Drawing on Niklas Luhmann's Social Systems Perspective* (Oslo, Abstrakt), 31–52.

Luhmann, N. (2004) *Law as a Social System* (Oxford, Oxford University Press).

Luhmann, N. (2008) 'Are there still indispensable norms in our society?' *14 Soziale Systeme* 18–37.

Luhmann, N. (2012) *Theory of Society*, vol. 1 (Stanford, Stanford University Press).

Luhmann, N. (2013a) *A Systems Theory of Religion* (Stanford, Stanford University Press).

Luhmann, N. (2013b) *Theory of Society*, vol. 2 (Stanford, Stanford University Press).

Luhmann, N. (2017) *Introduction to Systems Theory* (Cambridge, Polity).

Lukes, S. (1973) *Emile Durkheim: His Life and Works* (London, Allen Lane).

Lukes, S. (2019) 'Norms as social facts' *13 Ann. Int. Instit. Sociol. Soc. Sci. Crossroads* 67–81.

Merton, R.K. (1957) *Social Theory and Social Structure* (New York, Free Press).

Merton, R.K. (1967) *On Theoretical Sociology* (New York, Free Press).

Moeller, H.-G. (2012) *The Radical Luhmann* (New York, Columbia University Press).

Nassehi, A. and Saake, I. (2002) 'Kontingenz: Methodisch verhindert oder beobachtet? Ein Beitrag zur Methodologie der qualitativen Sozialforschung' *31*(1) *Zeitschrift für Soziologie* 66–86.

Neves, M. (2001) 'From the autopoiesis to the allopoiesis of law' *28*(2) *J. Law Soc.* 242–264.

Vogd, W. (2009) 'Systemtheorie und Methode? Zum komplexen Verhältnis von Theoriearbeit und Empirie in der Organisationsforschung' *15*(1) *Soziale System* 98–137.

Chapter 10

Integration and disintegration
Protest, social movements and legal interpretation

Celso Fernandes Campilongo

Introduction

Niklas Luhmann died at the end of the 20th century. He did not see the crisis of 2008, the Arab Spring, the expansion of social digital networks or the Brazil of June 2013. He could not guess the impact of these phenomena on the dynamics of law and on constitutions. His theory, however, is an evolving and self-constructing apparatus, and can open a new trend for the study of social movements beside consolidated lines of investigation, such as those around the concepts of 'collective action' or 'resource mobilisation' (see, eg, McCann 2006).

This chapter aims to test the possibilities of relationships between social movements and the legal system. Its hypothesis is that social movements install themselves in the legal and political systems as a reaction to functionally differentiated society, and that law in turn answers to the conflict that the social movements activate and perform.

The opening section considers the concept of 'integration' and the difference 'inclusion'/'exclusion' in Luhmann's systems theory. The second section is concerned with the distinction between movements of disintegration and movements of integration. The former react to functional differentiation from within, on its own terms, generally coding their structures through the form of organisations: institutionalising themselves as perennial hierarchical systems that distinguish among members and non-members, and approaching the state, the legislature or the courts through procedural channels. Movements of integration try to contrast functional differentiation from the outside – although they are an expression of a functionally differentiated society. These movements protest mainly against the established institutions and propose integration – 'order', be it the old or a new one – in the place of the distinction among law, politics, economy and other communication arenas.

The last section deals with interpretation as the operation leading to the evolution of the legal system. Interpretation is described as the legal construction of law's self-observation. Who interprets? Not the judge. What is interpreted? Not the case. The difference 'subject-interpreter'/'interpreted object' has no meaning in our perspective. Interpretation is an operation of the legal system. The system itself interprets. Interpretation is also a form of the self-description of law. It enlaces the necessary reference to texts, to statutes and case law, to the reconstruction of premises of fact. Interpretation, argumentation as observation among competing interpretations (Luhmann 1995) and finally the decision – as the scissors fixing a new authoritative premise – are interlaced steps referred to the symbol that connects legal communications: the validity of positive law. But interpretation also has a dimension external to the law. When law interprets, it not only observes itself. It also performs other-observation: the observation that the legal (sub)system does of the society as a whole (its environment). In this process, law also observes social movements, as systems, and is observed by them. Legal interpretation, therefore, is the technique of reintroducing the social environment into the legal system, or of re-casting society in the society's law.

Integration, inclusion and exclusion

The logic of paradoxes and tautologies runs through Luhmann's entire work. Perhaps no other author has so deepened the systemic distinction 'integration'/'disintegration' in the field of sociology of law as Raffaele De Giorgi, another author in this volume. What is social integration? A relationship between freedom and attachment? An obstacle to the self-reference of systems? The result of the difference between inclusion and exclusion? (De Giorgi 2006: 223–233).

In a functionally differentiated society, the greater the social complexity, the greater the resistance to the effects of differentiation itself. Functional systems often do not process, process poorly or process in such a way as to reinforce problems that they were intended to solve. The performance of their function generates paradoxes and indeterminacies within the systems. Redundancies (stabilised recursive structures) and variations (corrections and structural changes) emerge thereof. Integration is the reduction of the degree of internal freedom of partial systems. It is related to the adjustment of systems. This limitation of freedom can occur under conditions of co-operation or conflict. Integration does not mean unity, cohesion, obedience or coordination. It is a dynamic relationship between systems. Conflict can be generated by the very strong integration of functional systems. To react to conflicts, systems promote integration. The problem, perhaps, as Luhmann (2013: 25) points out, is to promote not (generally strong) integration but rather the 'sufficient disintegration' of partial systems (or the extension of their limits of freedom). Exclusion, therefore, integrates systems much more (ie, restricts their freedom) than inclusion. Exclusion from one system means a high probability of exclusion from other systems as well. Partial inclusion does not necessarily mean total inclusion.

What are the relationships between integration and disintegration on the one hand and courts and social movements on the other? At least two can be pointed out. If integration means limitation of the freedom of partial systems, on the side of social movements the flag of exclusion perceived as an unacknowledged right often rises. This exclusion also promotes integration among the excluded: limits to freedom. Does the mobilisation of rights by social movements promote 'conflict of integrations'? Does it diminish freedoms in both systems? This is one of the possible relationships: inflexibility blocking the communicative possibilities of both sides.

However, even more rarely, it is also possible to broaden the choice and build structural variability. The conflict can alert both systems to the need for adjustment: it would be a 'disintegration conflict'. Some would call this emancipation. Others would say this is restoring the system. In any case, here are the possibilities of expanding the horizon of selections and choices.

The binomial 'integration'/'disintegration' is related to the other, 'inclusion'/ 'exclusion'. Inclusion and exclusion form a unit permeated by paradoxes. To include means to exclude. The formation of a system is the result of exclusions. Inclusion is the internal part; exclusion, the external part. Exclusion can result in inclusion. It can work as rhetoric to think of participation, citizenship, public policies and access to justice as a virtuous and cumulative race to the inclusive side of difference – which is supposed to always reap the positive results of reciprocal incentives: more participation would imply more citizenship, which would result in a deepening of public policies, which would guarantee more rights … . These notions together form a fragile, obsolete and idealising semantics of inclusion. Instead of reflecting on or facing the problem of exclusion, they tend to hide or simply lament its existence. More participation in what? In flawed parties and electoral processes? In governments resulting from spurious coalitions? In access to media controlled by a few groups? In representative processes specialised in demobilising, fragmenting and deferring demands, and in the indeterminacy of time?

More participation may paradoxically result in the opposite, hence the expansion of forms of mobilisation (such as social movements) and of recipients of the themes (the courts) as more and more communicative addresses, with their own values and structural specificities capable of generating alternatives. More citizenship? Which one? The one that legalises and deepens differences? The one that creates dependencies in relation to government programs? The one that includes the citizen in scrapped schools? It is clear that the production of exclusions cannot be attributed to only one subsystem. Nor is there a system responsible for being the super controller of inclusions and exclusions, even if certain professional sectors have this illusion (just think of some of the Public Prosecutor's Office initiatives in countries like Brazil). The great themes provoke adhesion and applause. Zero hunger, zero pollution: is anyone against these? Of course not. However, an attentive and critical look at social policy selections – access to housing and real estate credit, agrarian reform, university access programs, social assistance, healthcare – reveals that inclusion in a policy may represent exclusion from it or from other policies. More investment in housing in the city may imply less money for land reform. Mortgage credit for those who have up to three income salaries may represent exclusion of those who earn four salaries. In other words: the 'inclusion'/'exclusion' difference is resistant and tends to reappear under various guises, including in the clothes of inclusion policies.

Social movements and the legal system also often operate on this shaky terrain: one achievement can generate several other unexpected others. Would people be concerned about access to justice if participation worked, citizenship were effective and public policies were responsive, without the paradoxes indicated? Why would collectivities mobilise for access to rights if the systems of functions operated in such a way as not to produce or distribute risk and indeterminacy? Would there be manifestations of protest in an imaginary world, in the idyllic society of stability of ideal conditions (economists would invoke the phrase 'coeteris paribus', jurists the dictum *pacta sunt servanda*', while intellectuals less affectionate for the practice of the functional systems would appeal to more noble and grandiose values)?

But none of this occurs: paradoxes are constitutive of communication systems; systems are unstable by definition; it would be too risky to imagine a society that takes no risk. Given these conditions, it would remain, as a last resort, to knock on the doors of the courts. More access to justice and yes, the virtuous cycle would be restored: participation, citizenship and public policies would be fulfilled promises. However, the paradoxes are reproduced: courts rehearse more rigorously the application of environmental law yet deforestation does not decrease. A courageous judicial measure in any area of public interest animates several possible plaintiffs, and this initiative congests the forums. The medicines granted in isolated cases make health policy impossible, and at the same time the judicialisation of this issue weakens the policy. In all these situations the paradoxes of modern society emerge. Pessimism? Disenchantment? Or do these situations not occur? Ignoring them may not be the best option for social movements.

In the face of so many problems, in regions of world society such as Latin America and specifically Brazil, inclusion and exclusion seem to gain different outlines. Luhmann (2013: 26), for example, mentions the hypothesis that the binomial 'inclusion'/'exclusion' may act in a kind of meta-code, linked to a 'secondary system of functions', which deals with the effects of exclusion produced by the systems of functions. Compensatory programmes, aid for development, international solidarity, popular legal assistance and the community economy, for example, would be manifestations of this precarious system in gestation. What would be at stake would not be benevolence, charity or old paternalism. Behind these initiatives, would there be attempts at structural change?

In a society differentiated into partial systems, integration does not mean positive value, something static, unity, obedience or relationship between the parts and the whole. Integration is the reciprocal reduction of the degrees of freedom of system selections. Integration is mutual respect between partial systems. In the context of systemic differentiation, each transformation of a partial system is, simultaneously, transformation of the environment of the other systems. A social system is always the environment for the other systems. In these terms, the internal transformation of one system affects the environment of all other systems. This requires mobility and dynamism of reciprocal adjustments. From the internal perspective of the systems, differentiation produces indeterminacy within them and the capacity for adjustment between them. Differentiation is the formation of systems within systems. The plurality of systems requires reactions. Integration consists of taking advantage of these internal indeterminacies and dynamism in reaction to environmental pressures. This requires increasing the independence of systems (protections that maintain their communicative operations) and, paradoxically, also increasing dependence on other systems, that is, sensitivity to the environment (Luhmann and De Giorgi 1995: 248–253).

Integration between partial systems triggers diverse causal relationships, depending on the system taken as reference. A judicial decision can have distinct and unexpected impacts on educational, scientific or family systems. Here are the problems and opportunities of integration: indeterminacy within systems. Taking advantage of these opportunities may increase or limit structural developments, may occur in a climate of cooperation or conflict. These chains of inter-systemic causal relationships have different effects, depending on the criteria of inclusion or exclusion. Integration does not occur in the same way when it comes to inclusion and exclusion. Inclusion is a selection of the system. Inclusion in one system may represent – or not – inclusion in others as well. However, when we speak of exclusion – or inclusion by 'secondary systems', 'parasitic inclusion networks', 'deficient inclusion criteria' – the opportunity for chaining exclusions into several other systems is greater. There is a reinforcing effect of exclusions (De Giorgi 1992, 1998).

Integration is related to these dynamic and changeable chains of adjustment to the indeterminacies of each system. Thus, the more exclusion, the more links that go through and spread to other systems: the greater the integration. 'Exclusion integrates much more strongly than inclusion', says Luhmann (2013: 25). As functional systems exclude, it is precisely exclusion that demands and produces stronger integration. Exclusion from one system communicates immediately to others: it promotes integration. It is contagious. Systems, from the perspective adopted here, are not actions: they are systems of communication. Therefore, integration and disintegration, inclusion and exclusion – as well as, within society, system and environment or, in terms of observation theory, first- and second-order observation – should be understood in terms of communication systems. The plurality of systems in a society differentiated by functions means that the regulation of inclusion is done in a fragmented way and adjusted to each system. Integration, inclusion and universal regulation – seen from this communicative perspective – have nothing to do with the idea of consensus among individuals in the public sphere for the formation of public opinion or the construction of legitimacy. Rather, the opposite: they call attention to the relevant fact, constitutive of modernity, that the negative opposites – disintegration, exclusion and partial regulation – must be observed and better understood conceptually.

It is trivial to perceive that functionally differentiated societies produce inequalities in the distribution of goods, asymmetry in the allocation of risks and imbalances in attempts at inclusion. An automatic and simplistic re-action is to criticise society: it is the fault of others! As if the critics, be they social movements, critical or alternative jurists or progressive intellectuals, did not take part in it. Less trivial is to seek instruments that describe ex-clusion and the structural effects of functional differentiation – in fact, to do so would require much more radical reactions than moaning, solemn de-clarations of solidarity and indignant denunciations, however important they may be. Inclusion and integration take place in a context of instability: they are not invariably positive values, much less unambiguous. Inclusion is an offer of possibilities (and also of restrictions): it involves choices in si-tuations with structural limits. These selections are, in general, ambiguous and bivalent. Morals, ethics, consensus, solidarity, beyond rhetorical com-fort and the aggregation of sympathy, are of little use for understanding the phenomenon (Corsi 1993: 279), can parasitically hide the paradoxes of in-clusion in poly-contextural situations (Luhmann 1998: 180) and act as ob-stacles to the self-reference of systems.

Social movements are always faced with these dilemmas. Criticism of society exposes them to choice. In the search for inclusion, they can find the opposite: reinforcing exclusion. But if in fact they are exposed to choices, they can also find what they seek. Whatever the point of arrival, new cycles of delimited selections are immediately reopened. This is also called con-tingency and complexity.

The distinction between inclusion and exclusion takes place within so-ciety. Communication systems observe, indicate, exclude and include. Differentiation is the formation of systems based on exclusions and inclu-sions. For a system, to include means to exclude, and to exclude something also involves including what is not left out. However, 'parasitic orders' may condition inclusion by cross-cutting criteria to functional systems – as seems to occur in some regions. Relationships of kinship, friendship, clientage, bossism/mandonism (*mandonismo*), *coronelismo*, patronage, mutual fa-vouritism, personality cult, stardom, careerism, charisma, informality, cor-diality and other well-known interactions between us dictate the pace of the choices of inclusion in the functional systems. In these cases, the functioning of the systems is compromised, communication is blocked and the possibilities of change and variation are removed. Even when designated under the digital name of networks, these practices continue to demand the same: hyper-integration among the functional systems of society.

Integrationist and disintegrationist social movements

In place of the individual actor or right holder – the militant or protester of the social movement or the legal professional (judge, lawyer, prosecutor or even party) – it is admitted by the methodology of systems theory that self-reference is the empirical property of communication systems themselves, not the construction of a subject observing them from outside. Social movements and law are communication systems, described, observed and produced through communications.

Communications are time-related events. They are mainly linked to two types of expectations or functional reactions over time: (1) adaptive reactions, tending to the assimilation of facts and learning that facilitate reversals, adjustments or compliance with disappointments; (2) reactions of non-conformity with what has occurred, tending to the non-acceptance of facts and the maintenance of the initial content of the promise, adjustment or rule. Of course, the law has little relation with the first reactions and very much with the others. Luhmann (2014) calls the former cognitive expectations and the latter normative expectations. Functionally, some are reviewed and others are kept intransigently over time. Despite the frustration of expectation, law makes its temporal maintenance possible and may eventually make its original realisation possible.

Both the legal system and social movements are systems that link normative expectations. But there is an important difference. If it is true that all normative expectations imply a lack of adaptation to facts, it is not correct that all normative expectations enjoy legal recognition. The normative expectations processed by the law are linked to limits of normative variety (constitutionality, legality, procedure and institutionality of decision-making powers), specific communicative codification (legal/illegal) and conditional-type communication programmes (hypothesis/consequence; if/then; illicit/sanction) that allow them to find in the legal system – and only in it – the communicative links capable of treating them functionally. Hence the function of law: congruent generalisation of normative expectations (Luhmann 2014).

Social movements also react to disappointments and do not accept the facts. They protest because they are negatively affected by the facts. They do not adapt, do not learn and are not willing to assimilate decisions – including legal ones – that are supposed to discriminate against them, harm them or exclude them from the distribution of social resources. These reactions may or may not characterise normative expectations. They are often clearly congruently generalised normative expectations that are faced with incomplete, insufficient or unattainable realisation. None of this detracts from the intrinsic legal nature of expectation. It only reveals serious problems of internal operationalisation of the legal system. For example, there is protest about the ineffectiveness of unquestionably valid rights. Some will assert an alternative or original interpretation of controversial, ambiguous claims, situated in an area of a penumbra of meaning. Movements also object to the revocation of valid rights which are incompatible with the law. In all these situations, when the protest of the social movements is taken to the courts, it is submitted to the temporal, social and material demands of judicial procedure. The participation of those affected must follow the ritual of producing rational evidence and arguments.

The case of the residents of Vila Itororó, on the outskirts of the city of São Paulo, illustrates these aspects. Seventy low-income families organised in an association of residents live in the architectural complex of the village, built in the 1920s and tumbled a few years ago. They stopped paying rent after the owner abandoned the property. Most of the families have lived in the village for over 30 years. Faced with the project of the city hall of São Paulo to create a cultural center with bars and restaurants on the site (the expulsion and eviction of residents is a direct consequence of the intervention), they filed a special action for collective usucapion , based on the City Statute (a federal statute regulating urban planning) and on constitutional law. Judicial decisions have disregarded the legal provisions of the City Statute, a recent and specific legislation for urban issues, initially little known and applied by the courts. In this case, the normative expectations find an obstacle in the difficulty the legal system has in following the variability of the law and the collective demand. In this case, the movement does not postulate an original interpretation. It claims only compliance with the law and recognition of the right. It thus seeks the recognition and cooperation of the legal system. At the same time, in this case the negatives of the courts caused disappointment and disbelief in the law. If at the beginning of the process the residents saw the legal system as an arena for the mobilisation of the law, after successive negatives they began to see City Hall and the judiciary as adversaries. The demand for housing brought to the legal system also changed the organisation of the residents. Its internal articulation followed the rhythm of the judicial process, and each new decision generated urgent meetings and moments of concentrated mobilisation. As a result of the lawsuits, the 70 families organised themselves into a formal residents' association and began to make contact with other movements that also fight for housing in the Bela Vista region of São Paulo city.

There are moments, however, when the protest is directed against a right that is valid and compatible with the legal system, in the name of a right that is not yet recognised or based on elements that are foreign to communications recognisable by the legal system. In such cases, social movements have little chance of judicial support. There is no normative expectation in the legal sense and no dialogue or reciprocity of communication between the social movement and the legal system. These are cases of closure of participation: 'we' (the protest movement) on the one hand and 'they' (society, the legal system and the courts) on the other. The communication available is that of reciprocal disqualification: for social movements, it is up to them to ride morally against functional systems or against the law; for the legal system, it remains to classify as inept, unreasonable and impossible the pretension brought in the face of a judge. No agreement is possible. The one side neither invites nor is invited by the other.

In the communication process it is always possible to say yes or no. Social movements can do both. They gain unity and internal consistency when they say no to society. They depend on that cohesion. Since they operate free from constraints or compromises with the functional systems and alienated from decision-making processes, they take advantage of the legal system's guarantees of freedom, in the clothing of the right to protest. However, society and its law need not accept the no from social movements, especially if the no is directed against valid law. Courts can also answer yes or no to claims, with the obvious difference in consequences. The addressees and those affected by final judicial decisions have no alternatives left, regardless of the quality or intensity of support or protest made. The amount of consensus assumed within social movements is infinitely greater than that expected from the courts or in relation to the law in general.

Communications structured by functional systems, ie, actions guided by stimuli of consolidated expectations, presuppose interactions and formal organisations with normally larger decision-making roles, and are therefore alien to social movements. Of course, face-to-face interaction systems and decision centers also exist in social movements. However, these are not the main features of protest-oriented communication systems. For politics, economy and law, the structuring of expectations offers other possibilities. Take, for instance, the participation of those affected. Contractual relations mark economic life. Contracts consolidate expectations, formalise consensus and constitute the participation of those involved in the formation, implementation, continuity and extinction of the adjustment (Macaulay 1963). The same can be said of the political-electoral process: voting guarantees the space for participation. The judicial process is not different. Presenting evidence, reasons and arguments, launching reasoned decisions, receiving and processing appeals – the steps of the judicial process guarantee the participation of those affected, including third parties (Fuller 1965).

Nothing prevents social movements – once structured as organisational systems – from signing contracts, assuming an electoral position or taking legal action. When they promote communications of this kind, they act as the generality of people and on the basis of available structures. They can also make all these actions forms of protest: contracts to be violated, protest votes or lawsuits as a mere form of stirring up issues. However, protest against society opposes those affected and decision makers. 'We do not participate in making the decision and we do not recognise it', protest movements say. In these cases, participation takes place outside the structures of consolidated, institutionalised expectations. It is about participation that denounces the lack of participation in the bodies that decide and calls for new forms of participation.

Unlike what happens in a contract, election or procedural dispute, the mode of participation of those affected who militate in social movements is paradoxical: they mobilise participation against decisions in which they did not participate. Decisions reveal that the courts in São Paulo have recognised the need for effective participation of social movements in hearings and consultations regarding transformations and interventions in the city. The great mobilisation against the revision of the master plan of the city of São Paulo has been translated into legal terms as a violation of the principle of democratic and participatory management of cities foreseen in the City Statute, a federal law. The hearings were cancelled by the judiciary, which demanded greater transparency and the creation of effective conditions for participation by the public administration. The lack of participation in many urban restructuring operations was also denounced. Also in this case, the legal system was receptive to the demands of social movements, recognising them as valid and necessary interlocutors so that major interventions in the city can be endowed with legality and legitimacy. In both cases, the legal system observes social movements as a demand for the functioning of the law itself.

Functional systems such as the law process a great number of communications and, therefore, of possibilities of action, superior to their capacity of implementing alternatives. This makes instability a constant of these systems. Several selections are always possible. Among them, some will be made, others not. Whoever receives the no hardly withdraws applause or reasonably conforms to the negative. They usually have arguments as good as those fought by the contenders. In the case of the legal system, this applies to those who seek it: both protests against society and the reactions of society to those who protest are exposed to positive or negative answers to the question 'Is it in accordance with the law?'

There is an important horison of unease. In difficult cases, where do you draw the rationale for decisions? Justice, morality, reason, principles and values dawn 'on the waiting list', as Luhmann ironically states (1996b: 160). In what way can the specificity of legal techniques help social movements? Without going into the merits of the themes and arguments, in thesis the responses of the legal system to the *quaestio juris* focus on the framing of cases (excess of possibilities), on normative structures and, from then on, on the typical operation of the system – producing or modifying the structure to produce redundancy or variation in an incessant and dynamic way.

Social movements can be divided into at least two large groups. One of them – which systems theory (Luhmann 1996a) calls 'protest movements' and to which it gives greater attention – seeks distance from society. Protest movements build their condition as communication systems, that is, they differentiate themselves from the environment by selecting a theme. Protest concentrates on a theme: the theme, together with the protest orientation, delimits and distinguishes the set of communications belonging or not to the system. The other group of social movements, more comprehensive and, in fact, unexplored by systems theory, has characteristics quite similar to those of the protest movements. But it also reveals differences that cannot be neglected. Here they will be called 'disintegration movements'. They also fight against systems of function, such as law, politics, economy or education. They point out their limits. They denounce transversality, corruption and the reinforcement of asymmetries that sequentially chain deficient exclusions and inclusions.

The concept of disintegration movements bridges the gap in the construction of systems theory. Inclusion, for Luhmann (1998, 2013: 16–27, 1998) and De Giorgi (1992, 1996), is the way society treats human minds and bodies as persons. Functional systems regulate inclusion: they observe persons in system communications. Partial or functional systems demarcate communicative environments in which people can act according to expectations recognised and stabilised by the systems. On the other hand, exclusion is synonymous with communicative disability: not being recognised as a participant in society. In the place of a person (ie, a communicative mark), there lie simply bodies (Luhmann 1998: 193)! Exclusion is violence, inefficiency of systems, indifference to the law, absence of conditions to take part in the communications constitutive of society. Inclusion is the internal, positive and preferential side of form. The external, negative and unspecified side is exclusion.

The theoretical effort of Luhmann and De Giorgi (1995) was directed toward enriching the theory of social differentiation. It points to the limits of typical forms of differentiation: stratificatory and functional. Social movements have in exclusion a motto for denunciations and attacks against the functionally differentiated society. They claim the word. They want to be included, preferably in a regenerated society, far from the pathologies of the present one. But the issue here is not people, subjects, individuals or bodies. It is in the collectivities, in the groups, in the communicative blocks, not in the frames of interactions. Systems theory can take new steps if it incorporates the arsenal of potentialities of the concepts of integration, disintegration, inclusion, exclusion and networks of inclusion in order to redraw social movements now.

The suggested difference distinguishes two types of social movements: protest movements, which could well be called parasitic systems of collective integration, corrupt systems of function; in contrast to this logic, movements of collective disintegration, which could well be called parasitic systems of disintegration, use functional systems to reconfigure, extend and restore the systems.

It is necessary to deepen and test the construction. In any case, it can be anticipated that the links of these two types of social movements with the legal system and the courts – systems and organisations that interest us in this work, not excluding analogous developments in other systems of functions – are completely different. Protest movements do not seek out the courts to enforce normative expectations. On the contrary: they do not believe in cognitive expectations or normative expectations. They feed 're-active' expectations. They disregard the others against whom they protest. It is not about understanding, negotiating or reflecting on functional systems. The protest is seen as morally superior to majorities and minorities, to the legal or illegal and to other codes of functional systems. They defend society from its functional systems: against the political system, against the legal system. At most, they make tactical and disdainful use of the functional systems. They are more interested in exposing the wounds of the systems than in treating them. The constitution itself is now seen as a provocation to provoke, as a cause for protest. These movements use one system to violate the other: they politicise courts; they judicialise politics.

Disintegration movements also protest. They do not want courts to act politically to disrespect their rights. They do not expect their issues to be recognised as valid because of friendship networks, personal bonds, idiosyncratic professional organisations that give them benevolence. They believe in the constitution, naive as this may seem. They do not see it as a provocation: they invoke it with the expectation of confirming what is expected of the law. In regions that Luhmann (2013: 127–131) calls 'developing' countries, social movements are of both types. It is worth pursuing and deepening this distinction.

The idea that people are treated, in some contexts, not as people but as bodies, is controversial and debatable. That this should occur and may involve significant portions of the population is not discarded. If it is correct that including can mean excluding, the opposite is also possible. Even in situations of extreme exclusion, some kind of inclusion always exists. The favelas of the big Brazilian cities – which Luhmann probably knew more from hearing about than empirically – are spaces that can only contain discouraging descriptions: a world of excluded people. But imagining them to be mere repositories of bodies is at an enormous distance. They are everything but that. The commitment to be heard, the difficulty of mobilising resources, the manipulation of participation, the inaccessibility to public services, the dependence on charity, all this is well known. However, when we talk about social movements – of protest or of disintegration – what we have in mind are communicative ensembles that seek conflict or cooperation, ie, that nurture expectations in relation to society. Partners or adversaries, critics or co-opted, social movements presuppose people, not bodies. Just think, among so many other Brazilian examples, of the case of the movement of residents of one of the largest favelas in the city of São Paulo,

Paraisópolis. The residents protest and mobilise the right to regularise the situation of their homes. Although they have a support network and specialised legal advice, the affected people themselves carry out communications oriented to protest. Paraisópolis is an example of a network of social movements and non-governmental organisations. It is worth highlighting the diversity of protests and themes of social movements in Paraisópolis: against violence, for women's rights, for the freedom of communication (radio and community press) and other forms of building communication systems far from the mere deposit of bodies.

First of all, what are social movements? In general, they are communication systems. In itself, this shows that they are not about bodies, biological or psychic systems, ie, the external environment of society. Unlike functional systems, though – economic, political, legal, scientific and others analysed in detail by Luhmann – social movements do not have a specialised, infungible, codified and programmed social function by binary schemas internal to the system. They are not functional systems. This does not mean that they are not autopoietic systems, ie, communication systems that produce and organise internally the elements and operations necessary for their reproduction and, from there, differentiate themselves from the environment. Social movements have a form; like every form, they have two sides: the inner side, constituted by the communications of those who protest, of those who do not conform, do not accept changes and react to them or propose and wait for them; and the outer side, against which they protest, constituted by functional and organisational systems of society questioned by the social movements. Society has instances and organisations that produce decisions. Social movements feel affected by these decisions. They imagine not having taken part in them. They complain. In the communicative way of framing the complaints, one can find the difference between protest movements and disintegration movements.

Systems of functions select alternatives. They produce denials. The number of communicative possibilities denied is invariably higher than those activated. Saying yes – as obvious and paradoxical as it may be – always implies saying no. Among other reasons, consensus is scarce. There are always good reasons for yes and no. It is illusory to believe that it is a problem of rationality that can easily be equated with the help of logical knowledge and available experiences. The no of functional systems is opposed to the no of social movements. Just as inclusion and exclusion are operations internal to society, systems of functions and social movements are also operations of communication internal to society. Bodies do not communicate, do not say no, let alone organise themselves into communicative systems formed around themes and alignments contrary to the no. Social movements do that. The internal side of the form 'social movements' is a no. They react to the external side of the form: from the perspective of the social movements, a no from society. On the side of social movements, the no of those who protest and are affected by decisions; on the functional systems' side, the choice (the yes) of who decides.

Social movements are not face-to-face interactions nor formal organisations. They presuppose interactions and organisations but do not extract their main sociological characteristics from these elements. Social movements leave out those who do not protest. Here there is a very important systemic difference between social movements and functional systems. Law, economics and politics work within the limits of operative schematics that allow them to process issues and allocate values based on specific programmes. For example, valid rules, prices and government plans allow for observations and operations that reflect on conditions internal to the respective systems (according to/not conforming to the law, in relation to the law; being/not being able to pay, for the economy; participating in the government/making opposition, in politics). Social movements lack an analogous internal reflexive mechanism. The functions are formed by values (licit, having and government, for example) and countervalues (illicit, not having and opposition) internal to the systems. These binaries stabilise communicative structures that delimit the scope and enable operationality and control of decisions. They impose limits on the freedom of systems. In the case of the legal system, the most important link lies in the normative validity offered by laws and precedents. Social movements do not have negative values or internal countervalues that stabilise criteria of repetition or variation of structures and allow them to self-observe their operations. They live on hetero-observations: references to the external side of social movements.

When the theories of law, economics or politics reflect on the operations of their respective systems, they construct self-descriptions of systems that cannot ignore the countervalue. They observe the paradoxical unity of internal and constitutive differences of systems (the binary schemas of codes). To what reflexive differences can the theory of social movements be reported? They are not internal to the communication system. They describe the unity between social movements and society. In this sense, social movements are a form of society's self-description which reacts to problems created by social differentiation. The theory of social movements is a theory of society.

Systems of functions operate in a closed mode because of the type of code and programmes they use. Social movements do not have this structure. The 'protest'/'theme' difference does not have the force of the 'code'/'program' difference. Functional systems also have means of communication that circulate throughout the system and condense into forms. Validity (law), currency (economy) and power (politics) are communicative symbols that transit throughout the systems and crystallise into forms. Social movements have an analogous symbol: themes, combined with the general attitude toward complaint. They are reservoirs of dissatisfaction with the weaknesses and negative consequences of modern society. There are no social movements – either of protest or of disintegration – with a general orientation toward satisfaction. Social movements do not align themselves with the class of the contented. Here, Pollyanna has no place. It is one thing to be dissatisfied and to use the system, to take advantage of its weaknesses, to stimulate its variability, to seek its change; another thing, quite different, is to take dissatisfaction to the extreme: to corrupt the systemic logic, to insist on impasse, to block the chain of communications. In the first case, one can speak of a creative use of functional systems; in the second, a destructive, unbelieving or uncompromising use of the systems of functions. In the first group we find disintegration movements: they insist on the use of functional systems. In the second are protest movements: they provoke the systems as a sign of rejection.

What functional systems do for society, only they are capable of doing. No other form of communication replaces or is interchangeable with legal, economic or political communication. This degree of specification does not occur with social movement systems. Dissatisfaction exists everywhere in the interactions of everyday life. They do not characterise social movements, but show how difficult it is to demarcate them. Moreover, social movements are not interactions. For the effects of the description sought here, psychological or emotional aspects of the participants or sympathisers of the movements are also irrelevant. These motives are unfathomable, at least from a sociological point of view. The question, therefore, is not objective dissatisfaction, the emotion of the adherents or the psychology of the masses, as it was imagined in the past. The question is to recognise a system of communication, not a psychic system. Functional differentiation is a way of organising communication. Reservoirs of dissatisfaction are in society as a whole, not just in social movements.

Social movements unfold in all areas of society. Where there is criticism of society, there is a high probability of social movements. In some functional systems, social movements seem especially active. Health care, education and law – they are not the only ones, but they deserve to be highlighted – exemplify the phenomenon. Why? Not, of course, for a hierarchical reason. Education is not above religion. Law is not above economics. Health care is not above family. When it comes to functional systems, there is no before and after, superior and inferior, general and special. That goes for the old theory of legal interpretation, or at least it did. A functionally differentiated society operates its systems simultaneously (ie, without before or after), without a vertex (ie, without superior or inferior) and without a management center (ie, without general and special). It operates on the basis of differences. Differences are not precedents, hierarchies or fundamentals. They are what they are: differences. These differences produce reactions. Among the most important are social movements.

Social movements and legal interpretation

The difference between integration movements and disintegration movements can be drawn from two premises typical of the systemic-theoretical approach to social movements. It is based on the assumption that society is formed by communications (or communication systems) – not by individual or collective actors – and that these communications are functionally differentiated, organised into self-referential systems. Therefore, if social movements criticise society, they can only be addressed to the partial systems that make up the functionally differentiated society. Social movements install themselves in the systems of function and establish modes of co-existence with the operations of functional systems in two ways. It is from this binary that the difference between movements of integration and movements of disintegration can be clarified. It is not possible, in this work, to develop the paradoxes of this idea in the fields of economy, politics and other systems of function. Within the legal system, taken as the focus of this chapter, this distinction is clear.

Integration movements seek to react to the functionally differentiated society by saying no to partial systems. They adopt the position of the excluded third. They do not submit themselves to the binary schematics of the partial systems. Taking the legal system as a reference, they criticise the limitations and perversions of the 'lawful'/'unlawful' code. They try to break these structural ties and integrate the communications of the legal system with other possibilities of communication. They intend to promote the coupling among communications from different systems or, better said, to ignore these differences and thus block the communication circuit of functional systems. Two forms of parasitic communication are introduced into the systems of functions with these objectives: the theme of attacking internal inequality and the theme of criticising external imbalances. An egalitarian and balanced society would be the negation of the functionally differentiated society. These are two utopian objectives. They serve as an unfolding of the real world in an idealised world, in which understanding among people, cooperation based on values and rupture of the limits of capitalist society present themselves as alternatives. Balance and equality are glimpsed as points of arrival but are not problematic as starting points for new imbalances and new differences. The values of equality and balance are explained by themselves.

The egalitarian and environmentalist guidelines (in terms of the general balance of society) enjoy a great advantage: disengagement with the real society at the level of operational systems or decisions. This disengagement is always illusory. Protesting involves the right to protest, even against the current law itself. In this sense, social movements are social systems parasitic to the legal system. They introduce their themes, demand resources from the host system, but do not commit themselves to the guest. The parasite is not a foundation, nor does it intend to replace the system. But it is capable of provoking, irritating and obtaining reactions from the guest system.

The metaphor of the parasite (Serres 1982) pre-supposes systems in operation. In the case of the legal system, communication varies between two poles – legal/illegal, valid/invalid – and outside this polarity is not capable of self-reproducing. The parasite exploits this binarism. In the case of integration movements, they posit themselves as the observer external to duality but internalised by the system. Their thematic proposals are utopian, difficult to process, in a word: indigestible. But they are not necessarily negative. The legal system, liking or disliking the themes of protest and the behavior of the parasite, must react to them. The instability typical of society and proper to the specific variability of the legal system has, in both topics, warning signs, stimuli for variation, engines that activate new stages of social complexity.

The themes are also potentially disorientating for the legal system. They favor the loss of focus on the specific function of the system and the ambition to go beyond the operational limits of the law. Encouraged by the themes, the legal system can react by breaking down boundaries. More than the guardian of the law of society – which is a lot – it becomes the guardian of society itself, which is too much. As if it were not enough to be equipped to respond to the economic, political, scientific and other challenges of the countless themes that arise from the expectations of equality and balance, the networks of social movements or 'the society of social movements' draw from the two inexhaustible sources of protest (Diani and McAdam 2003; Mosca 2007). Trying to face all this unstructured complexity, the legal system would lose the capacity to perform its own function. It would abandon opportunities to review its premises, update its operations and produce new events and information. In the optimistic expectation of extracting the maximum from the law by referring its operations out of the system, the legal system would make impossible the enormous arsenal of tools available to extract the maximum from the law by referring to the law itself. It is legally that the law modifies the law. It is legally that the law is part of differentiated society. Law can, for instance, guarantee compensation for dismissal but not maintenance of the worker's living conditions. The imposition of goals and purposes alien to the operation of the law may corrupt the 'lawful'/'unlawful' code and compromise the functional autonomy of the legal system. The inability of the law to determine the future becomes more evident when it is observed as a non-trivial machine. Non-trivial machines elaborate their own internal states. Therefore, they are not reliable for external claims of control and regulation (von Foerster 1984). In law, it is legally that social movements can aspire to any gain.

Otherwise, it is better to act politically or economically in politics or in economy. The opposite, acting politically or economically in the law, comes up against countless disadvantages, not only legal but also political and economic ones. Integration movements try to do this with themes: overlap and confuse law, politics and economy. Hence the transversality of their operation.

In contexts of high social exclusion, such as Brazil, the calls for integration are immense. From the sociological point of view, systems theory describes the phenomenon of integration as resulting from a chain of exclusions – as much as this may surprise sociologists who, according to the tradition inaugurated by Durkheim and consolidated by Parsons, associate this concept with positive representations. Those who are excluded from one system are also excluded from the others, which means that one of the possible reactions of social movements is widespread criticism or rejection of functional systems. This brings about the immobilisation of functional systems and tends to amplify exclusions and maximise differences (Luhmann 2009).

Integration movements are introduced into functional systems, forcing transverse connections between the legal system and the other functional systems. They react to the deficient functioning of the functional systems by deepening the deficiencies and compromising even more their weaknesses.

Some systems theorists have developed the concept of 'exclusion networks' (Corsi 1998a) to describe chains of reciprocity, friendship nets and exchanges of favours which, in the clothing of the functional systems and their decision-making organisations, transfer the seat of decision to communicative connections which also break or weaken the functional systems, without contestation to their clothing. These networks do not have the character of direct contestation to the functional systems, but also promote transverse connections which parasitically use the opportunities offered by the functional systems to look for gaps, shortcuts or ways out.

Disintegration movements also react to malfunctions of partial systems. Within the legal system, they introduce issues that promote necessary and processable instabilities under the binary coding of law, whereas integration movements make use of a communicative strategy aimed at blocking the system or merely self-irritating the law. Given the difficulties of response, comprehensiveness and unrealism of the pretensions of equality and balance that go beyond the limits of the legal system, integration movements tend to introduce more and more instability into the legal system. Inequalities and imbalances are introduced into the system under double wrapping: conflicts have a negative or positive meaning. They represent opportunities for change that allow for the anticipation and the legal conditioning of conflicts. Procedures, in turn, authorise processes of communicative restructuring of expectations. Inequalities and imbalances are thus introduced into the legal system in the form of proceduralised conflicts.

While integration movements attack and protect themselves from functional systems such as the law, disintegration movements make use of the legal system. Conflict is present in both forms of social movements. In the first case – integration – what is at stake are the limits of functional systems, pressured by demands for equality and balance. In the second case, the communicative integration of the conflicting parties – the double contingency of denials between the contenders – tends to be converted into procedures which tame the conflict and re-educate the expectations of the antagonists. Law plays a role in immunising society from conflicts, and thus also social movements in the face of their internal conflicts.

Social movements that introduce their orientation toward conflict into the legal system without expectations of learning, dealing with and restructuring conflicts – ie, without proceduralising them – refute the law. They do not want to know whether what they do or postulate is legal or illegal, allowed or forbidden. They want much more: equality and balance that the law cannot guarantee. The protest points to the overcoming of functional systems and to systemic hyper-integration: ie, de-differentiation. Conflicts are disguised as protest against society.

Social movements of disintegration introduce conflicts into the legal system in the form of normative legal expectations. They submit themselves to the restructuring of expectations typical of judicial procedures. They do not refute the law. They want to confirm whether their claims are permitted or forbidden, licit or illicit, constitutional or unconstitutional. They are communication systems that convert conflicts into proceedings. They expect equality before the law and due process, respect for differences and alternation between redundancy and variation. All this requires a legal system that is operationally closed and cognitively open, resistant to the pressures contrary to functional differentiation, but with high sensitivity to social conflict.

Functional systems operate within limited margins of choice. They behave endlessly according to communication themes, but they are not effective in dealing with these themes outside their mechanisms of coding, specific progra199mmes and communicative engagements of operations and observations internal to the system itself. Disintegration movements (such as the movement of landless people in Brazil – see, eg, Losano 2007) are aware of these differences. They use the functional systems – in the case we are interested in, the law – according to the elements of the system. On the tracks of the binary coding of the law and its limited margins of choice, they seek to produce information. On the reverse side, integration movements are hostile to binary coding. They are derailed trains. In Luhmann's mythological and fabular language (1996a: 175–200), they 'morally ride wild horses'. Without reins or halters in the corners of society: in the place of information, there is noise and irritation of society by society.

Saying that integration movements build themes based on the values of equality and balance, and that these themes would be utopian, can lead to serious misunderstandings if the terms are not well explained. In the usual language, no one doubts that most regions of world society are marked by inequalities and imbalances. There is unanimity on this. Everyone too, at least rhetorically, is in favour of promoting equality and balance. It is not only social movements of integration that elaborate on these issues. In a society criticised for being unequal and unbalanced, the greatest beneficiaries of these distortions usually subscribe to the waiting lists against these problems previously denied to those affected by the imbalances. Recurrent reforms in functional systems are nothing more than attempts at equalisation and rebalancing. In most cases, they are also the starting point for further reforms. Tax reforms and procedural law reforms are reforms that fuel new reforms. Reforms always come, go and are reborn in self-referential terms and in hetero-referential clothes. They present themselves to reform society and reform only the last reform of the system of reference. Social movements protest against functional systems and their reforms in the name of equality and balance, but the new measures inevitably generate new inequalities and imbalances (on reforms, see, eg, Corsi 1998b).

Nothing against equality and balance, therefore. However, no one imagines that a legal principle such as equality can serve or aim to eliminate any possibility of difference. It serves the exact opposite. Everyone is equal before the law. Because of that, it can be said that some pay more taxes than others, that the majority can make decisions contrary to the minority, that owners can exclude non-owners. To say that everyone has equal access to justice does not mean that everyone will win their case. Equal access to credit does not guarantee equal success in financed enterprises. Equal access to school does not mean equal performance of students and teachers. It seems obvious, but the semantics of equality and balance strive to cover up the dark side of differences. There is equality only as the other side of difference with in-equality. There is balance only where instability is possible. One side is a condition and a result of the difference with the other. 'Equality'/'inequality', 'equilibrium'/'imbalance' form units of difference (De Giorgi 2006: 137): the conditions of equality and equilibrium are the same as those of inequality and imbalance. One can protest against inequality and imbalance in both ways: by observing the unity of difference or by ignoring it. The levels of observation, the structures of the system, the dynamics of expectations, the treatment of conflicts, the usefulness of procedures and, finally, the paradoxes of legal interpretation are pressured by marked differences.

Luhmannian theory makes it possible to understand how, in addition to a benefit to the political system (legitimacy), the principle of equality can be observed from the function it performs for the legal system and the courts. On the one hand, the right to equality does not mean that everyone should have the same rights. The demand for equality can, at most, nullify the force of an individual subjective right – as in the case of the right to property and the requirement that its use must fulfil a social function. On the other hand, the recourse to the Aristotelian definition of justice also seems of little use: what does it mean to 'treat the equal equally' if there are no prior criteria for comparison and selection of what is equal and what is unequal? The 'equal'/ 'unequal' scheme is arbitrarily applied. How do you select what to compare? Exactly because this scheme does not provide guidance on what is equal and what is unequal, it becomes necessary to identify and justify criteria for unequal treatment. It generates a demand for criteria not solved by the scheme itself: equality is not a criterion of equality.

According to Luhmann (2004: ch. 5), the principle of equality, from the internal point of view of the legal system, requires that the law be generalised in its temporal dimension. Courts must therefore decide independently of the time at which the decision is taken. Without this kind of generalised equality in time, judicial decisions cannot be the subject of expectations or behavioural guidance (prevention). Moreover, it would not be possible to distinguish between discretion in applying the law in similar specific cases and legitimate modification or innovation of the legal order. Therefore, it is equality that guarantees the possibility of material change in the law: more than creating the right to eternal permanence, equality allows law's alteration and positivity. In this sense, the only difference allowed is the change of the law applicable to the case. Equality is not a mechanism for neutralising differences between individuals, but a criterion for creating normative expectations (if the case is equal to another one previously decided by the court, it should also be decided in a similar way). This bond to precedent does not create certainty of equality: the judge may decide that the new case is different from the previous one. This possibility of being diverse is the essential character of positive law.

It is then possible to distinguish between the political and the legal use of the principle of equality. Politics requires that persons be treated as equals. Law requires the courts to treat cases equally. From the point of view of systems theory, the principle of equality plays an important role: it maintains the operational unity of the law and reactivates functional differentiation. In applying the 'equality'/'inequality' scheme to decide which cases should be treated as equal and which ones as unequal, the legal system needs to compare them with previous cases, and this should be done by observing only the distinctions generated within the system, without recourse to external elements. By guaranteeing the unity of the legal system, the principle of equality assures the maintenance of a potential for functional differentiation in modern society and prevents the political colonisation of the courts. This is an abstraction indifferent to material inequalities.

It is possible to criticise the Luhmannian proposal on the basis of the experience of the courts on the periphery of modernity. Luhmann presupposes constant recourse to case law to apply the principle of equality of cases. In peripheral countries, the lack of jurisprudential consistency on some issues compromises the function of creating normative expectations and maintaining the legal security typical of precedents. What, then, could be the difficulty of the legal system in dealing with the issue of equality? Why, in the face of the mobilisation of so many resources and themes of new social movements, alongside the evident inequality and notorious imbalances, does the legal treatment of these themes suffer so many limitations? Why does a cardinal principle of modern legal semantics generate so much perplexity and disenchantment?

Jurists – and, in truth, the legal system itself – observe the difference 'equality'/'inequality' as subjective right, as a technical-legal question about pretensions or, alternatively, as mere expectations directed at the political system, as a conditional programme or a finalistic programme. In general, De Giorgi (2006: 142) says, they are discrete observers. Sociologists would be much more pretentious in the matter – perhaps because they do not know, for instance, the structural limits of the internal functioning of the law, perhaps because they have a field of observation outside the law – since they would have an ambition to indicate the obstacles to overcoming inequality. The moralists' attempt would be easier: they would have principles with 'denomination of controlled and guaranteed origin' capable of preventing, on the basis of rational agreement between the parties, the increase of inequality. In terms of principles, nothing to oppose. At the level of observing the concrete operations of the company, many doubts.

Equal opportunities or equal treatment? Material or formal equality? Equal distribution of public resources or unequal distribution in support of the unequal? Equal distribution of benefits and risks? It is enough to insist reflexively on the unity of the 'equal'/'unequal' difference for paradoxes and tautologies to reveal how difficult it is to find or maintain consensus. What about sociological observation of how courts observe social movements and their attacks on inequalities, and how judges use procedures to decide conflicts of this magnitude? Let us insist on one very important point: pointing out the paradoxes of inequality/equality does not mean, under any circumstances, taking the sides of inequality. On the contrary: the fight against inequality is the least that can be expected from the horizons of the law and the inevitable path to be taken by social movements. No one needs to say this to the judge and the activist. One expects something else from academic work. Sentences and pamphlets are expected from those who decide at the center of the system and protest from its periphery: judges and social movements. From an academic work, of course, one cannot expect a better-justified sentence than that of the judge, nor can one expect a protest more inflamed than that of social movements. One can only expect modes of observation with greater structural horizons. Examining all this, for the sociology of law or for second-order observation of the operations of interpretation and application of law, has another meaning: describing the complexity of modern society.

Another recurring theme in integration movements is environmental balance. This balance must be understood in two dimensions. From the perspective of the social system, at least in the description adopted here, everything that is outside the communication process is society's environment. Balance refers, then, to the 'system'/'environment' relationship. Of course, there is no dialogue or any possible communication between society and the environment. The environment can be the subject of communication. It will never be a communicative operation. The environment does not communicate anything. This does not detract from its relevance. Without environment there is no system. Society has operational limits: it is not confused with the environment and can only treat it communicatively. Society produces 'ecological communication' (Luhmann 1989).

How to observe the 'system'/'environment' relationship and describe it from within without a managing and producing center capable of a great self-description of the society? The fragmentation caused by social differentiation does not allow the stabilisation of such a center. In place of hierarchies, strata, segments and geographical differences, multiple specialised communication systems appear. By self-observation, society is left to promote the critique of functional systems. This is what social movements do. This was the strong mark – and continues to be, although channeled and, today, added to protests against globalisation – of the environmental movement until the mid-1990s. The reactions of these movements are largely based on premises foreign to the functional systems. Hence the moralistic, fundamentalist and simplistic character of protest movements, especially the environmental one. The new social movements would divide the world into good and bad, us and them. The rhetoric of these movements would be alarmist: instead of uncertainty about actual situations, the certainty of fear: the threat of ecological disaster. With this, they would provoke the blocking of the communicative chains of the functional systems that deal with the environment. In the condition of supposed carriers of the true and good social morals, as an Olympian body and without commitment to the decisions of the functional systems, they would act as true courts of exception: they do not decide, but denounce who does. Their success would be in creating difficulties and embarrassments to functional systems, in stiffening their own dynamisms and, in this way, breaking down their boundaries and integrating them into new structures or new forms of social differentiation capable of rebalancing the 'system'/'environment' relationship. And all without a global theory that would reflect on these actions, different from what happened in a previous generation with the socialist movement.

Still with regard to equilibrium, one can also think of it as a functional system in relation to the others. Law is the environment for politics. Politics, in turn, is the environment for law. The same system, depending on the reference of observation, can be system or environment. Social integration movements criticise the negative effects of this social organisation. They seek to rebalance the relationships between systems and their environments by questioning differentiation and forcing a process of assimilation, absorption and inter-systemic catalysis.

Finally, the theme of balance also refers to aspects totally internal to the system. Within functional systems there is an environment in which the operations of the system are reproduced. The symbolically generalised means of communication circulate in this internal environment. For instance, the market is the internal environment in which currency circulates and economic communication is programmed by the pricing self-reference. Public opinion is the environment of the circulation of power and the teleological programming of politics. Codes, programmes and functions of the systems adjust to and rely on auxiliary systems and formal organisations. Despite Luhmann's dense and refined description of the legal system (1990, 2004, 2014), there is no precise indication of the symbolically generalised means of communication or the internal environment of the legal system.

Courts occupy the core of the legal system (Luhmann 2004: ch. 7). Social movements are present transversally in various functional systems, as well as conflicts and procedures. However, because of their deliberate refusal to identify themselves or the desire to replace these systems, social movements do not evoke the role of a substitute, nor the decision-making powers of formal organisations. In this sense, although often organised, they do not decide as functional systems. Within the legal system, orthogonal to its structures, programmes and operations, social movements play this parasitic role in the host system. They can compromise the function of the legal system, as seen. But they can also contaminate the very internal environment of the legal system: the area throughout which valid law circulates, subjective rights are claimed, citizenship rights are evoked, human or constitutional rights are recognised and access to justice is demanded. This dynamics can also lead to a 'hypercontact' between functional systems (Campilongo 2011). The internal environment of the legal system is related to these issues and to the rule of law. Integration movements unbalance this environment. Disintegration movements presuppose these environmental conditions. Therefore, conflicts and procedures (see Luhmann 1982, 1984) are perfectly suited to disintegration movements, although the answers of the legal system are not always those expected.

It is enough to point out that integration and disintegration movements operate on binaries also: 'balance'/'imbalance', 'equality'/'inequality', 'against'/'for the movement', 'constraint'/'freedom', 'convention'/'invention', 'regularity'/'creativity', 'rigidity'/'decomposition', 'repetition'/'improbability'. Atlan (1986) would say: between crystal and smoke. This characteristic of social movements is particularly important to understand the projection of these binaries, through the mobilisation of law, within the legal system. Variation and redundancy, ie, the dynamism and evolution of the legal system, condition the ecological relationship with social movements and are conditioned by it. Of course, this does not mean certainty as far as the results of mobilisation are concerned. The legal system can consider the claim lawful or unlawful. It can recriminate or criminalise social movements. It may not know the demands, for lack of legal basis. However, it can also offer new interpretations and broaden the horizons of possibility of legal structures.

The ecological interface between social movements and law involves at least four possibilities: cooperation, competition, predation or parasitism. Social movements of disintegration are much closer to the first type; those of integration, the remaining three. This distinction can be illustrated by at least three behaviours. The first is the attitude toward conflict. The second is the perception of the position of the courts by the social movement. The third is the expectation of judicial provision.

Position in face of conflict

With regard to conflict, disintegration movements seem to be more involved with issues of a distributive nature, eg, more or less investment in a public policy. In such conflicts, the possibility of negotiation or compromise is always open. There are real chances of variation in the legal system and construction of precedents. So-called strategic litigation is an example of this. From the point of view of procedural and extra-procedural legal techniques, the different forms of negotiation, self-composition and hearings (eg, amici curiae) illustrate the formulas for stabilising these structures and generating redundancy.

In such cases, the adaptive capacity of the legal system to non-routine issues and original communicative events expands in the form of programs with high cognitive capacity, despite – or perhaps exactly because of – the explosiveness of the conflict, considering the relevance of the themes, the intensity of the preferences of movements, the mass media impact of the issues, the complexity of the causes and the number of people involved. Hence the proliferation of agreements. In short, conflicts rooted in disintegrating social movements have a high readiness for consensus, negotiation and compromise.

The stance of integration movements toward conflict is less flexible. Claus Offe (1985: 830), referring to then-new social movements, describes this posture in terms of profound antagonisms: 'they/we, the desirable and the intolerable, victory or defeat, now or never'. What is at stake are not distributional issues or issues that can be allocated with mere criteria of economic efficiency. It is difficult for the legal system or even the other functional systems (worth mentioning politics and economics) to adapt to this dynamic of little willingness to compromise. These are conflicts driven by dissent. Ideas, truths and values, generally elevated to the altar of principles, are not the object of bargaining, do not admit gradation or price. The feminist movement does not admit the exploitation of women. The pacifist movement does not tolerate wars. The anti-nuclear movement does not tolerate atomic power plants. Cultural movements do not give up their identities. There is nothing to negotiate. The game is all or nothing. These movements have nothing to trade. That's why they are labeled as irrational or intransigent. Logically, the procedural and extra-judicial techniques of dispute composition are useless for people with interests of this kind. There is not much to expect from the behaviour of the legal system. Two possibilities remain: simply to stop protesting (which, in theory, is available to the integration movement, but at the same time hinders its legitimacy and means its end) or to maximise protest – in communicative terms, to block communication by ending the movement or radicalising the conflict. The tendency is deadlock or transgression (Foust 2010). Integration movements migrate to their own denial.

Perception of the role of courts

Another behaviour that distinguishes the legal mobilisation of disintegration and integration movements is the perception of the role of courts. For disintegration movements, the bet is that the judge is the third party, removed and impartial in relation to the conflict. A triadic relationship is established between litigants and the judge. The litigants are, in general, decision-makers and the affected. The judge is neither of them. Social movements hope to have the judge as an ally, sometimes showing that the judge too, like all of society, is affected by a perverse decision-making process.

Disintegration movements, when they mobilise the law, cannot be certain of the judicial decision. This is not different from what happens with any citizen who seeks justice. Many times, they know that the lawsuit functions as an experiment. Repeated attempts can result in condensation of legal structures. However, if defeats are stabilised without perspectives of variability, the typical advantages of legitimation by procedure are undone: temporalisation and deferment of issues (Luhmann 1984). The law will present its other face: an obstacle to social change. We must not lose sight of the fact that this is also a constitutive characteristic of the legal system. When disintegration movements grasp this, they can become disenchanted with the law and migrate to new forms of protest, such as integration movements that denounce the structural limits of the law.

Integration movements do not see the judge or the courts as reliable interlocutors. Instead of the triadic relationship, the communicative dynamic that is established is dyadic: on the one hand, the movements of integration; on the other hand, the courts and their true allies – the order of the functionally differentiated society. In this relationship no sympathy is expected from the courts. Protest is directed at the defendants and the judges. Society's law is used against law and society (Aubert 1963, 1967). The challenge to the law has an evident paradoxical dimension. Involuntarily, the protest confirms the meaning of the law. When protest movements seek to disorganise society or promote the integration and overcoming of systems that function differently and achieve this goal, they must organise themselves. Disorganisation leads to organisation. Disorder brings a new order (Estrada Saavedra 2010: 914; Freund 1994: 47). The enchainment that characterises the conflictive society of social movements, ie, the complex and functionally differentiated society, is the following: organisation that disorganises and reorganises itself. Incessant evolution and indeterminate results are the characteristics of this type of society.

Expectation in relation to the judicial decision

A third distinction concerns the social movement's expectation of a judicial decision. In disintegration movements, the game takes place according to the rules of a functionally differentiated society. In this sense, the actions of social movements are proactive, not only because of the willingness to negotiate but also because of the trust placed in the legal system and its decision-making core. It is up to the courts to give legal value to the demands of the movements. The commitment, then, is to technically substantiate the requests, observe the validity of legal norms and stimulate creative interpretations, generating variation. In short, the movements collaborate and strive to make the decision feasible. Analysed from the difference between system and environment, the relationship between the legal system and social movements of disintegration is one of cooperation and respect for the operational limits of each system.

The mobilisation of law promoted by integration movements deals with another type of reaction. Social movements react to a functionally differentiated society. The difference lies in the reaction strategy. Protest brought to justice involves a relationship (between a system and its environment) of competition, predation or parasitism. In the case of competition, integration movements go to the judiciary against functional systems. They compete with functional systems, including the legal system, not because they want to replace with identical logic the decisions of the courts. It is not a question of taking the place of the judge. The substitution imagined is not that of an alternative law, but of an alternative to the law. The ambition of substitution goes beyond the legal system (De Giorgi 1998: 149–163).

Integration movements may also adopt a predatory stance toward the judiciary. They are not, in this case, seeking alternatives to the law. They simply intend to denounce its bias and discredit its authority. The predator takes advantage of and exposes the limits of the system. It denounces its own contradictions without pretending to suppress them. The intention is simply to weaken the system. The principle-based, universalising and undetermined character of legal normativity diminishes the opportunities for this type of action. It is more strategic to use principles in the courts, even if risky, than simply to use law against law. This is indicative of the growing relevance of the legal system and the courts in modern society. The mobilisation of the law can occur through predation, cooperation or other forms. But under the structural conditions of modern law, predatory logic loses its strength. It seems outdated and incompatible with the evolution of a functionally differentiated legal system.

The parasite attaches itself to the host in order to feed on its energies. Integration movements, even though they may have an opponent in the courts, can still use the judicial arena to be heard. The question – to use, by analogy, famous economic terminology (Hirschman 1970) – is not of 'exit' from the courts or of 'loyalty' to them but simply of seeking a 'voice' option. The question boils down to addressing a protest even to those who, in the specific case, are not willing to listen but are obliged to do so (since courts cannot deny justice – prohibition of non liquet). No one can be penalised for the regular exercise of rights. The legal system offers support to the voice without charging loyalty. Seeking out the courts appears to indicate trust in the organisation as if integration movements refused to leave this institutional space. But in this case, it does not involve the slightest loyalty to judicial organisations or commitment to their decisions. It is not the hypothesis of 'widespread readiness' for decisions of uncertain content; readiness refers only to protest (Luhmann 1996a).

Concluding remarks: Fixed unrest

Social movements pursue the goal of changing the law – and in extreme cases, not only the law but society. Within the legal system, the pretension to change, as indicated, takes different orientations: (1) simply ridiculing and protesting against the law; (2) betting on the law solely because of the space it offers for its modification; (3) seeing in law a system that can stabilise expectations and promote the restructuring of expectations.

Modern constitutions offer sufficient guarantees for all three perspectives. Pluralist democracies incorporate different values in their texts. This could suggest that only hermeneutical resources external to law – metaphysical principles, human nature, social ethics, majority consensus, relevant interests etc. – would be able to fill the gaps or inconsistencies in the legal system. But this does not seem to be the case, either from a legal perspective or from the perspective of the sociological description of legal interpretation.

The search for grounds to validate interpretation external to the legal system comes up against a paradox: it is based on the assumption that the legal system is inoperative or incomplete to construct the decision. The plurality of values in the constitutions presupposes, rather, the inverse: a legal system capable of legally constructing interpretative meaning to the plurality of values. Social movements contrast the vision of one group with that of other groups. Collective conflicts and group contraposition are common and salutary. It is not ruled out that opposing groups dispute the prevalence of their interpretation of values. The criteria for resolving these controversies cannot be private. It is not a question of opting for the right of one group against the right of another. The criteria must be sought and constructed in law and by the law itself. This may imply various types of response to social movements and opposing groups. Denial or acceptance of the changes claimed in the law, ie, redundancy or variation of the system, is what is at stake. The reorientation of expectations may occur, but because of internal operations – among them interpretation – of the system itself.

Neither social movements nor anyone seeking the judiciary – nor a socio-logical observation describing the operations of legal interpretation – is in-terested in speculating on the subjective reasons or personal elocutions that lead judges to a decision. The duty to justify the decision legally immunises the judge – and indeed the parties – from attacks on the personal conditions of those involved. Except in cases where the personal aspect compromises due process – ie, illegitimacy of the party or suspicion of the judge – the operations of the legal system must be marked by the system itself. What to do in grey areas and hard cases? What about when the law does not offer answers? In such cases, the need is greater for interpretation to be found in the system and not outside. Recourse to principles is generally misleading: a hermeneutical or moral safe haven is sought in them, and what is found is generally paradoxical.

Modern society lacks stability. Social movements do not know how the courts will decide. The courts cannot control the reaction of social move-ments. It would be no different if, instead of social movements, companies or individuals sought justice. What, then, is the specificity of the presence of social movements in the courts? It inheres in at least three aspects:

  i. the magnitude, complexity and visibility of the conflict;
 ii. the intensity of the preferences of those affected: the maxim 'one for all, all for one' integrates and consolidates the social movement. This exacerbates the conflict, the uncertainty of expectations and social instability. Inevitable and positive: without instability, there is no continuity;
iii. the conspicuous function of conflicts and social movements consists in communications tending to conflict; in the incessant production of instability lies the paradoxical continuity of communication: a stable relationship with instability is established, constant instability.

All this can undermine the credibility and consistency expected from both sides: courts and social movements. It is up to the former to interpret the law and decide the conflict, and the latter to maintain the instability. Only a society in need of instability, ie, a modern society, welcomes and reproduces the relationship between law, stable expectations and conflicts. Social movements attest and guarantee the continuity of instability. Legal interpretation offers the normative correlate anchored in positive law: variety that produces redundancy, which exposes the new variability. Modern law and society would not resist a stable legal order and the absence of protest. Together, they would attest to the self-destruction of complexity.

If the relativisation of centres and hierarchies, with the change in the role of nation-states and the proliferation of sources of juridicity, did not empty constitutions, they are changes that gave them new dynamics. Hence the verbiage of attempts to reconstitute the concept: societal constitutionalism, trans-constitutionalism, inter-constitutionalism, neo-constitutionalism, new Latin American constitutionalism – and so on.

At the same time, symptomatically, social movements – often acting in the name of the realisation of constitutional rights – have undergone significant modifications. Organised in the form of large global networks online, they introduce into society unprecedented capacity for connection, processing, speed and communicative intelligence. Here too, poly-centrism and heterarchies operationalise the mobilisation of social resources: the formation of communities, energy, time and money for protests, opinions, actions ....

What explains the protests in Brazil in 2013, for example? Were we not, until that date, the emerging country, with the incorporation of millions into the market, a strong currency and full employment? President Dilma Rousseff saw, weeks before June 2013, peaks of approval from her government! In August 2016, the Senate removed her from office, in a controversial impeachment procedure based on the accusation of fiscal and budgetary manoeuvres as a 'crime of responsibility'.

We are a democracy, and that is the key to trying to understand what happened. Because of that democracy, many escaped poverty. They climbed the ladder. They wanted more. The new consumers wanted citizenship – that is, more rights. Growth generated aspirations and asymmetries. The streets protested for rights, not pennies. The price of bus tickets was one of those rights. As Manuel Castells (2015) says about social movements in the internet age, when everyone is overloaded with frustrations, they open their dream boxes.

In 2013, what where the frustrations? Seeing millions of reais transformed into tax incentives for the cheapening of individual transport on the one hand, and very little quality in public transport on the other? Millions invested in stadiums for the soccer World Cup, but hospitals relegated to neglect? Lack of resources for education, but scandals of corrupt political-entrepreneurial links exploding daily? How, in the face of these repeated situations, can one be convinced that the right belongs to everyone, not to a sector? In functioning, Brazil has not realised that it has forged mismatches, perversions and new inequalities. The lack of this perception may have led the Dilma administration and that of her successor to great misunderstandings. Inclusion, paradoxically, generated new exclusions.

What dreams? The usual ones: more humane cities, less violence; a more just and egalitarian country; sustainable development and respect for differences. The new social configuration makes clear the limits and the inability, at the pace of current politics, to have full access to well-being that translates into rights. Hence the explosion of hope: everything – frustrations and dreams – demanding changes in institutions and ways of governing. These are problems of this order, which have arisen with disparate particularities in movements such as Occupy Wall Street (USA), the Pots and Pans Revolution (Iceland) and the Outraged (Indignados; Spain).

Protests are warnings. They show that patience has limits. In recent times, demonstrators have taken to the streets of Brazil. They have exercised their freedom to demonstrate, but not always peacefully. They have reacted to stupid police violence in some cases; to political scandals in others; to corruption, to staggering judicial decisions, to regulatory demands, and so on, almost incessantly. There is no news of demonstrations that have spread through as many cities at once as those in 2013 or the 2018 truckers' strike. This reveals that we are not facing a routine. This is not localised protests. This is what is called a network and an interconnection of protests. Much more costly than the bus fare or truck freight will be the 'interconnection fare' between these 'protest networks' and the governments, if the authorities don't show seriousness, transparency and creativity proportional to the challenge. We are facing the greatest political manifestations of democratic Brazil. We must keep this in mind. Testing the resistance of a 30-year old constitution in the face of this new framework is the great task.

A wave of inter-connected movements and organisations emerged after 2013 and the manifestations for the impeachment of Dilma Rousseff or the arrest of her predecessor, Lula da Silva, condemned of corruption crimes under Operation Car Wash. The expectations are not univocal but very volatile. In 2013 the main claim was for public investment (eg, in urban mobility), which was diagnosed as an expectation of deepening of the social-democratic spirit of the 1988 constitution – a charter that largely amplified the expectations of social movements dammed by the military dictatorship (1964–1985). However, the economic crisis deepened by the political crisis signalled in 2013 was attributed to the interventionist policies of the Workers' Party. The government that emerged from the impeachment process implemented neo-liberal policies, such as labour-rights 'flexibilisations'. Now some movements have been axes for manifestations also against the democratic constitutional order: clamouring for a military intervention (repeatedly from 2017 until now, 2020) or organising wide support and social media platforms (with massive shots of 'fake news') for the election of Jair Bolsonaro in 2018 (a former low-rank military, right-wing populist with radical neo-liberal policies). Today, in 2020, some of Bolsonaro's supporters protest against the Congress and the Supreme Court, demanding the closure of these institutions. On the other hand, the economic measures and reforms (such as the 'downsizing' of social security and social assistance policies) did not provoke a massive reaction and the organisation of protests, but only punctual claims in the face of courts.

The difficulties are not only on the side of traditional policy sectors. Protest has limits. Demonstrators cannot judge themselves above or outside society. Protest movements that 'morally ride wild horses', as Luhmann says (1996a: 175–200), can block not only traffic and roads but also the functioning of politics, the economy and the struggle for rights. Without presenting plausible organisational and decision-making alternatives, protests will stop society and fall into disrepute as being as noisy as ineffective. The wave of violence and looting that accompanied the demonstrations in 2013, no matter how minor and dissonant, and the roadblocks for more than a week in 2018 with popular support and wide use of social networks are worrying. Moreover, daily mass demonstrations are unsustainable for long periods, as 2013 and 2018 also showed.

Brazil has not matured to protests. It has not realised its vitality. The first reactions to the movements revealed astonished rulers. In 2013, the initial violence against demonstrators and journalists and the intolerant rhetoric about the freedom of demonstration were remnants of our unease with democracy. In 2018, the individual interest of the truck drivers – who cornered the government – was met with strange and masochistic support from the population: the strike sparked widespread dissatisfaction. Once again, the government's response to the protests was shaky, with the illegal tabling of freight.

It is not the vague notion of the common good that limits law. As Gargarella (2006) reminds us, it is the rights that define the limits of the common good claims. Rights are at the centre of the scene. In 2013, it was necessary for the press to denounce the disproportionate nature of the repression so that the authorities would realise that the greatest value at stake belongs to the right to demonstrate, not to the evasive excuses that criminalise the protest. The confrontation between social rights always emerges in moments of collective protest. It is in these situations that freedom of expression must be the object of special protection, not the first right to be sacrificed. It is criticism of rulers that deserves protection and priority ears.

Only in democracy can the growth of consumption patterns be contrasted by the demand for rights. Only in democracy does protest against authority have a turn. Democracies exclusively show the effervescence of the scenes that Brazil has shown in recent years. The re-arrangement of social structures opens space for the re-formulation of the semantics of rights and politics. Protests are paradoxical causes and effects of this correlation. Constitutions, in turn, cannot get rid of this paradox: they 'fix unrest', as Luhmann reminds us (2004: 409), quoting Schlegel. They are liberating, but at the same time they stop revolutions! Would they be resilient to the point of fixing the unrest of the new social movements of the 21st century? Would they have the adaptive capacity to catalyse dreams and frustrations?

Uncertainty about the future can lead either to integration or disintegration. Decision-making, as Corsi (2000) reminds us, is only the tentative control of consequences at the level of each organisation – the nation-state, for instance. Society, though, is widely the consequence of evolution, not of good or bad intentions.

Exclusion generates chain effects: being excluded from the economy, for example, involves the risk of exclusion from politics or law as well. However, protests sometimes occur at a historical moment of inclusion in the economy. In this respect, our already-historic June 2013 bears similarities (although not many) to May 1968 in France. The chain effect, then, is the opposite: inclusion in the economy generates pressures for inclusion in health, education, urban mobility, combating corruption, control and quality of public spending, respect for differences, finally, under a countless number of flags, posters and constitutional rights presented in the fragmentary claims of the protests. Here, the operational differences between law, politics and the economy sweat their dissonant sweats with all intensity. And the constitution can reveal their freshness or mold in promoting functional differentiation.

From within society, protests exhale what seemed only dormant: society's reflection on itself. The elites are amazed. The extended middle class raises their voices. The periphery complains. That is one of the novelties of protest. The other is that we protest in a consolidated (and always threatened) democracy, not against dictatorship or against mishaps of democratic transition. The differences are not few. The box of democratic dreams is very open. If the new risks generated cannot be translated and processed by the democratic institutions themselves, they turn into a danger to democracy, pressuring the differentiation of the political system and its coupling with the rule of law.

References

Atlan, H. (1986) *Entre le cristal et la fumée: Essai sur l'organisation du vivant* (Paris, Points).

Aubert, V. (1963) 'Law and conflict. Competition and dissensus: two types of conflict and of conflict resolution' *7*(1) *J. Conflict Resolut.* 26–42.

Aubert, V. (1967) 'Law and conflict: courts and conflict resolution' *11*(1) *J. Conflict Resolut.* 40–51.

Campilongo, C.F. (2011) *Política, sistema jurídico e decisão judicial*, 2nd ed. (São Paulo, Saraiva).

Castells, M. (2015) *Networks of Outrage and Hope: Social Movements in the Internet Age*, 2nd ed. (London, Polity).

Corsi, G. (1993) 'Inclusione: la società osserva l'individuo' *1 Teoria Sociológica* 279–301.

Corsi, G. (1998a) 'Redes de la exclusión' in Sabino, F. and Vázquez, A. (eds), *Redes de inclusión: La construcción social de la autoridad* (Ciudad de México, Porrúa), 29–43.

Corsi, G. (1998b) *Sistemi che apprendono: Studio sull'idea di riforma nel sistema dell'educazione* (Lecce, Pensa).

Corsi, G. (2000) 'Protest and decision-making in a society of blame' 6(3) *Democr. Nat.* 361–374.

De Giorgi, R. (1992) *Il disagio del'inclusione* (Lecce, Conte).

De Giorgi, R. (1996) 'Redes de la inclusión' in Sabino, F. and Vázquez, A. (eds), *Redes de inclusión: La construcción social de la autoridad* (Ciudad de México, Porrúa), 17–28.

De Giorgi, R. (1998) *Direito, democracia e risco: Vínculos com o futuro* (Porto Alegre, Fabris).

De Giorgi, R. (2006) *Temi di filosofia del diritto* (Lecce, Pensa).

Diani, M. and McAdam, D. (eds) (2003) *Social Movements and Networks: Relational Approaches to Collective Action* (Oxford: Oxford University Press).

Estrada Saavedra, M. (2010) 'La anarquía organizada: las barricadas como el subsistema de seguridad de la Asamblea Popular de los Pueblos de Oaxaca' 28(4) *Estudios Sociológicos* 903–939.

Foust, C.R. (2010) *Transgression as a Mode of Resistance: Rethinking Social Movement in an Era of Corporate Globalisation* (Plymouth, Lexington).

Freund, J. (1994) *Diritto e politica: Saggi di filosofia giuridica* (Napoli, Edizione Scientifiche Italiane).

Fuller, L. (1965) 'Science and the judicial process' 79 *Harvard Law Rev.* 1604–1628.

Gargarella, R. (2006) *Carta abierta sobre la intolerancia: Apuntes sobre derecho y protesta* (Madrid, Siglo XXI).

Hirschman, A. (1970) *Exit, Voice and Loyalty: Responses to Decline in Firms, Organizations, and States* (Cambridge, Harvard University Press).

Losano, M. (2007) *Il movimento Sen Terra del Brasile: Funzione sociale della proprietà e latifondi occupati* (Reggio Emilia, Diabasis).

Luhmann, N. (1982) 'Diritto e conflitto' 2(2) *Laboratorio Politico* 5–25.

Luhmann, N. (1984) *Legitimation durch Verfahren* (Frankfurt, Suhrkamp).

Luhmann, N. (1989) *Ecological Communication* (Chicago, University of Chicago Press).

Luhmann, N. (1990) *La differenziazione del diritto: Contributi alla sociologia e alla teoria del diritto* (Bologna, Il Mulino).

Luhmann, N. (1995) 'Legal argumentation: an analysis of its form' 58(3) *Modern Law Rev.* 285–298.

Luhmann, N. (1996a) *Protest: Systemtheorie und soziale Bewegungen* (Frankfurt, Suhrkamp).

Luhmann, N. (1996b) 'Quod omnes tangit: remarks on Jurgen Habermas's legal theory' 17(4–5) *Cardozo Law Rev.* 883–899.

Luhmann, N. (1998) 'Inclusión y exclusión' in Luhmann N., *Complejidad y modernidad: De la unidad a la diferencia* (Madrid, Trotta), 167–195.

Luhmann, N. (2004) *Law as a Social System* (Oxford, Oxford University Press).

Luhmann, N. (2009) 'Causalidad en el sur' 27(79) *Estudios Sociológicos* 3–29.

Luhmann, N. (2013) *Theory of Society II* (Stanford, Stanford University Press).

Luhmann, N. (2014) *A Sociological Theory of Law*, 2nd ed. (New York, Routledge).
Luhmann, N. and De Giorgi, R. (1995) *Teoria della società*, 7th ed. (Milan, FrancoAngeli).
Macaulay, S. (1963) 'Non-contractual relations in business: a preliminary study' *28*(1) *Am. Soc. Rev.* 55–67.
McCann, M. (ed) (2006) *Law and Social Movements* (Aldershot, Ashgate).
Mosca, L. (2007) 'Dalle piazze a la rete: movimenti sociali e nueve tecnologie della comunicazione' in Nardis, F. (ed), *La società in movimento: I movimenti sociali nell'epoca del conflitto generalizzato* (Roma, Riuniti), 189–218.
Offe, C. (1985) 'New social movements: challenging the boundaries of institutional politics' *52*(4) *Soc. Res.* 817–868.
Serres, M. (1982) *The Parasite* (Baltimore, Johns Hopkins University Press).
von Foerster, H. (1984) *Observing Systems*, 2nd ed. (Seaside, Intersystems).

Chapter 11

Politics, law and legitimacy

Re-constructing Brexit from a systems theory perspective

John Paterson

Introduction

Recent years have seen key jurisdictions in the English-speaking world face considerable challenges in relation to the performance of their political systems. At one level explained simply as the rise of populism, even this glib assessment begs questions about the nature and functioning of politics in countries traditionally regarded as leaders in the design and operation of robust and legitimate political institutions. As politicians and commentators struggle to make sense of these upheavals (Frum 2018; SD King 2018; Kirchick 2017) the question raised by this chapter is whether systems theory might offer a distinctive and useful contribution.

The United Kingdom's exit from the European Union presents many challenges for academics. These range from efforts to understand why a majority of those voting in the 2016 referendum opted to leave the European Union to those directed toward understanding the many consequences of the decision. Perhaps the most striking aspect of the Brexit phenomenon, however, has been the protracted period of apparent paralysis on the part of politics in relation to implementing the result of the referendum. At the time of writing at the very start of 2020, it is expected that the UK will finally leave the EU on 31 January – three and half years from the original decision. As one political commentator has expressed the sentiments at this time: 'the rolling constitutional crisis of 2016–2019, testing the limits of convention, is over' (Rentoul 2020). This may or may not be true, but understanding what led to this crisis will be a critical issue in the months ahead.

The referendum produced a clear result; Article 50 was activated; the withdrawal agreement was negotiated; and then what seemed at times like an interminable parliamentary process ensued. There were points when it appeared possible that extended periods agreed by the EU would expire without the withdrawal agreement being ratified by Parliament, meaning that the UK would leave in a disorderly manner – a so-called no-deal Brexit. Even if this situation has been avoided, the period of protracted debate on Brexit within Parliament has surely exposed significant flaws within the UK's constitutional order.

A conventional account might focus, for example, on the folly of seeking to resolve an internal political party problem by means of a referendum whose result was not predictable, or perhaps on the tension arising from an unfortunate mismatch between a majority for 'Leave' in the country and a majority for 'Remain' in the Parliament.

This chapter proposes that a systems theory approach offers a distinctive perspective which, while not offering a solution, does help in understanding *how* the extraordinary division and paralysis has appeared. In particular, by drawing on Luhmann's unique and sophisticated account of the political system, it shows how constitutional confusion in the UK about the nature, role and significance of a referendum leads in turn to confusion of the distinction 'government'/'governed' that constitutes one dimension of the system's binary code. This observation is further developed via consideration of Luhmann's account of legitimacy: first, in terms of the idea that the political system achieves legitimacy by endowing itself with a form which enables it to create a degree of certainty regarding its communications and thus to establish the validity of its processes; and second, in terms of the idea that the degree of participation implied by a referendum could, unless carefully circumscribed, result in the system being potentially overloaded to a damaging degree. This approach does not have normative implications for the resolution of the Brexit impasse, but it likely does have a contribution to make in terms of future constitutional design in the UK – albeit much more modest than might be imagined.

This chapter begins by outlining Luhmann's understanding of the functioning of the political system in terms of its unique double binary code and the importance of legitimacy. It then goes on to provide an overview of key events in the Brexit process, with emphasis on those which appear to expose the tension between people, Parliament and judiciary. The following section seeks to reinterpret those events from a systems theory perspective before conclusions are drawn.

The chapter, therefore, makes no observation on whether Brexit is a good thing or a bad thing, nor on whether the UK requires a written constitution. It does, however, reinforce the need for the existing clear legal principles of UK constitutional law to be appropriately recognised so that they can operate to underpin the smooth functioning of the political system.

Luhmann on politics

At first sight, systems theory – and perhaps particularly Niklas Luhmann's approach – might seem an unusual source to turn to in order to make sense of a situation which has produced surely unprecedented confusion within British politics and given rise to contentious legal interventions. On the one hand, Luhmann's theorising is often perceived to be complex in its formulation, not lending itself to the ready provision of clear conceptualisations of a particular problem. On the other, is it not the case that his approach is even characterised by its very non-normativity? In other words, if the desire is for an easily applicable solution, systems theory could be characterised as both unduly complex and substantively inappropriate. This chapter proposes, however, that a proper understanding of Luhmann's treatment of politics within his overall social systems theory reveals an approach that is in important ways both *adequately* complex and actually dependent upon particular dispositions if politics is to be able to perform its function within society.

In a world where political debate can sometimes appear to monopolise the more serious news media, it can actually be refreshing to find that Luhmann understands politics as performing a rather specific and narrowly defined – albeit vitally important – role. In particular, in a society understood as composed of autopoietic systems (Luhmann 1995), each proceeding on the basis of unique and immutable binary codes, there are clearly issues which are by definition matters for discussion and resolution within one or another of those individual systems. Thus, issues which are apt for consideration in terms of the scientific code ('true'/'false') or the legal code ('legal'/'illegal') do not require or engage politics. It is immediately apparent, however, that there are issues which can engage both science *and* law, for example, and which may be treated in ways in each case that are essentially mutually contradictory. It is here that the role of politics in the context of autopoietic functional differentiation emerges: the production of collectively binding decisions in situations where issues cannot be resolved by the application of the binary code of one of the other social subsystems. This in turn implies that politics must have at its disposal the power to enforce those decisions – indeed, that it is uniquely able to deploy power in this way (Ashenden 2006; Clam 2006). In other words, the role of politics is indeed specific and narrowly defined, but it is one that ensures that the system as a whole is able to continue to function and not to descend into either aporia or conflict (Luhmann 1977). It would be easy at this point to object that Luhmann's approach risks the politicisation of other systems, but properly understood it can be seen rather to ensure that functional differentiation is preserved, with problems of potential damage inflicted by one system on another being avoided by the intervention of politics. That is not to say that this is an easy function to perform – think, for example, of the challenge presented by the financial crisis of a decade ago, the ramifications of which for other systems continue to test politics to this day (Kjaer et al. 2011) – nor that situations cannot arise which politics struggles to resolve by the deployment of power (think, for example, of Brexit).

But insofar as Brexit appears precisely to be the sort of problem which has left politics in a position where it is unable to perform its function, what is it about such problems that renders them so insoluble? In order to address this question, it is necessary to look in greater detail at how, from Luhmann's perspective, politics actually performs its function. It has already been seen that what distinguishes functionally differentiated social systems is their unique and immutable binary *codes* ('legal'/'illegal', 'true'/'false', 'payment'/ 'non-payment' etc), and it can be mentioned that autopoiesis theory also posits mutable *programmes* by which individual subsystems can proceed (Luhmann 1995: 203–204). In the case of politics, however, things are a little more complicated, insofar as Luhmann suggests that here there is what might be described as a dual coding. In the first instance, the binary code is 'government'/'governed', ie, drawing a distinction between those who are engaged in the process of governing and those who are not (but who are subject to the power wielded by those who are). This in turn implies that a distinction exists between those matters which are properly the preserve of government and those which are not. Second, it is then the case that one side of the initial binary distinction (government) is subject to a second distinction: 'government'/'opposition', which in practice plays out in the contest between political parties who then characterise that contest in terms of binary distinctions such as 'conservative'/'liberal' etc (Luhmann 1990: 167–186; see also Hornung 2006).

The implications of this characterisation of politics are profound (M King and Thornhill 2003: 72). First of all, by defining itself on the primary distinction 'government'/'governed', 'politics ensures that it only transmits power through the circles of government', excluding 'most social bodies from participation in the direct exercise of power' and restricting 'the number of themes which it perceives as relevant to politics'. Second, via the secondary distinction 'government'/'opposition', politics 'ensures that the application of power remains focused in bodies which are (for whatever reason) most equipped for its effective implementation'. This in turn reveals the extent to which political parties have a vital 'role to play in enabling the political system to describe to itself the most appropriate way in which power should be applied'.

Insofar as the function of the political system is to produce collectively binding decisions and insofar as this involves the deployment of power, it also follows that (absent a situation of naked coercion) politics requires legitimacy. In other words, the subsystem must produce justifications for the decisions it makes and explain them in ways which will be acceptable to the governed. In societies which are not characterised by full functional differentiation, it is possible for legitimacy to be achieved by referring to, say, religious sources to justify collectively binding decisions and to offer explanations in religious terms which will be both understandable and acceptable to the governed. In the context of modern societies in which full functional differentiation has been achieved, however, such an approach will not work, and a more sophisticated account of the attainment of legitimacy will be required. There is, of course, no shortage of political theories seeking to account for legitimacy in terms of, for example, an implicit social contract or the engagement of citizens in democratic processes or indeed the qualities of leadership, but Luhmann is unimpressed by all of these. There is no necessity, from his perspective, for the political subsystem to fit with any external model (Thornhill 2006). Rather, it is a matter in each case of politics successfully establishing a coherent and persuasive explanation of its operations and its reasons for operating in that way – usually related to some version of the public interest. There are clearly many ways in which such an explanation could be achieved, which in turn reveals the extent to which the legitimacy of the political subsystem is contingent. It can thus be concluded that a legitimate political system is one that can explain that it is legitimate and be accepted as such. Critics will, of course, be nervous that such a contingent approach leaves open the possibility that the substantive content of what counts as legitimate might include things that would run contrary to what many, say, contractarian political theories would regard as acceptable – or even essential. Luhmann's answer would simply be that this is certainly the case. And to be fair, it would have to be acknowledged that the diversity of what counts as legitimate in different societies which to all intents and purposes would be characterised as fully functionally differentiated would tend to suggest that Luhmann has a point. By way of reassurance, perhaps, it is equally clear that legitimacy is a dynamic rather than a static quality; as such, it has to be established on an ongoing basis, and politics cannot take legitimacy for granted. It is for this reason, no doubt, that Luhmann's position is not one of 'anything goes' relativism. The recognition of the contingency of political legitimacy in conditions of functional differentiation means that there is a greater likelihood of certain forms of government being successful in the long term than others. It might be suggested, therefore, that a political system will be legitimate to the extent that it can clearly differentiate itself from other systems and restrict itself to the function of producing collectively binding decisions only where these are clearly perceived by the governed to be both necessary and acceptable. In other words, legitimacy will be in question where there is any sense in which politics has become beholden to other systems or has engaged with questions that are properly the preserve of those other systems and where no conflict has arisen requiring a political solution (M King and Thornhill 2003: 72–76; Luhmann 1995: 201).

With this admittedly brief overview of the key attributes of the political system, its coding and the importance of legitimacy (its 'contingency formula') in mind, the next section moves on to examine some of the key aspects of the Brexit debate through these lenses, with a view to discovering whether this offers any novel insights.

Brexit: People, Parliament, party and courts

The idea that there should be a referendum on the question of whether the UK should remain in or leave the European Union was mooted in a speech by then Prime Minister David Cameron in early 2013. Whilst articulating a pro-EU stance, Cameron nevertheless pointed to challenges in the shape of the Eurozone post-crisis, a lack of international competitiveness and the democratic deficit which, if not addressed, he suggested, would prompt the British people to 'drift towards the exit'. His call was then for reform of the EU, not least the introduction of greater flexibility and a recognition that further integration threatened 'democratic consent for the EU in Britain', which was by then 'wafer thin'. He indicated that a referendum was inevitable but that it should not be held immediately, but rather only once there had been an opportunity 'to put the relationship right'. Cameron then went on to utter what would turn out to be very fateful words: 'It is time for the British people to have their say. It is time to settle this European question in British politics. I say to the British people: this will be your decision' (Cameron 2013). Some two years later, the Conservative Party manifesto for the 2015 general election included the commitment to hold an in-out referendum by the end of 2017 (Conservative Party 2015: 30), which commitment was fulfilled with the passage into law of the European Union Referendum Act 2015 in December of that year. Section 1(4) of the act specified that the question to be put in the referendum would be 'Should the United Kingdom remain a member of the European Union or leave the European Union?', whilst section 6 required the government to publish in advance of the referendum a report detailing the outcome of negotiations between the member states as well as 'the opinion of the Government of the United Kingdom on what has been agreed'. The Act was silent, however, on what should happen specifically in the event that the result of the referendum was that the UK should leave the EU.

During 2015 and 2016, negotiations were held between the UK and the European Council addressing the UK's concerns. These resulted in a draft decision on a new settlement (European Council 2016) and the publication by the UK government of a document explaining the UK's new status within the EU in the context of that new settlement (UK Government 2016). The opinion of the government required by the 2015 act is detailed in section 4 of the report, but iseasily articulated in the executive summary: 'The UK is stronger, safer and better off in a reformed EU' (UK Government 2016: 11). Despite this clear position on the part of the government, it remained the case that the decision would be for the people; as the prime minister expressed it in his foreword to the report: 'this will be a once-in-a-generation moment to shape the future of our country. Whatever the British people decide, I will make it work to the best of my abilities' (UK Government 2016: 5).

The referendum was held on 23 June 2016, resulting in a majority (51.9%) in favour of leaving and the remainder (48.1%) in favour of remaining (Electoral Commission 2019). Although legally the referendum result was not binding, given the doctrine of parliamentary sovereignty, the clear statements of the prime minister in advance that the result would be treated in that way meant that from a practical point of view there was no other option now but to move forward to withdrawal. The prime minister announced his intention to resign the following day, and he was replaced by Theresa May on 13 July 2016. In her speech to the Conservative Party conference on 2 October 2016, she acknowledged the considerable disquiet that existed around the decision but was unwavering in her determination to implement it, saying 'to those who claim he was mistaken in calling the referendum, we know there is no finer accolade than to say David Cameron put his trust in the British people. And trust the people we will. Because Britain is going to leave the European Union' (May 2016). These sentiments were very strongly echoed when she went on to address the further contention that had arisen in relation to how Article 50 of the Treaty on European Union should be triggered, thus beginning the process of the UK's departure. May was unequivocal that it was not a matter for Parliament, but rather for the government alone. Her reasoning was as follows: 'When it legislated to establish the referendum, Parliament put the decision to leave or remain inside the EU in the hands of the people. And the people gave their answer with emphatic clarity. So now it is up to the Government not to question, quibble or backslide on what we have been instructed to do, but to get on with the job.' It might have been argued to the contrary that Parliamentary sovereignty required a different approach, but May was unmoved, stating that 'those people who argue that Article Fifty can only be triggered after agreement in both Houses of Parliament are not standing up for democracy, they're trying to subvert it' (May 2016).

Notwithstanding the prime minister's certainty in this regard, a businesswoman, Gina Miller, had raised an action in the High Court challenging this position. The court gave its judgment against the government on 3 November 2016, finding that it could not use prerogative powers to trigger Article 50. In reaching that decision (*R[Miller] v. Secretary of State for Exiting the European Union* [2016]), it is interesting to note that the judges quoted with approval one of the classic statements of parliamentary sovereignty which specifically addresses the issue of the will of the people: 'the judges know nothing about any will of the people except in so far as that will is expressed by an Act of Parliament' (Dicey 1915: 38). And while the court was clear that it is a 'settled feature of UK constitutional law that, as a general rule applicable in normal circumstances, the conduct of international relations and the making and unmaking of treaties on behalf of the United Kingdom are regarded as matters for the Crown in the exercise of its prerogative powers' (para. 30), the impact of triggering of Article 50 on domestic law was a more important consideration in the instant case. In this last regard, the court referred to 'the powerful constitutional principle that the Crown has no power to alter the law of the land by use of its prerogative powers' (para. 86), and the 'wide and profound extent of the legal changes in domestic law created by the [European Communities Act] 1972 makes it especially unlikely that Parliament intended to leave their continued existence in the hands of the Crown through the exercise of its prerogative powers' (para. 87). The court also took the opportunity to state clearly its understanding of the law regarding the relationship between the prerogative power and the 2015 Referendum Act, even though the government had not sought to base its claim on that foundation. In this regard, it stated that the

> Act falls to be interpreted in light of the basic constitutional principles of Parliamentary sovereignty and representative parliamentary democracy which apply in the United Kingdom, which lead to the conclusion that a referendum on any topic can only be advisory for the lawmakers in Parliament unless very clear language to the contrary is used in the referendum legislation in question. No such language is used in the 2015 Referendum Act. (para. 106)

The court also drew attention to the fact that the act itself was passed in the context of a briefing to Parliament, which made it clear that 'the referendum would have advisory effect only' (para. 107). All of that said, however, the court was also at pains to stress that this analysis was as to the legal effect of the referendum, and did not in any way 'question the importance of the referendum as a political event, the significance of which will have to be assessed and taken into account elsewhere' (para. 108).

The government immediately announced that it would appeal this decision (Attorney-General's Office 2016), and leave was given to leapfrog the Court of Appeal and go straight to the Supreme Court. The case was heard in early December before all sitting justices of the Supreme Court (for the first time in the Court's history). While the case was being heard, Parliament voted to respect the outcome of the referendum (UK Parliament 2016). The Supreme Court in early 2017 rejected the government's appeal by a majority of 8–3 (*R [on the application of Miller and Dos Santos] v Secretary of State for Exiting the European Union and associated references* [2017]). As in the Court of Appeal, among the issues addressed by the majority was the impact of the principle of parliamentary sovereignty on the government's ability take action under the prerogative power. In this regard, the court was unimpressed by the government's arguments, stating that if

> prerogative powers could be invoked in relation to the EU Treaties despite the provisions of the 1972 Act, it would have been open to ministers to take such a course on or at any time after 2 January 1973 without authorisation by Parliament. It would also follow that ministers could have taken that course even if there had been no referendum or indeed, at least in theory, even if any referendum had resulted in a vote to remain. Those are implausible propositions. (para. 91)

The court was similarly unimpressed by the government's argument that the fact of the result of the referendum changed the normal position in relation to the role of Parliament. In other words, the suggestion was that while the 2015 Act had been passed by Parliament, the result was a matter for ministers – in effect, that there was a popular mandate for ministerial action. Responding to this proposition, the court proceeded by examining the various pieces of legislation that had been involved in previous referenda in the UK and noted that in each case, with the exception of those relating to the referenda on the UK's relationship with Europe, Parliament had specified what action should be taken by ministers following the announcement of the result. The two statutes relating to European referenda,[1] by contrast, were silent in this regard. As a consequence, where the result of the referendum required a change in the law (as in the case of the 2015 Act), this 'must be made in the only way in which the UK constitution permits, namely through Parliamentary legislation' (para. 121). The court acknowledged that the statute in question (a notice under Article 50) might be very short indeed, but pointed out that there is 'no equivalence between the constitutional importance of a statute, or any other document, and its length or complexity' (para. 122).

The court made some important observations about the distinction between the political and the legal in the context of this discussion. The referendum of 2016

> did not change the law in a way which would allow ministers to withdraw the United Kingdom from the European Union without legislation. But that in no way means that it is devoid of effect. It means that, unless and until acted on by Parliament, its force is political rather than legal. (para. 124)

> The court nevertheless observed that the way in which the proposed referendum was described in public statements by ministers, however, differed in the two cases. The 1975 referendum was described by ministers as advisory, whereas the 2016 referendum was described as advisory by some ministers and as decisive by others, but nothing hangs on that for present purposes. Whether or not they are clear and consistent, such public observations, wherever they are made, are not law: they are statements of political intention. Further, such statements are, at least normally, made by ministers on behalf of the UK government, not on behalf of Parliament. (para. 119)

Finally, the court reminded the government of the way in which the legal significance of a referendum result in the context of UK constitutional law had been discussed during an earlier House of Lords select committee consideration of the matter. The committee's recommendations included the following: 'because of the sovereignty of Parliament, referendums cannot be legally binding in the UK, and are therefore advisory. However, it would be difficult for Parliament to ignore a decisive expression of public opinion' (House of Lords Select Committee on the Constitution 2010a: para. 197). The government's response to this was to the effect that it 'agrees with this recommendation. Under the UK's constitutional arrangements Parliament must be responsible for deciding whether or not to take action in response to a referendum result' (House of Lords Select Committee on the Constitution 2010b: 12).

Within two days of the Supreme Court's decision, on 26 January 2017, the government published an extremely brief draft bill (The European Union [Notification of Withdrawal] Bill) to trigger Article 50. This received royal assent on 16 March 2017, and before the end of the month Theresa May wrote to the president of the European Council notifying him of the United Kingdom's intention to leave the European Union (May 2017a). The requirements in relation to Article 50 had finally been met, although it had involved a tortuous constitutional journey which had required the highest court in the land to set out for the government the limits of the legal and the political. Despite that newfound clarity, a political act was about to set the stage for almost three more years of uncertainty and impasse. The general election called by the prime minister on 18 April 2017 to be held on 8 June produced a hung parliament. What had been designed to produce a larger Conservative majority with a view to enabling such a government to push through Brexit with a minimum of opposition resulted instead in a situation where no party had an overall majority. The stage was thus set for the considerable further delay and confusion that ensued, although a Parliament sitting for two years (instead of one, as would normally be the case) might have given early warning of what was to come.

The European Union (Withdrawal) Bill was introduced on 13 July 2017. If passed, this would be the legislation that would repeal the European Communities Act 1972 (which took the UK into Europe in the first place) and also, significantly, give members of Parliament (MPs) the power to approve or reject the withdrawal agreement to be negotiated between the UK and the EU setting out the terms on which the UK would leave. It passed its second reading in the Commons on 12 September 2017, allowing the prime minister to conclude that Parliament had decided 'to back the will of the British people' and allow the government to move on with negotiations with the EU (May 2017b). The bill ultimately received royal assent on 26 June 2016. During the intervening period, the government announced that there would be a new bill enacting the withdrawal agreement between the UK and the EU, and the first draft of that agreement was published on 26 February 2018 (European Commission 2018). Whilst the parties initially hoped that the negotiation would be concluded by the end of October, agreement in principle was reached in mid-November. In the intervening period, the secretary of state for exiting the European Union, Dominic Raab, reminded Parliament that passage of the European Union (Withdrawal) Act 2018 confirmed its 'ultimate role in delivering on the will of the British people', while conceding that approval 'of the final deal will be the responsibility of the House of Commons alone'. Whereas it was clear that the government expected this delicate balancing act to be completed with Brexit on whatever terms it was able to negotiate, others within Parliament – and indeed within the governing Conservative Party itself – understood that they 'would be enabled to express a desire for alternatives when voting to reject or accept any deal' (UK Parliament 2018a). The government published the Withdrawal Agreement and the Outline Political Declaration (setting out the basis upon which the future relationship between the UK and EU would rest; Department for Exiting the European Union 2018a). But by the time these documents had been endorsed at a special meeting of the European Council on 25 November 2018 (European Council 2018), it was already clear that the government faced very considerable difficulties.

First of all, the secretary of state for exiting the EU resigned (along with other ministers), citing concerns with the content of the Withdrawal Agreement. A key worry emerging (not least among members of the Conservative Party) was the effect of the so-called backstop agreement designed to deal with the complications of the border between Northern Ireland and the Republic of Ireland following Brexit. It was known that the attorney-general had given the government legal advice on the implications of the backstop, but the government refused to publish this. Following protracted arguments in the Commons, three defeats for the government and its ultimately being found in contempt of Parliament (UK Parliament 2018b), the advice was published. This revealed that the attorney-general had concluded that the backstop arrangements meant that departure from the EU was not solely in the hands of the UK (Department for Exiting the European Union 2018b). The original plan to hold the meaningful vote (ie, the vote on the terms of the agreement negotiated with the EU) under the European Union (Withdrawal) Act 2018 on 10 December was accordingly postponed (UK Parliament 2018c).

Early 2019 brought no respite for the government, which first of all lost a vote on an amendment to the Finance (No. 3) Bill, which had the effect of limiting its financial powers in the event that the UK were to leave the EU without a deal (UK Parliament 2019a). Thereafter, as five days of debate on Brexit got underway, the government lost a vote on an amendment which meant that in the event that it lost the delayed meaningful vote on 15 January 2019, it would be required to return to Parliament with a new plan within three days (UK Parliament 2019b). The meaningful vote was indeed lost (UK Parliament 2019c), but before the prime minister could present the required new plan, she had to face a vote of no confidence, which she survived (UK Parliament 2019d). The degree of difficulty facing the government was further demonstrated in the debate on the required new plan at the end of January 2019. Votes on amendments indicated that a majority of MPs were opposed to the UK leaving the EU without a deal and to the backstop arrangements relating to the border on the island of Ireland (UK Parliament 2019e). The government was defeated again in mid-February when it sought the support of MPs in its negotiations with the EU (UK Parliament 2019e). The prime minister thereafter promised Parliament that, in the event that the government lost the second meaningful vote, it would hold a vote on a no-deal Brexit and, were that also to be rejected, a further vote on a delay to Brexit (UK Parliament 2019f). The government did then lose the second meaningful vote, on 12 March 2019 (UK Parliament 2019g), whilst MPs then voted in favour of ruling out a no-deal Brexit (UK Parliament 2019h) as well as seeking an extension to Brexit beyond 29 March 2019 (UK Parliament 2019i). The Speaker of the House of Commons then further constrained the government's freedom of action by making a statement to the effect that it could not bring forward a motion for a third meaningful vote that was the same or substantially the same as the previous one (UK Parliament 2019j). The prime minister then wrote to the president of the European Council requesting an extension under Article 50 (May 2019a), which request was agreed to at a meeting of the council on 21 March 2019, albeit imposing a tighter time frame (European Council 2019a). The difficulty of the prime minister's position was made all the clearer when she indicated at the end of March 2019 that she would resign before negotiations on the future relationship between the EU and the UK commenced, thereby attempting to bolster support from the more Eurosceptic wing of her party (Mairs 2019a). The month closed with the government losing the third meaningful vote (UK Parliament 2019k).

The following month was to bring no more cheer for the government, but two votes held on 1 April 2019 indicated the extreme complexity of the situation for Parliament as a whole. First of all, a motion that would have required any Brexit deal passed by Parliament to be confirmed by a public vote was defeated (UK Parliament 2019l). Such a lack of enthusiasm to return the question to the people might have been assumed to indicate a desire instead to place matters more firmly in the hands of Parliament, but a second motion, which sought an extension to the period under Article 50 or, failing that, a choice for Parliament between no deal or the revocation of Article 50, was also defeated (UK Parliament 2019m). Results such as these indicated the extent to which Brexit was not a party political issue in any traditional sense. The following days brought news of another request for an extension to the Article 50 period, to 30 June 2019, which letter also indicated that the UK was making preparations for the event that it might be required to participate in the forthcoming elections to the European Parliament (May 2019b). The president of the European Council, with perhaps a greater sense of realism, asked EU leaders for a flexible extension up to a maximum of one year (Tusk 2019). In the event, an extension to the end of October was agreed, with the possibility of an earlier departure assuming ratification of the Withdrawal Agreement (European Council 2019b).

May 2019 brought two opportunities for the people as a whole to express their views on the progress of Brexit, in the shape of, first, local government elections and, second, the elections to the European Parliament. Whilst neither of these votes constituted a second referendum on the question first posed in 2016, few doubted that this issue was uppermost in the minds of the electorate. In the local elections, the Conservative Party lost over 1,300 councillors, with the beneficiaries being mainly the (pro-Remain) Liberal Democratic and Green parties (BBC 2019a). But if pro-Remain parties were encouraged by those results as they entered the European elections later in the month, they were to be disappointed – and perhaps even shocked – when the Brexit Party won the largest number of votes and 29 of the available 73 seats (House of Commons Library 2019). With Theresa May announcing just before the European elections that she would resign on 7 June, prompting a leadership contest in the Conservative Party, the future for the next leader and prime minister looked anything but certain. In the event, Boris Johnson – famous for having apparently decided only at the last minute which position he would take in the 2016 referendum (Singh 2016) – won the contest easily (BBC 2019b) and on assuming office promised to 'to fulfil the repeated promises of parliament to the people and come out of the EU on October 31' and to 'do a new deal' (Johnson 2019a). Repeating these promises in Parliament on 25 July, just before it rose for the summer recess, he crucially refused to rule out the possibility of a no-deal Brexit, thus putting the government at odds with the expressed (though non-binding) will of the House (UK Parliament 2019n). As the summer wore on, the new prime minister wrote to the president of the European Council stating that the backstop in its current form was unacceptable to the UK and proposing instead an essentially looser commitment as to what would happen in that regard during and at the end of a transition period (Johnson 2019b).

In advance of the reopening of Parliament, Hilary Benn published the European Union (Withdrawal) (No. 6) Bill, which set two new deadlines. The first of these was 19 October 2019, specified as the point by which the prime minister would have to have achieved one or another of a number of itemised options: (1) succeed in getting a withdrawal agreement passed in Parliament; (2) succeed in getting MPs to agree to a no-deal Brexit; (3) write to the president of the European Council requesting a further extension to the Article 50 period. A schedule to the bill set out the text of this letter, which included reference to the second deadline, 31 January 2020, which would be the new withdrawal date, assuming agreement from the European Council (UK Parliament 2019o). This bill made rapid progress when Parliament re-convened, prompting the prime minister to seek (unsuccessfully) to call an early general election (UK Parliament 2019p), whereupon the bill became law as the European Union (Withdrawal) (No. 2) Act 2019. Shortly afterwards, however, in accordance with the schedule earlier announced by Boris Johnson, Parliament was prorogued on 9 September and was not due to sit again until the state opening on 14 October. This was seen by many as an attempt to limit the time available to Parliament to deal with Brexit, but the government's position was, to the contrary, that after an exceptionally long session it was appropriate to have a longer break and also allow the preparation of the Queen's speech (setting out the agenda for the new session).

In the event, however, this turned out to be the occasion of yet another twist in the ongoing tale of constitutional crises that had become almost normal since the referendum of 2016. Whilst a challenge launched in the High Court by Gina Miller was unsuccessful, with that court ruling that the prorogation was lawful on the grounds that this was an essentially political matter (*R [on the application of Miller] v The Prime Minister* [2019] EWHC 2381 [QB]), a similar challenge launched in the Court of Session in Scotland by a Scottish National Party MP and others was successful (*Joanna Cherry QC MP and Others v Lord Advocate* [2019] CSIH 49, P680/19). The lord president observed that 'the circumstances demonstrate that the true reason for the prorogation is to reduce the time available for Parliamentary scrutiny of Brexit at a time when such scrutiny would appear to be a matter of considerable importance, given the issues at stake' (para. 53). Therefore, the government's advice to the Queen to prorogue Parliament was 'unlawful and thus null and of no effect' (para. 60). Both cases were appealed to the Supreme Court, where a full bench unanimously found against the Government (*R [on the application of Miller] [Appellant] v The Prime Minister [Respondent], Cherry and others [Respondents] v Advocate General for Scotland [Appellant] [Scotland]* [2019] UKSC 41). The court based its decision on the principles of parliamentary sovereignty and parliamentary accountability. In relation to the first, of course, the idea is that only Parliament is able to make the law, whilst in relation to the second:

> Ministers are accountable to Parliament through such mechanisms as their duty to answer Parliamentary questions and to appear before Parliamentary committees, and through Parliamentary scrutiny of the delegated legislation which ministers make. By these means, the policies of the executive are subjected to consideration by the representatives of the electorate, the executive is required to report, explain and defend its actions, and citizens are protected from the arbitrary exercise of executive power. (para. 46)

On the basis of these understandings of the two principles, the court was clear that the prerogative power to prorogue Parliament cannot be unlimited, but noted that the question then was how the limit on the power could be defined so as to make it compatible with the principles. The court answered the question by noting that

> for the purposes of the present case, therefore, the relevant limit upon the power to prorogue can be expressed in this way: that a decision to prorogue Parliament (or to advise the monarch to prorogue Parliament) will be unlawful if the prorogation has the effect of frustrating or preventing, without reasonable justification, the ability of Parliament to carry out its constitutional functions as a legislature and as the body responsible for the supervision of the executive. In such a situation, the court will intervene if the effect is sufficiently serious to justify such an exceptional course. (para. 50)

The court was not unaware that such an intervention would be controversial, but was clear that it was not something that should be regarded as unduly challenging: 'the extent to which prorogation frustrates or prevents Parliament's ability to perform its legislative functions and its supervision of the executive is a question of fact which presents no greater difficulty than many other questions of fact which are routinely decided by the courts' (para. 51). Adopting this approach, the court stated that

> it is impossible for us to conclude, on the evidence which has been put before us, that there was any reason – let alone a good reason – to advise Her Majesty to prorogue Parliament for five weeks, from 9th or 12th September until 14th October. We cannot speculate, in the absence of further evidence, upon what such reasons might have been. It follows that the decision was unlawful. (para. 61)

It therefore 'follows that Parliament has not been prorogued and that this court should make declarations to that effect' (para. 70).

This was in many respects a stunning blow for the government, and whilst it was welcomed by the Speaker of the House of Commons (Honeycombe-Foster 2019), the prime minister was very critical, stating that he 'strongly disagree[d] with this judgement' and going on to suggest that he read it in a way which is difficult to square with the careful constitutional reasoning of the court: 'we in the UK will not be deterred from getting on and delivering on the will of the people to come out of the EU on October 31st' (Johnson 2019c). Be that as it may, he could certainly be forgiven in due course for assuming that any additional time available for discussion in Parliament would make it more difficult for him to achieve the objective of a timely Brexit. By 19 October, a lack of progress meant that he was obliged by the European Union (Withdrawal) (No. 2) Act 2019 to write to the president of the European Council seeking a further extension to the Article 50 period. In the event, a rather creative interpretation of the act was adopted in which no fewer than three letters were sent: an unsigned photocopy of the letter required by the act (UK Prime Minister 2019a), a letter of explanation from the UK's ambassador to the EU (UK Representation to the EU Brussels 2019), and a personal letter from the prime minister explaining why he did not in fact want a further extension (UK Prime Minister 2019b). It was thus clear that having been on the receiving end of unprecedented judgements from full benches of the Supreme Court had not in any way diminished the government's willingness to test the limits of the UK's flexible constitution.

The following days brought yet further indications of the complexity of Parliament's attitude toward Brexit. On the one hand, there was progress in the sense that the bill that would ratify the Withdrawal Agreement passed its second reading in the Commons with a reasonably healthy majority on 22 October (UK Parliament 2019q). On the other hand, however, MPs immediately rejected the timetable for the bill (UK Parliament 2019r). The prime minister responded by pausing the progress of the legislation, indicating that preparations for a no-deal Brexit would now be accelerated and consulting with EU leaders (UK Parliament 2019s). The president of the European Council announced on 28 October that the EU was willing to agree a further extension of the Article 50 period, to 31 January 2020 (Mairs 2019b), and the UK subsequently accepted this offer – although in the same letter the prime minister indicated that he felt that Parliament would continue to seek to delay Brexit insofar as it had the opportunity to do so. Accordingly, he added, he would be seeking a general election in December (Johnson 2019d). On the following day, whilst an effort to hold such an election failed in terms of the Fixed-term Parliaments Act 2011 (insofar as the required special majority was not attained; UK Parliament 2019t), the government then introduced the Early Parliamentary General Election Bill, which, requiring only a simple majority, thus neatly sidestepped the obstacle placed by the 2011 Act (UK Parliament 2019u) – ironically, a classic example of parliamentary sovereignty in action.

The run-up to the election on 12 December 2019 was of course a period of very considerable speculation. In the event, fears on the part of the government that they would suffer a humiliation of the sort that had attended the 2017 election proved to be misplaced. Instead, they were returned with a very solid majority, meaning that all obstacles in the way of Brexit on 31 January now appeared to have been removed. And indeed, the European Union (Withdrawal Agreement) Bill passed its third reading in the House of Commons on 9 January 2020, meaning that, at the time of writing, it is now all but certain that the UK will leave the EU on 31 January 2020.

Analysis

At the outset, David Cameron characterised the UK's problems with the EU as, at least in part, an issue of democratic legitimacy that, if not addressed, would become terminal for the country's membership in the union. Insofar as the issue is thus characterised as being in no small measure about the location of sovereignty and thus the ability to deploy the resource of power, this is by definition a political problem. It is possible to see, however, that, in systems theory terms, it is more precisely a problem of how the political system itself operates, as opposed to a problem that politics would be required to engage with because of, for example, the differential treatment of the same issue in two other social systems. Right from the outset, accordingly, systems theory appears to signal that caution is required in determining how this particular problem should best be solved.

The then prime minister's response of handing the decision directly to the people is thus a bold one, but also one that looks problematic from the outset. For a start, it ignores the legal position (which his own government has explicitly acknowledged in the context of the report on referenda by the House of Lords Select Committee on the Constitution) that such a decision can only be advisory and that it will ultimately be for Parliament (see also Douglas-Scott 2016). From a systems theory perspective, it can be suggested that there was at this point a confusion of the binary code 'government'/'governed'. In a representative democracy, such as the UK, the governed (by definition, it might be suggested) do not decide; rather, they get to choose who will decide (Sumption 2019). By contrast, as soon as a referendum is established and the result is in effect described as binding, the governed have become the government. Now, if this is done explicitly, then there is no reason why it cannot be taken forward successfully. Where there is confusion from the outset, however, then the sort of delay and dispute that characterised the following three and half years has a certain inevitability about it. This is not because there is any doubt as to what the law requires, but rather, we may now say, because the means by which politics achieves legitimacy on an ongoing basis has been jeopardised. The courts cannot say anything other than what is lawful constitutionally (Baghai 2015; Nobles and Schiff 2013, 184–195), but even they are aware that statements made which misrepresent the law nevertheless have political effects – in this case undermining legitimacy on the basis, bluntly, that the people have been promised one thing and now another seems to be happening.

To this extent, it could be suggested that Theresa May's efforts to trigger Article 50 by means of prerogative powers and sidelining of Parliament poured fuel on the fire rather than water. What those efforts did achieve, however, insofar as they brought the courts into the process, was to open the way for clear judicial statements of the fundamental constitutional position in a representative democracy. Thus, the courts could only know the will of the people insofar as that was expressed in an act of Parliament, and a decision in a referendum did not operate as a mandate for executive action but rather as advice to Parliament – unless Parliament itself had directed otherwise.

It was not, therefore, surprising that Parliament continually fought to re-assert itself in the way that it did (for example, by seeking to rule out a no-deal Brexit or to obtain extensions of the Article 50 period to allow adequate debate and planning). It could be argued that the actions of successive prime ministers at this time might best be characterised as a wholesale inversion of the binary code of politics: the government became the governed and vice versa. On the other hand, it can equally be seen that with the expectations of the people having been raised in the context of the legally misdescribed referendum, the very legitimacy of politics was jeopardised on every occasion where there was effort to re-establish the normal ordering of the binary code. Any autopoietic system must mask its foundational paradox by avoiding the application of its binary code to itself; it can now be seen that this was in essence what was happening in the context of the ongoing Brexit debate.

It would be wrong, however, to suggest that in re-asserting itself in the way that it did Parliament thereby spoke with one voice. As indicated by some of the apparently contradictory votes already discussed, it simply did not. But those very contradictions expose another way in which Brexit challenged traditional political thinking. Whereas the dual binary code of politics sees the government arm of the initial distinction further elaborated by the code 'government'/'opposition', Brexit was not an issue that could easily be thematised in that way. There were Leavers and Remainers in both the government and main opposition parties, meaning that the usual party discipline that could be relied upon to ensure efficient decision-making was practically impossible to achieve. Nor was this aspect of Brexit an emergent phenomenon which, as it were, blindsided politics once the referendum had been called. It could very plausibly be argued that it was the long-standing presence of a substantial Leave group within the governing Conservative Party (which was otherwise essentially pro-Remain) that led to the referendum being called in the first place. Thus, David Cameron might be understood to have sought to silence the Leave wing of the party by giving them the referendum they wanted, but in the expectation that the popular vote would be to remain. That expectation could go a considerable way to explaining the otherwise inexplicable confusion over the legal status of a referendum and the silence of the 2015 Act on what should specifically and practically happen in the event that the result was to leave. In this way, it can be argued that although there undoubtedly was disquiet in the country about the nature and direction of the UK's relationship with the EU, this was not actually the motivation for the referendum. Instead, it could be argued that insofar as the motivation was an internal party problem, this was precisely not an issue that should have engaged the wider political system.

Conclusion

From the foregoing analysis, it might be concluded that there were in essence multiple ways in which the Brexit referendum process subverted or inverted the normal functioning of the political system. There was a lack of clarity about the nature of the problem in the first place – whether it was actually a problem that engaged the political system in the normal sense or whether it called for an exceptional approach. Assuming that it did engage the political system but – because it was in essence a question of the location of sovereignty and thus of the ability to deploy power – did call for an exceptional approach, there was nevertheless a critical lack of clarity about the nature and significance of that approach, ie, the referendum. When that lack of clarity emerged as a key problem in the ensuing impasse, efforts to provide legal certainty thus had the effect of inflaming political sentiments among voters who felt (paradoxically, but understandably) that their normative expectations were thereby disappointed – the exact opposite of the function of the legal system.

This chapter does not, therefore, contribute to the debate about Brexit in terms of whether it is a good thing or a bad thing. It does not even contribute to the debate about whether the Brexit events lead to the conclusion that the UK needs a written constitution. What it does do, importantly, is reinforce the need for the existing clear legal principles of UK constitutional law to be appropriately recognised, because given the chance, they operate, as they should, to underpin the smooth functioning of the political system irrespective of preferences or party allegiances. As Luhmann himself put it: 'the politization of power centralizes the decision of conflicts, and it thereby makes conflict with those who decide conflicts hopeless, save by recourse to law' (1995: 377).

Note

1 Following its accession to the then European Communities on 1 January 1973, the UK held a referendum seeking the confirmation of the people, which was duly given.

References

Ashenden, S. (2006) 'The problem of power in Luhmann's systems theory' in King M and Thornhill C (eds), *Luhmann on Law and Politics: Critical Appraisals and Applications* (Oxford, Hart), 127–144.

Attorney-General's Office (2016) *High Court ruling on Article 50: Statement*. 3 November 2016 [online] Available at: https://www.gov.uk/government/news/high-court-ruling-on-article-50-statement (accessed 8.01.20).

BBC (2019a) *England Local Elections 2019* [online] Available at: https://www.bbc.co.uk/news/topics/ceeqy0e9894t/england-local-elections-2019 (accessed 12.01.20).

BBC (2019b) *Boris Johnson Wins Race to be Tory Leader and PM* [online] Available at: https://www.bbc.co.uk/news/uk-politics-49084605 (accessed 12.01.20).

Cameron, D. (2013) *EU Speech at Bloomberg, 23 January 2013* [online] Available at: https://www.gov.uk/government/speeches/eu-speech-at-bloomberg (accessed 7.01.20).

Clam, J. (2006) 'What is modern power?' in King M and Thornhill C (eds), *Luhmann on Law and Politics: Critical Appraisals and Applications* (Oxford, Hart), 145–162.

Conservative Party (2015) *General Election Manifesto* [online] Available at: http://
ucrel.lancs.ac.uk/wmatrix/ukmanifestos2015/localpdf/Conservatives.pdf (accessed
14.03.20).

Department for Exiting the European Union (2018a) *Policy Paper: Withdrawal
Agreement and Political Declaration* 25 Nov. [online] Available at: https://www.
gov.uk/government/publications/withdrawal-agreement-and-political-declaration
(accessed 7.01.20).

Department for Exiting the European Union (2018b) *Policy Paper: Exiting the EU:
Publication of Legal Advice* 5 Dec. [online] Available at: https://www.gov.
uk/government/publications/exiting-the-eu-publication-of-legal-advice   (accessed
12.01.20).

Dicey, A.V. (1915) *An Introduction to the Law of the Constitution*, 8th ed. (New
York, Macmillan).

Douglas-Scott, S. (2016) 'Brexit, Article 50 and the contested British constitution'
79(6) *Modern Law Rev.* 1019–1089.

Electoral Commission [UK] (2019) *Results and Turnout at the EU Referendum* 25
Sep. [online] Available at: https://www.electoralcommission.org.uk/who-we-are-
and-what-we-do/elections-and-referendums/past-elections-and-referendums/eu-
referendum/results-and-turnout-eu-referendum (accessed 12.01.20).

European Commission (2018) *European Commission Draft Withdrawal Agreement on
the withdrawal of the United Kingdom of Great Britain and Northern Ireland from
the European Union and the European Atomic Energy Community, TF50 (2018) 33
– Commission to EU 27* [online] Available at: https://ec.europa.eu/commission/
sites/beta-political/files/draft_withdrawal_agreement.pdf (accessed 12.01.20).

European Council (2016) *Draft Decision of the Heads of State or Government,
meeting within the European Council, concerning a New Settlement for the United
Kingdom within the European Union, Brussels, 2 February 2016, EUCO 4/16* [on-
line] Available at: https://www.consilium.europa.eu/media/21980/decision-new-
settlementen16.pdf (accessed 7.01.20).

European Council (2018) *Special meeting of the European Council (Art. 50)
(25 November 2018) – Conclusions, EUCO XT 20015/18* [online] Available at:
http://data.consilium.europa.eu/doc/document/XT-20015-2018-INIT/en/pdf   (accessed 13.01.20).

European Council (2019a) *Special Meeting of the European Council (Art. 50)
(21 March 2019) – Conclusions, EUCO XT 20004/19* [online] Available at:
https://www.consilium.europa.eu/media/38744/21-euco-art50-conclusions-en.pdf (accessed 12.01.20).

European Council (2019b) *Special Meeting of the European Council (Art. 50) (10
April 2019) – Conclusions, EUCO XT 20015/19* [online] Available at: https://www.
consilium.europa.eu/media/39042/10-euco-art50-conclusions-en.pdf   (accessed
12.01.20).

Frum, D. (2018) *Trumpocracy: The Corruption of the American Republic* (New York,
Harper).

Honeycombe-Foster, M. (2019) 'John Bercow orders Commons to reopen after
Supreme Court rules Boris Johnson's shutdown "unlawful"' *PoliticsHome* [online]
Available at: https://www.politicshome.com/news/uk/political-parties/conservative-
party/news/106799/john-bercow-orders-commons-reopen-after (accessed 12.01.20).

Hornung, B.R. (2006) 'The theoretical foundations and context of Luhmann's legal and political sociology' in King M and Thornhill C (eds), *Luhmann on Law and Politics: Critical Appraisals and Applications* (Oxford, Hart), 187–216.

House of Commons Library (2019) *European Parliament Elections 2019: Results and Analysis* [online] Available at: https://researchbriefings.parliament.uk/ ResearchBriefing/Summary/CBP-8600 (accessed 12.01.20).

House of Lords Select Committee on the Constitution (2010a) *Referendums in the United Kingdom, 12th Report of Session 2009-10, HL Paper 99* [online] https://publications. parliament.uk/pa/ld200910/ldselect/ldconst/99/99.pdf (accessed 12.01.20).

House of Lords Select Committee on the Constitution (2010b) *Government Response to the Report on Referendums in the UK, 4th Report of Session 2010-11, HL Paper 34* [online] Available at: https://publications.parliament.uk/pa/ld201011/ldselect/ ldconst/34/34.pdf (accessed 12.01.20).

Johnson, B. (2019a) *Boris Johnson's First Speech as Prime Minister*. 24 July 2019 [online] Available at: https://www.gov.uk/government/speeches/boris-johnsons-first-speech-as-prime-minister-24-july-2019 (accessed 12.01.20).

Johnson, B. (2019b) *PM Letter to Donald Tusk*. 19 August 2019 [online] Available at: https://www.gov.uk/government/publications/pm-letter-to-donald-tusk-19-august-2019 (accessed 12.01.20).

Johnson, B. (2019c) *PM Speech at Hudson Yards Business Event*. 24 September 2019 [online] Available at: https://www.gov.uk/government/speeches/pm-speech-at-hudson-yards-business-event-24-september-2019 (accessed 12.01.20).

Johnson, B. (2019d) *Prime Minister's Letter to President Donald Tusk*. 28 October 2019 [online] Available at: https://www.gov.uk/government/publications/prime-ministers-letter-to-president-donald-tusk-28-october-2019 (accessed 12.01.20).

King, M. and Thornhill, C. (2003) *Niklas Luhmann's Theory of Politics and Law* (Basingstoke, Palgrave Macmillan).

King, S.D. (2018) *Grave New World: The End of Globalization and the Return of History* (New Haven and London, Yale University Press).

Kirchick, J. (2017) *The End of Europe: Dictators, Demagogues and the Coming Dark Age* (New Haven and London, Yale University Press).

Kjaer, P.F., Teubner, G. and Febbrajo, A. (2011) *The Financial Crisis in Constitutional Perspective: The Dark Side of Functional Differentiation* (Oxford, Hart).

Luhmann, N. (1977) 'Differentiation of Society' 2(1) *Can. J. Sociol.* 29–53.

Luhmann, N. (1990) *Political Theory in the Welfare State* (Berlin, de Gruyter).

Luhmann, N. (1995) *Social Systems* (Stanford, Stanford University Press).

Mairs, N. (2019a) 'Top Tory backbencher Sir Graham Brady "told Theresa May MPs want her to quit" over Brexit' *PoliticsHome* [online] Available at: https:// www.politicshome.com/news/uk/foreign-affairs/brexit/news/102722/top-tory-backbencher-sir-graham-brady-told-theresa-may (accessed 12.01.20).

Mairs, N. (2019b) 'Donald Tusk says EU leaders have agreed to 31 January Brexit extension' *PoliticsHome* [online] Available at: https://www.politicshome.com/ news/uk/political-parties/conservative-party/news/107580/donald-tusk-says-eu-leaders-have-agreed-31 (accessed 12.01.20).

May, T. (2016) *Britain after Brexit: A Vision of a Global Britain, Speech to the Conservative Party Conference*. 2 October 2016 [online] Available at: https://www.

politicshome.com/news/uk/political-parties/conservative-party/news/79517/read-full-theresa-mays-conservative (accessed 12.01.20).

May, T. (2017a) *Prime Minister's Letter to Donald Tusk triggering Article 50* [online] Available at: https://www.gov.uk/government/publications/prime-ministers-letter-to-donald-tusk-triggering-article-50 (accessed 12.01.20).

May, T. (2017b) *PM Statement on EU Withdrawal Bill.* 12 September 2017 [online] Available at: https://www.gov.uk/government/news/pm-statement-on-eu-withdrawal-bill-12-sept-2017 (accessed 12.01.20).

May, T. (2019a) *Letter to Donald Tusk, President of the European Council, 20 March 2019* [online] Available at: https://www.consilium.europa.eu/media/38668/20190320_may_letter_tusk_extension.pdf (accessed 12.01.20).

May, T. (2019b) *Letter to Donald Tusk, President of the European Council.* 5 April 2019 [online] Available at: https://assets.publishing.service.gov.uk/government/uploads/system/uploads/attachment_data/file/793058/PM_letter_to_His_Excellency_Mr_Donald_Tusk__1_.pdf (accessed 12.01.20).

Nobles, R. and Schiff, D. (2013) *Observing Law Through Systems Theory* (Oxford, Hart).

Rentoul, J. (2020) 'Boris Johnson has "got Brexit done" – and politics will now move on to be about "other things"' *The Independent* [online] Available at: https://www.independent.co.uk/voices/brexit-bill-boris-johnson-vote-commons-latest-a9276906.html (accessed 12.01.20).

Singh, A. (2016) 'Boris Johnson's secret pro-EU article revealed, expressing doubts over Brexit' *Independent* [online] Available at: https://www.independent.co.uk/news/uk/politics/boris-johnson-secret-pro-eu-article-revealed-expressing-doubts-brexit-a7363781.html (accessed 12.01.20).

Sumption, J. (2019) *Trials of the State: Law and the Decline of Politics* (London: Profile Books).

Thornhill, C. (2006) *Niklas Luhmann's political theory: politics after metaphysics.* In M King and C Thornhill (eds), *Luhmann on Law and Politics: Critical Appraisals and Applications* (Oxford, Hart), 75–99.

Tusk, D (2019) *Invitation Letter to the Members of the European Council (Art. 50) Ahead of Their Special Meeting on 10 April 2019* [online] Available at: https://www.consilium.europa.eu/en/press/press-releases/2019/04/09/invitation-letter-by-president-donald-tusk-to-the-members-of-the-european-council-art-50-ahead-of-their-special-meeting-on-10-april-2019/ (accessed 12.01.20).

UK Government (2016) *The Best of Both Worlds: The United Kingdom's Special Status in a Reformed European Union Presented to Parliament Pursuant to Section 6 of the European Union Referendum Act 2015* [online] Available at: https://assets.publishing.service.gov.uk/government/uploads/system/uploads/attachment-data/file/502291/54284EUSeriesNo1WebAccessible.pdf (accessed 12.01.20).

UK Parliament (2016) *The Government's Plan for Brexit* [online] Available at: https://hansard.parliament.uk/Commons/2016-12-07/division/242B1EA4-AFA1-4F6D-9C74-CDBFBDC10C5A/TheGovernmentSPlanForBrexit?outputType=Names (accessed 12.01.20).

UK Parliament (2018a) *Leaving the EU: Meaningful Vote* [online] Available at: https://hansard.parliament.uk/commons/2018-10-22/debates/18102210000002/LeavingTheEUMeaningfulVote (accessed 12.01.20).

UK Parliament (2018b) *'Contempt Motion' on Publishing of Legal Advice* [online] Available at: https://www.parliament.uk/business/news/2018/december/contempt-motion-on-publishing-of-legal-advice/ (accessed 12.01.20).

UK Parliament (2018c) *Exiting the European Union* [online] Available at: https://hansard.parliament.uk/Commons/2018-12-10/debates/45B04B71-E595-4C17-AA41-686E96BF70E3/ExitingTheEuropeanUnion (accessed 12.01.20).

UK Parliament (2019a) *Finance (No. 3) Bill* [online] Available at: https://hansard.parliament.uk/commons/2019-01-08/debates/1EC25998-330C-40DB-BEFB-1EF707727120/Finance(No3)Bill (accessed 12.01.20).

UK Parliament (2019b) *Business of the House (Section 13(1)(b) of the European Union (withdrawal) Act 2018) (No. 2)* [online] Available at: https://hansard.parliament.uk/Commons/2019-01-09/division/053420DE-69A6-4C68-BE10-467A90F9D8E9/BUSINESSOFTHEHOUSE(SECTION13(1)(B)OFTHEEUROPEANUNION(WITHDRAWAL)ACT2018)(NO2)?outputType=Names (accessed 12.01.20).

UK Parliament (2019c) *European Union (Withdrawal) Act main Motion (Prime Minister)* [online] Available at: https://votes.parliament.uk/Votes/Commons/Division/562 (accessed 12.01.20).

UK Parliament (2019d) *No Confidence in Her Majesty's Government* [online] Available at: https://votes.parliament.uk/Votes/Commons/Division/565 (accessed 12.01.20).

UK Parliament (2019e) *European Union (Withdrawal) Act 2018* [online] Available at: https://hansard.parliament.uk/commons/2019-01-29/debates/BB8A5769-12B4-4D0E-9B4E-158F89F9FCDE/EuropeanUnion(Withdrawal)Act2018 (accessed 12.01.20).

UK Parliament (2019f) *Leaving the European Union* [online] Available at: https://hansard.parliament.uk/commons/2019-02-26/debates/B5B3B17F-E96D-4093-ADE4-E5A8F4F3C58B/LeavingTheEuropeanUnion (accessed 12.01.20).

UK Parliament (2019g) *Section 13(1)(b) of the European Union (Withdrawal) Act Main Motion* [online] Available at: https://votes.parliament.uk/Votes/Commons/Division/623 (accessed 12.01.20).

UK Parliament (2019h) *Main Motion, as Amended by Amendment (a), on UK's Withdrawal from the European Union* [online] Available at: https://votes.parliament.uk/Votes/Commons/Division/628 (accessed 12.01.20).

UK Parliament (2019i) *UK's Withdrawal from the EU: Prime Minister's Motion* [online] Available at: https://votes.parliament.uk/Votes/Commons/Division/633 (accessed 12.01.20).

UK Parliament (2019j) *Speaker's Statement* [online] Available at: https://hansard.parliament.uk/commons/2019-03-18/debates/AB031E78-C906-4833-9ACF-291998FAC0E1/Speaker%E2%80%99SStatement (accessed 12.01.20).

UK Parliament (2019k) *United Kingdom's Withdrawal from the European Union* [online] Available at: https://votes.parliament.uk/Votes/Commons/Division/664 (accessed 12.01.20).

UK Parliament (2019l) *Votes in Parliament* [online] Available at: https://votes.parliament.uk/Votes/Commons/Division/668 (accessed 12.01.20).

UK Parliament (2019m) *Votes in Parliament* [online] Available at: https://votes.parliament.uk/Votes/Commons/Division/669 (accessed 12.01.20).

UK Parliament (2019n) *Priorities for Government* [online] Available at: https://hansard.parliament.uk/commons/2019-07-25/debates/D0290128-96D8-4AF9-ACFD-21D5D9CF328E/PrioritiesForGovernment (accessed 12.01.20).

UK Parliament (2019o) *European Union (Withdrawal) (No.6) Bill: Commons stages* [online] Available at: https://www.parliament.uk/business/news/2019/september/commons-european-union-withdrawal-no6-bill/ (accessed 12.01.20).

UK Parliament (2019p) *That There Shall Be an Early Parliamentary General Election* [online] Available at: https://votes.parliament.uk/Votes/Commons/Division/715 (accessed 12.01.20).

UK Parliament (2019q) *Second Reading: European Union (Withdrawal Agreement) Bill* [online] Available at: https://votes.parliament.uk/Votes/Commons/Division/722 (accessed 12.01.20).

UK Parliament (2019r) *Programme: European Union (Withdrawal Agreement) Bill* [online] Available at: https://votes.parliament.uk/Votes/Commons/Division/723 (accessed 12.01.20).

UK Parliament (2019s) *European Union (Withdrawal Agreement) Bill* [online] Available at: https://hansard.parliament.uk/commons/2019-10-22/debates/277C5A20-456D-469B-A415-D04AFFD83248/EuropeanUnion(WithdrawalAgreement)Bill#contribution-262B1873-A85F-418E-A94D-62BE152F1CDC (accessed 12.01.20).

UK Parliament (2019t) *That There Shall Be an Early Parliamentary General Election* [online] Available at: https://votes.parliament.uk/Votes/Commons/Division/731 (accessed 12.01.20).

UK Parliament (2019u) *Early Parliamentary General Election Act 2019* [online] Available at: https://services.parliament.uk/bills/2019-19/earlyparliamentarygeneralelection.html (accessed 12.01.20).

UK Prime Minister (2019a) *Letter from UK to EU Council* [online] Available at: https://assets.publishing.service.gov.uk/government/uploads/system/uploads/attachment_data/file/840665/Letter_from_UK_to_EU_Council.pdf (accessed 12.01.20).

UK Prime Minister (2019b) *Letter to Donald Tusk* [online] Available at: https://assets.publishing.service.gov.uk/government/uploads/system/uploads/attachment_data/file/840660/PM_to_Donald_Tusk_19_October_2019.pdf (accessed 12.01.20).

UK Representation to the EU Brussels (2019) *Letter to the Secretary-General of the Council of the European Union* [online] Available at: https://assets.publishing.service.gov.uk/government/uploads/system/uploads/attachment_data/file/840666/Cover_letter_from_Sir_Tim_Barrow.pdf (accessed 12.01.20).

Chapter 12

A historical sociology of constitutions and democracy

An interview

Chris Thornhill

Introduction

Chris Thornhill is a Professor and former Head at the School of Law at the University of Manchester, UK. He was also the Niklas Luhmann Distinguished Visiting Professor in Sociological Theory at the University of Bielefeld, Germany. Professor Thornhill was interviewed at the University of São Paulo Law School on 23 August 2019 by Lucas Fucci Amato and Marco Antonio Loschiavo Leme de Barros (editors of this volume) and Carina Rodrigues de Araújo Calabria (a PhD candidate at the University of Manchester, UK). He commented on his intellectual endeavour of connecting legal, historical and sociological research, and emphasised the need to combine nationally located trajectories with transnational comparisons of historical dynamics. This is exemplified by his recent work on constitutions and democracy (Thornhill 2011, 2016, 2018), which define a framework of analysis deeply influenced by Luhmann's systems theory. However, these works would go further than Luhmann in describing the emergence of a global legal system. Despite adopting the vocabulary of a 'world society', Luhmann describes social systems such as law and politics within a national imagination. Luhmann's critique of the welfare state also becomes problematic if we think that social inclusion brought by public policies is a requirement for functional differentiation and that exclusion, crises and systemic integration (ie, de-differentiation) are deeply connected phenomena.

We would like to know a little more about your academic trajectory and specifically how Luhmann entered into your studies and how you discovered the systems theory.

The question about how Luhmann entered my intellectual field of vision is an interesting story. I realise now, going back to my earlier writings, from my 20s and 30s, that I was always just really experimenting to find a method to address the questions I would like to ask, maybe in some ways I had not even formulated the questions I would like to ask. I used to write a lot of commentaries on other thinkers. I wrote a book about the history of political theory in Germany and I wrote about Luhmann in this context (Thornhill 2000). I think it is also possible to read Luhmann as a political theorist. People would say that he did not have really a theory of politics, but he clearly does. My educational background was very much in the field of critical theory, so I have been strongly influenced by the first generation of the Frankfurt School and to a lesser degree by its second generation. When I was first reading Luhmann, I was very critical of him. I did not like him. Many aspects I really did not understand. I am not particularly proud of the first things I wrote about Luhmann. But a dilemma began to present itself to my mind. I had to think about key political questions and key constitutional questions. Then I came to a dilemma between my anthropological way of thinking and more positivistic or functionalist forms of thinking. I did not know which path to pursue. As a process of intellectual engagement with myself, I wrote two books at the same time: one was on existentialism (Thornhill 2002) and the other on systems theory, joint with Michael King (King and Thornhill 2003). These seem, within the context of 20th-century philosophy, the most diametrically opposed positions: one very strongly relying on ethical and anthropological assumptions about political questions, questions of legitimacy, and the other based on extremely anti-anthropological preconditions, namely Luhmann. When I was writing these books at the same time, it was a kind of dialogue with myself, during my 30s. Which way should I go, intellectually? And I surprised myself, because my purpose was to write very critically about Luhmann, but during the writing of this book I became much more sympathetic to his ideas. This is really how Luhmann came into my field of vision. He is a theorist like Hegel or Marx in some way: if you engage closely with the theory, it is hard to disengage. Even if you do so, your way of thinking will be necessarily defined by it. I have never really thought of myself as a Luhmannian or as a systems theorist. There are a number of other theorists that influenced me just as much as Luhmann, but there are some paradigmatic elements in Luhmann's thinking that remain very fundamental to the way in which I try to pursue legal analysis and political analysis. Much of what I do now is very critical of Luhmann, and particularly of some of his historical analyses, but I am critical of him in a Luhmannian way. I do not have any problem with this ambiguous relationship; I do not feel I am too close or too far away from Luhmann. This is really what happened. After the book on Luhmann (co-authored with Michael King) published in 2003, it was very clear that this theoretical basis provided a way to address the questions that always interested me. I wrote a book when I was in my late 20s and which I never published, about the secularisation of law. I never completed and finished it. I realized that I did not have the methodology for writing the book, despite having a lot of material on religious contests in Europe, the investiture controversies and the legacy of religious conflicts in European history. It was a book about religion and law, but I was really searching for a methodology to write that book in a way that was not purely reconstructive. After the book on Luhmann, I started to use Luhmannian frameworks to approach similar questions. A book that I published much later, *A Sociology of Constitutions* (Thornhill 2011), was in some way a kind of a re-written version of that earlier unfinished work, using a more Luhmannian framework. This happened very often: there is a lot of material I wrote when I was younger and I never published, but I re-wrote all again, with a different form, about 15 years later, using this framework with which I became familiar.

It is very common that people start by criticising Luhmann and then become much more sympathetic to him. And there is a perspective on how Luhmann works with history in his writings but also about how his theory can work with history. You can really disagree with his interpretation of some historical argument, but still use his theory to work out your own argument. But what are the main authors, besides Luhmann, that form your way of thinking?

I started working on cultural sociology, on the intellectual history of the Frankfurt School; I was trying to look at the cultural theorists that influenced the early Frankfurt School. But halfway through my PhD I read Carl Schmitt. I did not have any legal training at that time. My formation was in philosophy, cultural sociology and languages. I had a stay as a researcher at the University of Frankfurt, and I lived in Germany when I was a teenager. So I had access to German material from quite an early age. When I read Carl Schmitt I was about 25. I finished the PhD quickly after this, but I realised that cultural sociology was an area of research that was completely dead for me from that point on. I started to think about constitutional questions, the relation of constitutional legitimacy to social formations, social conflict. In connection with this, I developed a strong interest in the constitutional theories of the Weimar Republic, such as in Hermann Heller. A strange intellectual trajectory took me out of cultural sociology into legal sociology and constitutional theory. Nothing was the same again after reading Carl Schmitt. I had to work in cultural sociology after that, but I never found that it was a productive environment for me. But Luhmann did not influence me when I was young, I had not read him until I was in my 30s. The starting point was really the constitutional theories of the Weimar Republic. If you have a deep foundation in constitutional theory and practice of that time, you will have the best intellectual foundation for understanding constitutional law, because almost every constitutional problem or challenge of today has some kind of precedent in that time. Other theories influenced me over the years: Karl Marx since I was a teenager, although I never thought of myself as a Marxist. People say that they can see in my writings that I take Marx very seriously. I am very respectful when engaging with his theory, specially his early political writings. I think *The Eighteenth Brumaire of Louis Napoleon* (1852) is a masterpiece in political thinking. When I was an undergraduate, I wrote a dissertation on Hegel. I read Hegel before Marx. This is not the usual way. And I think Hegel's influence on me is greater than Luhmann's. I was working on Hegel when I was 21 or 22, and this was very deep in my thinking. I do not know why I decided to go into cultural sociology, because when I was working on Hegel it was always the political and legal writings that I found so important (on German political thought, see Thornhill 2007). And classical sociology also has been an influence: Weber, Simmel, of course Durkheim; I came to appreciate more Durkheim when I was older. When you read Durkheim when younger it is not so obvious what is the point, but then I came to consider him of extreme importance. And when I was younger a great influence was literature, more than philosophy: Proust, Balzac, Kafka. Balzac is a sociologist!

In Brazil we have the influence both of Luhmann and other European authors that worked with Luhmann, in Italy for instance, and now we feel the influence of Anglophone authors, such as you, today. Did you notice any difference of uses, methods or themes that are approached here with systems theory but which do not have the same emphasis in Germany, Britain or in Europe in general?

You cannot talk about an Anglo-American context in this respect. American lawyers and British lawyers do not speak to each other. There is more convergence in sociology, but the interest in Luhmann in the USA is almost non-existent. In Britain it is quite intense, but almost always amongst lawyers. There are very, very few sociologists using Luhmann. We find some people in the sociology of culture, of media. But Luhmann is not established in sociology departments. He belongs to the canon of classical sociology, but he is not established in British Sociology departments, which are very good. I think this is due to the connection between Luhmann and Parsons. I myself like Parsons, specially his political writings, but this association with Parsons was problematic for the reception of Luhmann in British sociology. In British legal schools, the understanding of Luhmann is quite widespread, although marginal. Every law school has some people that know Luhmann very well, and there has been a proliferation of research using Luhmann in different areas of law (see King and Thornhill 2006). I write in constitutional law, Gunther Teubner in private law, Michael King is a specialist in family law. There are also people using Luhmann in medical law. The influence is quite pervasive. Intellectual and political intensity leads to an engagement with Luhmann, as you can feel in some symposia: there are people using his theories to explain very pressing problems of the legal profession and political institutions. And one area that Luhmann became influential in Britain is law and literature, law and cultural studies. However, I myself try to use

Luhmann to address problems of political formation, questions of legitimacy, and these concerns are closer to the uses of Luhmann in Brazil and other Latin American countries.

When you come to Brazil and go to a library, what is the kind of research that interest you? What are the missing points, the kind of research that people should do and that you would find interesting to read?

I always search for historical research. I think that the quality of historical research in Brazil has improved over the years. I find that there are some really crucial areas, crucial topics that are fundamental to understand Brazilian society. And you can compare these works with historical research in Germany, France or other European countries. I am always trying to connect sociological, legal and historical research, and historical sociology has developed as an important discipline in Brazil. There are a number of important works in this area on Brazilian history. But the volume of research in this area remains too small. This is an area of research that can be strongly developed. What is missing is sometimes big structural analysis of long-term historical shifts, historical epochs, rather than very generalised research on particular themes. A deep structural analysis of historical process seems to be lacking, although there are some very good researchers working in these areas, but maybe not so many. And I also find in historical research some over-dependence upon works originally written in English, which have been translated, usually translations of what has been written by Americans. The original works may be good, but Brazilians can do it better! I find a deep split between legal research and other social sciences; this is also a problem in Brazil. If you go to a law bookshop, a law library, you find textbooks on legal questions – even in constitutional law the focus is on constitutional commentary – so the interweaving of legal research with history and social sciences is also a path to be strengthened. Brazil is not alone in this. And good books stay in print for a short period of time in Brazil, so they have a very short life and cannot gain influence. Hence the problems are some lack of historical research, coupled with an excessive dependence on scholarship actually situated in other national intellectual contexts, and then a lack of inter-penetration between legal scholarship and other social sciences.

Usually law schools in Brazil are isolated from other social sciences. The spatial isolation contributes to the lack of dialogue.

You have very good lawyers and very good sociologists, but there is not very much relationship between them

Some have observed that Luhmann's vision about functional differentiation is a good description for the West Germany of his time, during the welfare state, which assured a potentially complete social inclusion, and then the differentiation between power, money, law etc. – although Luhmann (1990) was very critical of it, pointing out the risks of 'politicisation and bureaucratisation of society. Do you agree with this, ie, that wider inclusion is a pre-requisite for functional differentiation? Luhmann (2013: 14) himself said that his scheme about the forms of differentiation in Theory of Society (Die Gesellschaft der Gesellschaft) was based on European history. Marcelo Neves (1992), for instance, accused Luhmann of 'empirical provincialism'. As someone that researched the history of constitutionalism in Europe and abroad, what would you say about the concepts of a single world society and functional differentiation as its prevailing form of reproduction?

Europe and Latin America are more similar than some Latin American theories are inclined to believe. Legal and sociological scholars in Latin America, on the one hand, adopt a view that is close to Latin American exceptionalism. On the other hand, they see Europe too favourably. This seems to be connected to the idea that in Europe you have stable democracies while in Latin America you have unstable democracies; and the idea that democracy in Europe is old and democracy in Latin America is new. I would say that democracies are always unstable. It is very hard to find a stable democracy. I have been saying this for many years, but now this is in front of our eyes. Latin American democracies went into a period of high instability, and European democracies as well. I do not think that on that level it makes sense to distinguish a central and a peripheral modernity, if democratic stabilisation and legal inclusion are taken as criteria for determining this difference. I reject this categorisation. I think that it is born from that dialectical attitude of Latin America towards Europe, which both insists on Latin American exceptionalism but is excessively rosy in the view of Europe. You could turn it the other way around, and I would say that in Latin America democratisation and legal inclusion – if these are criteria by which we measure the distinction between peripheral and central modernity – are actually surprisingly consolidated, given that the historical preconditions are far less propitious. In Europe, we had institutions that became progressively embedded and reached deeper and deeper into the society. The preconditions for national inclusion and the establishment of early forms of citizenship were quite consolidated by the 18th century. Then we had states committed to the semantics of democratic legitimacy in the late 18th century, which was preserved through the 19th century, as serfdom was abolished, personal ownership of people was abolished. The basic preconditions for democracy were given at a relatively early stage in Europe, but European societies are not still fully democratic. Many have only precarious claims to democratic legitimacy. And none of them, except for in Scandinavia, became full democracies before 1945. Therefore, the actual temporal difference between democratisation in Latin America and Europe is not very big. Most European states had propitious preconditions for democratisation, but are not very democratic. And Latin American states had less propitious preconditions for democracy, but are surprisingly democratic. Therefore, I do not accept this centre-periphery distinction. We can also talk about economic criteria, or the universalisation of legal norms, and we can arrive at similar conclusions. I would say to fellow scholars in Latin America: think more critically about Europe. Because this idealising engagement with European history is so prevalent in Latin America that it is a block for understanding Latin America.

The other point I would make is that Luhmann made this groundbreaking development, he pioneered the concept of world society in the early 1970s, and at the end of his life (in the 1990s) he argued that every social system is part of a world society. But in Luhmann there is always a distinction between the sociological terminology and the sociological description. We can say that there is a world society in many ways, we can talk about a world system of health, a world system of law and probably a world system of sports, media etc. However, Luhmann did not provide a thick description of what a world system of law might look like. He had a global sociological vocabulary, but a national imagination. The phenomena which he describes in law and politics are still very national. And this is extraordinary, because the globalisation of law and the emergence of global legal institutions were quite advanced from the 1970s; he should have described this more accurately. Gunther Teubner, on the contrary, has an understanding of the global legal system. Luhmann's descriptions are very much embedded in national experience. In particular, his description of the political system, in which we have administration, legislation and the public, which is only legitimised if the welfare responsibilities of the administration do not become too heavy, is an anti-Keynesian view, belonging to the 1970s. On this point Luhmann is clearly wrong. The idea that in some way the assumption of excessive social responsibilities by the political system contaminates the political system and the economic system, and possibly also the legal system at the same time, is incoherent. It is most correct to see it the other way around: the establishment of guarantees for social inclusion becomes a precondition for social differentiation, in the legal system, in the political system and in the economic system. Without some degree of material inclusion for all citizens, these systems cannot work well. We have empirical evidence in the last 10 years that legal, political and economic systems tend to enter a kind of convergence crisis when social inclusion is reduced. Luhmann is mistaken about that, and this mistake was strongly determined by the environment in which he was working, where people were turning against Keynes after the oil crises.

On democracy, Luhmann refused to view it as an ideal and tried to characterise it by some institutional features. Sometimes he said that democracy rests upon the submission of the higher power to the lower power (like in the paradox of sovereignty, or popular sovereignty); other times he emphasised that democracy is based on a decomposition of decisions on other decisions, through representation or participation, which may overburden the system. And finally, he sometimes defined democracy by the division of state power between government and opposition. How would you characterise democracy? Can its elements be different from context to context and from time to time? Do we sometimes overestimate the constitutional evolution of the rich countries? In a course here in Brazil, you mentioned the evolution of political rights in Britain. So here in Brazil, slavery was abolished in 1888, men's universal suffrage was guaranteed in the 1890s and women's vote in the 1930s. We tend to see this as an eccentric evolution, while we idealize other countries, believing that everything was solved since the 17th or 18th century, let's say, with Glorious Revolution in Britain, American independence and the French Revolution. How do you see this historical idealisation?

If we take as a threshold concept of democracy – so that anything above this can be considered democracy, even if it is incompletely democratic, and anything below this is not really a democracy – my threshold definition would be: one person, one vote; competitive elections; no discrimination on grounds of ethnicity or gender or social class. Anything below that is not a democracy. And anything above this is a democracy. Of course that democracy can take different forms, and we can say that some system is more democratic than another, there may be a better system of media, there can be a better education system in one society, access to the public sphere may be easier in some places, but all these factors concern the quality of democracy. If we take that threshold concept of democracy, there is not such a difference between Europe and Latin America. There is a huge sociological literature on processes of democratisation, but these processes are very similar in virtually every country (see Thornhill 2018). Virtually all states that were independent in the 19th century followed the same path. You had a very incomplete representative system in the 19th century, which allowed the exercise of political rights by a small number of men, and then after the First World War there was a rapid process of transition to full male democracy, and in some cases (like Germany) to female democracy. But in a few years this system of mass democracy collapsed and was replaced by some form of authoritarianism, extreme or very extreme authoritarianism, the more extreme forms including genocide. After 1945 there was a gradual reorientation, between 1945 and 1960 democracy was consolidated in North and Western Europe (see Madsen and Thornhill 2014). It is only by this time that we can see democracy as a type of political system that was emerging as a generalised political form. And in Latin America there was a delay; for a number of different reasons, democracies did not become consolidated until the 1980s. I do not think that Brazil between 1945 and 1964 was fully democratic – it became more democratic but still had a restricted franchise. Argentina was more democratic than Brazil in that stage. In Latin America there was a volatile pattern of democracy, and democracy came to be consolidated after 1983 in Argentina and after 1985 in Brazil. However, the process of re-democratisation in Latin America is very similar to the process of de-mocratisation in Europe after 1945. The foundations were very similar. There is a difference of about 30 years. It is deeply erroneous to look at European history and say that the basic principles of democracy were al-ready consolidated in the 18th century. Britain is usually seen as the oldest European democracy, but it was not really a democracy until 1950; before then plural voting was retained, so that privileged people could vote more than once; and in no way before 1928, because all women could not vote before that. Virtually every society that was perceived as democratic had some characteristics before 1945 that do not meet with that basic, threshold definition of democracy. The USA was an apartheid system until 1964, 1965. A small percentage of non-Caucasian men in the southern states could vote. Now we would say that it was apartheid. Canada had ethnic exclusion until 1960, Australia had ethnic exclusion until 1962. Only Scandinavia had earlier democracies, probably Sweden, Finland, Norway were democratic by the 1920s. The most pessimistic constructions about Latin America would need to recognise only a gap of 30 years with de-mocratisation in Europe. Democracies in Europe demanded a higher price, in terms of the number of people who actually died. It seems paradoxical that people in Latin America have this view that their societies are very violent, while historically European societies are far more violent than Latin American. The number of people who died in either domestic conflict or inter-state conflict in Europe totally eclipses the figures in Latin America. An informed relativisation of this contrast is required when comparing these regions.

You recognise that law and politics may constitute a single partial system, commanded by the code 'rights'/'non-rights'. Could you advance this idea?

I do think there is an issue in Luhmann's thinking. This is partly my own opinion, a position that strategically deviates from Luhmann's work. I do think that there is an issue in Luhmann's work, that he never developed a complete understanding of the political system. The relationship between the political system and the legal system in Luhmann's work is always very anomalous. He does not really develop an idea of a political code. Very often, the code and the programme in the political system are closely related to each other. But much more important than this, Luhmann argues that the political system always relies on a secondary code. So that is why I call it a 'transmission code': that political power can only be distributed through society insofar as it undergoes a process of secondary coding, so that it is coded as law. The political system does not actually transmit power. It requires law, it requires a structural coupling with law, actually in order for political decisions to be implemented through society. The secondary coding occurs as a parallel process, defining the 'law'/'not-law' form. This typically takes place through the construction of a constitution. The constitution works as a medium, a pre-condition that translates power into law so that power is translated into a form that can be distributed throughout society. I think Luhmann himself in effect always said that law and politics are the same system. He was always very uneasy about writing about the political system. If you look at his writings and how he develops it throughout the years, he always changed the descriptions of the political system. Even the description of the political code changes over the years.

But this is not so important for me. What is important for me is that, when we look at global society, I do not think there is a global political system. I think there is a global legal system and the global legal system assumes certain political functions. I would also say that at the level of national society, the differentiation of political systems only took place through the increasing inter-penetration of the legal system and the political system. National political systems on their own never actually became differentiated. It was only through the constant displacement of political functions into law that the political systems began to become differentiated. This takes place through an overlying or a secondary codification of political decisions, through the binary opposition 'rights'/'not-rights'. It is as political questions are formalised in accordance with this code that political functions have become differentiated. But I think that Luhmann himself said this, through his concept of the constitution. He says that the secondary coding of the political system takes place through the constitution. What is the code of the constitution? The code of the constitution is 'rights'/'not-rights', in essence. If we were to imagine the constitution as a subsystem which has its own particular coding, this would have to be 'rights'/'not-rights'. This is what constitutions do. They say this decision can be categorised as compliant with rights expectations, that decision has to be characterised as not compliant with rights expectations. So I think that probably Luhmann already said this, but I really developed, expanded this argument. This is now heretical for Luhmannians, but I do not think that law and politics are differentiated. I think they are the same system. In fact, I do not think that societies develop political systems on their own. They only develop political systems through the inter-penetration of law and politics. I would like to know what this political system is that is not law. But this is what Luhmann probably writes as well. You almost can hear in the semantics of his argument that he has a lack of confidence when he talks about the political system, and some of the things that he says about politics are so banal. All the stuff about the welfare state, you know, this is like journalism. Some of the stuff he writes about politics – it is very banal and it is very misguided. I really think that he just really did not understand the political system, in the same way that I think that he did not understand the more globalised parts of the legal system. He did not have in this respect the same sophistication with which he was able to talk about other forms of social communication. There is a discrepancy between this and this sort of neo-conservatism that he expresses in his discussions of the welfare state.

It is the same when he talks about 'favelas' (eg, Luhmann 1998).

Yes, but he obviously did not spend much time in South America, and his opinions on South America would follow some authorities. I think that some of this is very questionable. But it is really in his positions on the welfare state, I think, that we can see flaws. The argument that in some way the welfare state inhibits the functional differentiation of different social systems is so absurd. It simply reproduces very simplified understandings or critiques of political collectivism. Whereas we really would have to say now, on an empirical basis, that the welfare state is at the core of processes of differentiation. It generates patterns of individualisation, which promote individual inclusion, which promote the differentiation of different systems, I would say. One of our colleagues was talking last night about pushing against Luhmann in empirical research. I mean, if you want to do welfare state research from a systemic-theoretical perspective, we have to completely push against these crude claims that come out in Luhmann's work, for instance in *Die Politik der Gesellschaft* (*Politics as Social System*; 2000). Obviously, this was published posthumously, and I think that some of this stuff he would never have published if he had been alive. It is just like a neo-conservative talk. My argument is always that he did not establish a reliable construction of the political system.

What do you think about these ideas of transnational constitutionalism that claim that we can have a legal system coupled with an economic system without the national political system? And could we call these constitutions, for example, constitutions of transnational enterprises, constitutions in legal orders without the state?

I do not see why you cannot say this. I think this is a completely sustainable view. We can talk about transnational constitutional norms, certainly. The problem that I always identify is, for me, a historical problem, because this argument, in its different articulations, pre-supposes that there was a period of nation-state constitutionalism, or national states and robust systems of constitutional norms, which regulate activities in their own societies, and that this period is finished. My view is that the problem lies in this periodisation of democratisation, of constitutional formation. I say that the transnationalisation of constitutional law is simultaneous with the nationalisation of constitutional norms. We only had national constitutional law in a small number of constitutional texts until recently. Constitutional law only really began to penetrate deeply into national societies in the very recent past, since the 1960s. And this is connected with the transnationalisation of constitutional law. The transnationalisation and the nationalisation of constitutional law took place as the same process (see Thornhill 2016). I would also see the construction of transnational constitutions as a much more generalised process than many theories of transnational constitutional norms. I do not think that we really need to look at individual areas of social practice or functional exchange. I think that we can see some universal norms, relatively universal norms. It is on the foundation of these norms that national constitutions have acquired their own constitutional orders, at least in a meaningful sense. So my argument regarding transnational constitutional law is that we need to see a much deeper dialectical interaction between the construction of national constitutional norms and the construction of transnational constitutional orders. There is plenty of evidence of this. And here we do need to think sociologically, not legally. Obviously, there have been many national constitutions since the late 19th century, but the question is what did they actually do? The extent to which constitutional norms or the fact that constitutional norms now do in many settings penetrate quite deeply into society is not separable from processes of normative globalisation.

We would like you to discuss the relation between empirical research and systems theory, and to comment on how you actually conduct this in your work.

I still have certain Luhmannian aspects in my analysis of social formation and legal formation, but I also disagree with Luhmann a lot now. I suppose I do empirical research in two ways. For instance, when Carina Calábria and I focused upon identifying legal processes, we conducted empirical research in the sense of the re-construction of case law, and in some cases we also conducted rather exploratory research in which we tried to observe immediately the impact of case law within national societies. We have done empirical research in this respect. But the more empirical research I do on my own is more historical; it is historical phenomenology rather than classical empirical research. I always call it historical phenomenology. I am not being arrogant or presumptuous when I use this term, but I do think this is the kind of research that I have developed over the years and in which I feel most comfortable, where I try to attach macro-sociological processes to particular phenomena. I do use elements of sociological phenomenology in pursuing this; I use Luhmann's descriptions of differentiation as a basis for historical phenomenological research. I also think that Luhmann's descriptions of processes of differentiation are not very accurate. I think they are accurate at an intuitive level. He grasps macro-sociological processes very well, but the empirical detail is not very reliable. He talks about the differentiation of the legal and the political systems in the 18th century. I would say that it is actually the opposite. The legal system and the political system by the late 18th century, he argues, approached a reasonably advanced level of differentiation. I would really say the opposite. The legal system and the political system by this time became more closely connected. At least at the legitimation level, which is really the determining aspect of both. I try to develop historical phenomenological and sociological-phenomenological analysis to examine these processes of differentiation. Sometimes the analysis runs very clearly against Luhmann.

I guess the more contemporary empirical research I have done, very often with Carina Calábria, is focused on questions of differentiation as well. I am not saying that we have the same kind of methodology, but there is some kind of convergence. In conducting empirical research with other people, there is not really an expectation of orthodoxy. We try to establish some sort of working principles, and conduct research on broad shared foundations, but without an expectation of complete congruence on different methodological approaches. I think that what we try to do is to look at ways in which a legal system, that is, the differentiation of the legal system, is articulated with the international level. I think that the empirical work that we have done can be broadly examined as an attempt to provide a re-construction of the pre-conditions of differentiation of the legal system at the global level. This can be empirically analysed, in a way, for example, that Luhmann did not imagine. I am always really struck by this, because Luhmann understood the law very well, but he did not understand legal differentiation at the global level – although he always said that law is a world system. Law is probably *the* most globalised system. Maybe with the economy. It is more globalised than education, although there are some global aspects in education. It is much more globalised than the political system. But if we want to look at, if we really want empirically to analyse the world systems, then we need to look at the economy and the law. Luhmann did not even begin to imagine what the actual global elements of the legal system would be. This always seems extraordinary, given that he actually had empirical expertise in law in a way that he did not have in politics, or aesthetics, or sport.

I would say that I find that Luhmann's work opens up two avenues for empirical socio-legal research, both essentially focused on providing a richer empirical analysis for processes of differentiation. It allows us to exemplify processes of differentiation, and also to provide empirical analysis of contagion between two different systems.

If you had to list three truisms or assumptions that are commonly spread in contemporary legal theory and that you highly dispute, which ones would they be?

First, I would say the assumption that we can divide different political or legal systems into simple categories, which can be positioned on an easy spectrum of democratic quality, a straightforward spectrum of democratic quality. The assumption that there are stable, better democracies in some parts of the world and weak, fragile or precarious democracies in other parts of the world. This I always dispute. I always think democracy is fragile and the constitutional foundation of democracy is fragile.

Second, I contest the assumption that the constitutional vocabulary of democratic legitimacy provides an adequate description of how democracy is created. We still use these concepts, these semantics of constitutional democracy, from the 18th century – popular sovereignty, citizenship and collective self-legislation – while we can provide both a better normative construction and a more sociologically sustainable description of democracy. I think that for us really to understand constitutional democracy we actually have to abandon a lot of the vocabulary of democracy. So I would challenge classical constitutional theory both at the normative and sociological level.

And then third, I think democracies do not have a national foundation. I do not think that national societies created democracy. This is not to say that democracy is created in a completely stable transnational society either. It is only through transnationalisation of legal systems that we begin to see the emergence of the stabilisation of democracy. Therefore, I challenge this basic conceptual and normative conflation of democracy and national society. My third challenge contains a much broader sociological question. This is again something that I started writing about 10 years ago, and actually now a lot of people agree with this point, so that you see this argument in quite a lot of recent literature. But in my construction it is not only democracy that is very recent and that pre-supposes a transnational foundation, to the extent that we have to abandon the classical normative vocabulary of democracy; it is actually really the nation-state that is recent. We are not really living in a period in which the nation-state is redundant. We still live in a period in which the nation-state is being consolidated, and this is very closely connected to transnationalisation. If we understand the nation state as something more than a legal title – obviously the sovereign legal title of the nation-state can be traced back to early modern Europe, or processes of decolonisation in Latin America and later in Africa. But if we see the nation-state as a sociological reality, in which there are reasonably uniform processes of citizenship construction and social integration, and legal norms have reasonably even purchase in different parts of national territories and national societies, then the nation-state is still in the process of development and it has not actually reached completion yet. But the acceleration in the completion of the realisation of the nation-state and national societies as a whole has also a transnational foundation. There are some deep commonplaces in sociological, historical, political scientific research; for example, the belief that there are historical variations in the development of democracy and Europe got there first. I can never see where this idea comes from.

The second claim refers to the fact that there is a constitutional vocabulary which is based on notions of national citizenship and national self-legislation and assumes that this can be used to define democratic constitutional systems. This I would like to deeply question. And I would like really to offer – I am working on this now – a comprehensive revision of the basic vocabulary of constitutionalism on a sociological foundation. This is intended to reflect the fact that national sovereignty and national citizenship always developed on a transnational basis. It is only through the articulation between national agency and international norms that democracy begins to become real as a constitutional phenomenon.

My third claim is that, actually, national societies themselves did not approach their realisation on national foundations. It is only through the influx of global norms into national societies that the processes of integration that national societies pre-suppose become real. These are three big claims. The first two, I just think they are empirically demonstrable. The first one about the inaccuracy of most periodisation of democratic formation: the evidence is so clear that the overlap, the temporal overlap between democratisation in different parts of the globe is actually very close. I am not saying there is no difference at all. But democracy did not even really exist before 1945. And it was not a widespread phenomenon before the 1960s. Then it was not consolidated as a global expectation until the 1980s. If we take that periodisation, the differences between different parts of the globe begin to look rather exaggerated.

Is there anything else that we did not ask and that you would like to add?

Thank you very much for your interest on my work. I am always really honoured that people are interested in my work in Latin America. I never quite know why this is. Maybe it is partly because I try to push against what seems to me to be a sort of pathology of self-depreciation in Latin America. I try to push against this. And I do not have the very favourable view of European democracy that a lot of European intellectuals have. But whatever the reason is, I am very pleased that people in Latin America find my work important and I am very honoured that you wish to conduct this interview. Thank you very much indeed.

References

King, M. and Thornhill, C., (2003) *Niklas Luhmann's Theory of Politics and Law* (New York, Macmillan).

King, M. and Thornhill, C. (eds) (2006) *Luhmann on Law and Politics: Critical Appraisals and Applications* (Oxford, Hart).

Luhmann, N. (1990) *Political Theory in the Welfare State* (Berlin, de Gruyter).

Luhmann, N. (1998) 'Inclusión y exclusión' in Luhmann N., *Complejidad y modernidad: De la unidad a la diferencia* (Madrid, Trotta) 167–195.

Luhmann, N. (2000) *Die Politik der Gesellschaft* (Frankfurt, Suhrkamp).

Luhmann, N. (2013) *Theory of Society II* (Stanford, Stanford University Press).

Madsen, M.R. and Thornhill, C. (eds) (2014) *Law and the Formation of Modern Europe: Perspectives from the Historical Sociology of Law* (Cambridge, Cambridge University Press).

Neves, M. (1992) *Verfassung und Positivität des Rechts in der peripheren Moderne: Eine theoretische Betrachtung und eine Interpretation des Falls Brasilien* (Berlin, Duncker & Humblot).

Thornhill, C. (2000) *Political Theory in Modern Germany: An Introduction* (Cambridge, Polity Press).

Thornhill, C. (2002) *Karl Jaspers: Politics and Metaphysics* (London, Routledge).

Thornhill, C (2007) *German Political Philosophy: The Metaphysics of Law* (London, Routledge).

Thornhill, C. (2011) *A Sociology of Constitutions: Constitutions and State Legitimacy in Historical-Sociological Perspective* (Cambridge, Cambridge University Press).

Thornhill, C. (2016) *A Sociology of Transnational Constitutions: Social Foundations of the Post-National Legal Structure* (Cambridge, Cambridge University Press).

Thornhill, C. (2018) *The Sociology of Law and the Global Transformation of Democracy* (Cambridge, Cambridge University Press).

Index

Act of Parliament 229–30
'action orientations' 83
Amato, Lucas Fucci 247
Andersen, Åkerstrøm 176, 185n11
anti-Keynesian view 253–4
Article 50, 223, 229–35, 237–40
Atlan, H. 211
attractors 55–6
autological theory 27
autopoiesis 25; constructivist position of 37–45; and empirical research 37–42; and empiricism 59–62; maps and mapping 42–5; redefinition of empirical work 33–4; structural hiatus between theory and empirical research 34–7; structurally coupled, processes of difference minimisation 58–9; usefulness of cognitive mapping 45–53; *see also* empirical legal autopoiesis
Axelrod, Robert 44–5

Baecker, D. 150
Bakken, T. 71
Balzac 250
Barros, Marco Antonio Loschiavo Leme de 247
Bateson, G. 16
Becker, Dirk 149
Begriffsjurisprudenz 13
Benn, Hilary 235
Berger, Johannes 185n16
Bertalanffy, L. 184n3
Berührungsangst 33
bifurcation and attractors 55–6
binary coding: in action, analysing 75–6; empirical mapping tool 71, 75–6;

integration movements and 205, 206
binding institutions 57–9
binding precedents or general repercussion 162n11
Bird 97, 102
'black box' 98, 112, 115
blind spot and self-observation paradox 166, 174–6
Bloor, David 60
Blumer, Herbert 167–8, 177–8, 184n4
Bolsonaro, Jair 218
Borges, J.L. 9
'bounded rationality' 117
Brazil 116, 148, 188, 190–1, 199–219, 250–1, 254–5
Brazilian constitutional law 161n3, 162n11, 163n14, 163n23
Brazilian Federal Supreme Court 163n23
Brexit 5, 223–4, 241n1; Article 50 of the Treaty on European Union 223, 229–35, 237–40; Cameron and 227–8, 238–9, 240; Parliament 223, 224, 229–40; referendum 227–32, 235, 236, 239–40; Supreme Court of UK on 230–2, 236–8
bureaucratic organisations and technological innovation 162n8
Burns, T. 143, 161n8

Calábria, Carina 258–9
'A calculus for self-reference' (Varela) 36
Cameron, David 228–9, 238–9
Campos, M. 148–9
case study: use of the concept of normative expectations 178–83
Castells, Manuel 217